DATE DUE

DEMCO 38-296

Vietnam
Joins the
World

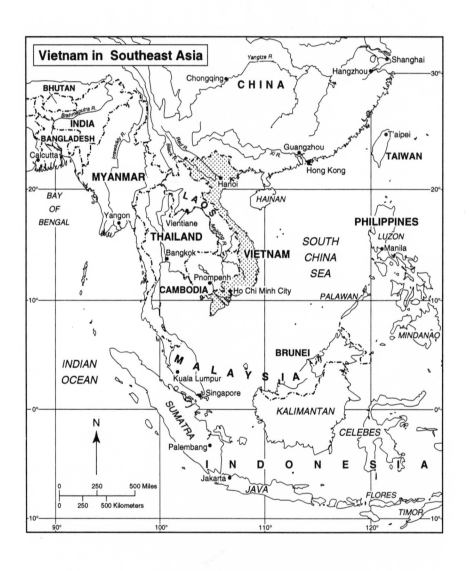

Vietnam in Southeast Asia

Vietnam
Joins the
World

James W. Morley and
Masashi Nishihara, Editors

Richard K. Betts   Tatsumi Okabe
John Bresnan   Yoshihide Soeya
Frederick Z. Brown   Seki Tomoda
Masahiko Ebashi   Donald S. Zagoria

An East Gate Book

M.E. Sharpe
Armonk, New York
London, England

An East Gate Book

Copyright © 1997 by M. E. Sharpe, Inc.

Library of Congress Cataloging-in-Publication Data

Vietnam joins the world / James W. Morley and Masashi Nishihara, editors.
p.   cm.
"An East Gate book."
Includes index.
ISBN 1-56324-974-X (alk. paper).—ISBN 1-56324-975-8 (pbk. : alk. paper)
1. Vietnam—Foreign relations.
2. Vietnam—History—1975–   .
I. Morley, James William, 1921–   .
II. Nishihara, Masashi.
DS559.912.V5427   1996
327.597′009′049—dc21
96-39809
CIP

Printed in the United States of America

The paper used in this publication meets the minimum requirements of the
American National Standard for Information Sciences—
Permanence of Paper for Printed Library Materials,
ANSI Z 39.48-1984.

BM (c)   10   9   8   7   6   5   4   3   2   1
BM (p)   10   9   8   7   6   5   4   3   2   1

Contents

Preface

This book is the outgrowth of a joint project on the former Indochina states inaugurated at a meeting in New York in 1990 of the ten authors here presented, together with selected other scholars and officials from Japan, the United States, and various Southeast Asian countries. At that time Cambodia was bogged down in a devastating civil war. Vietnam was grappling with ways to transform itself that were little understood abroad. And the two most influential countries in the Asia-Pacific region, Japan and the United States, appeared to be moving down different tracks.

Japan recognized the Sihanouk-led government of the three opposition factions in Cambodia and sustained its long-time relations with the government in Vietnam. The United States, on the other hand, refused to recognize either Cambodian government and, with Vietnam, refused to permit even commercial or humanitarian contact. While Japan and the United States were exchanging views with each other and showing some understanding of each other's interests and perceptions, the United States worked inside the circle of the permanent five members of the United Nations Security Council; Japan, outside.

It seemed obvious to the group assembled in New York that unless Japan and the United States could come to a more common understanding of the situation in this area and achieve a greater harmony of views, they were in danger of frustrating positive developments there. They were in danger also of weakening their own partnership and impeding the development of the broader Asia-Pacific community both desired.

Was there something that concerned citizens could do to help ward off these possibilities? The Research Institute on Peace and Security, an independent research center in Tokyo, and the Pacific Basin Studies Program, a teaching and research program of the East Asian Institute and the Center on Japanese Economy and Business of Columbia University in New York, decided to try.

The five Japanese and five American specialists who have contributed chapters to this volume were recruited as country core groups. A multiyear research program was devised that has involved each core group's making periodic visits to Cambodia and Vietnam (the Japanese group also visited Laos and China) to interview officials and private persons, gather materials, and form firsthand impressions. Following each of these dual visits, the two groups have met together and in consultation with knowledgeable officials, scholars, and businesspeople who have shared their impressions. After each such session, the two core groups have then worked privately to draft a common report of their findings and recommendations. These have been circulated to interested persons and discussed with appropriate government and business leaders in each country. Five such reports have been issued, the last in January 1994.

Fortunately, over these years, the situation in the peninsula has greatly improved—in Cambodia, the Agreement on a Comprehensive Political Settlement, the UN intervention, and the establishment of a legitimate government; in Vietnam, the economic liberalization, the opening of the country, and the resumption of humanitarian and commercial relations by the United States. In the course of these developments Japan and the United States have come to a clearer perception of their common interests in the area and have worked more and more constructively together.

The situation in Cambodia is still fragile. The new coalition government is insecure, the Khmer Rouge insurrection goes on, and the country lies in desperate need of international assistance. But we have chosen in this volume to focus on Vietnam. There a historic new era is about to begin as Vietnam struggles to throw off its old controlled economy and bring itself into the modern world, and as the United States, having established diplomatic relations, prepares for full normalization, and Japan, being relieved of the many inhibitions it has been operating under in deference to its American ally, reinvigorates its thrust into Southeast Asia.

It is particularly urgent at this time, therefore, that the American and Japanese people know more about Vietnam. What kind of country is it becoming? Will its market reforms work? Will its society benefit? Will the Communists remain in power? Will it succeed in establishing cooperative relations with its neighbors? What interest do Americans and Japanese have in it and what should be our policies toward it?

The authors of this volume do not claim to have definitive answers to these and other important questions. The future is always unknowable. In any event, the facts about Vietnam are elusive and the judgments are uncertain. Nevertheless, the future does not wait. Important decisions are pressing. And having had the privilege of observing Vietnam at first hand over the past several years, we should like to make what contribution we can to the wider public discussion that is now required.

We begin with a brief overview to provide the reader with a foretaste of what is to come and a framework in which to fit the subsequent detail. In the chapters that follow, individual authors take up first the changes that Vietnam is bringing about in its political system, its economy, and its society, then its efforts to open to the outside world. The focus is on the recent reform period, from 1986 to the present, with an eye to the future. The responses of Japan and the United States are then assessed, and in a concluding chapter we offer some recommendations as to how our two governments can best engage this new entity in the Asia-Pacific equation.

Each chapter stands on its own, but all have been influenced by the materials we have exchanged and the countless impressions we have shared with each other and so many other knowledgeable people over the past five years. Each of us, therefore, would like to express his debt to the others in this project and to thank again the many citizens and officials of Vietnam who gave us such a warm welcome on our visits and the citizens and officials of our own and other countries who participated in our conferences, shared with us their views, and listened to ours. The number is too great to acknowledge here by name all of the persons who over the past five years have helped us, but we would be remiss if we did not express our special thanks to those who attended our last conference, in Maui in January 1995, and who there critiqued early drafts of the papers that form this book: Muthiah Alagappa, Evelyn Colbert, Nguyen Ngoc Dien, Robert E. Driscoll, Russel Heng, Hiroshi Kadota, Than T. Nguyen, Marvin C. Ott, Kusuma Snitwongse, Bui Than Son, Jonathan R. Stromseth, Carlyle A. Thayer, William S. Turley, Toshiyuki Yasui, and Hiroyuki Yushita.

Finally, we are especially grateful to the Research Institute on Peace and Security and the Pacific Basin Studies Program, which sponsored our work, to the Institute of International Affairs in Hanoi, which hosted our visits and whose members engaged us in such useful dialogue, and to the U.S.-Japan Foundation, which so generously provided the necessary financial support.

James W. Morley
Masashi Nishihara

Contributors

Richard K. Betts is Professor of Political Science and Director of International Security Policy Studies in the School of International and Public Affairs at Columbia University. He is the author of *Military Readiness* (1995); *Soldiers, Statesmen, and Cold War Crises*, 2nd edition (1991); *Nuclear Blackmail and Nuclear Balance* (1987); *Surprise Attack* (1982); and co-author of *The Irony of Vietnam* (1979). Until 1990 he was a Senior Fellow at the Brookings Institution. He has also taught at Harvard and Johns Hopkins universities and worked on the staffs of the Senate Select Committee on Intelligence and the National Security Council, and he currently serves as a member of the Military Advisory Panel to the Director of Central Intelligence.

John Bresnan is a Senior Research Scholar of the East Asian Institute of Columbia University. He is also Executive Director of the Pacific Basin Studies Program of the university. A former senior executive of the Ford Foundation, Mr. Bresnan served as head of its Office for Asia and the Pacific from 1973 to 1981. He earlier served the Ford Foundation as representative in Indonesia and in various other positions from 1953. He is editor of *Crisis in the Philippines: The Marcos Era and Beyond* (Princeton, 1986) and the author of *Managing Indonesia: The Modern Political Economy* (1993) and of *From Dominoes to Dynamos: The Transformation of Southeast Asia* (1994).

Frederick Z. Brown is a Fellow at the Foreign Policy Institute of the Johns Hopkins University School of Advanced International Studies, where he directs the Henry Luce Foundation program in Southeast Asia studies. Mr. Brown was a Department of State foreign service officer from 1958 to 1984, with assignments in France, Thailand, the Soviet Union, Vietnam, and Cyprus. From 1984 to 1987 Mr. Brown was professional staff member for East Asia and the Pacific of the United States Senate Committee on Foreign Relations. He was a senior associate at the Carnegie Endowment for International Peace from 1987 to 1988. Mr. Brown is a graduate of Yale (B.A.) and the University of Colorado (M.A.). He was a diplomat-in-residence at the University of Minnesota and Macalester College, St. Paul, 1978–80. He is the author of *Second Chance: The United States and Indochina in the 1990s* (1989), as well as numerous chapters in books on U.S. policy towards East Asia and the Pacific. He recently edited *Rebuilding Cambodia: Human Resources, Human Rights, and Law,* published by Johns Hopkins School of Advanced International Studies.

Masahiko Ebashi is Professor of International Economics at Meiji Gakuin University. Professor Ebashi worked for the Japan External Trade Organization (JETRO) from 1969 to 1987. While with JETRO, he was a consultant to the United Nations Economic and Social Commission for Asia and the Pacific (ESCAP) for the Asia Pacific Project and special assistant to the Japanese Ambassador to the Philippines. Professor Ebashi graduated in law from Waseda University. His recent articles include "Industrialization in Southeast Asia" in *Economy of Southeast Asia* (in Japanese, 1990), "A Structure of Poor Economic Growth in the Philippines" (in Japanese, 1991), and "New Zealand Links with Asia" (in English, 1992).

James W. Morley is Ruggles Professor Emeritus of Political Science at Columbia University and Co-chairman of its Pacific Basin Studies Program. Born in 1921, he received his B.A. from Harvard College in 1942, studied at the Fletcher School of Law and Diplomacy, 1942–43, and received his M.A. degree from the School of Advanced International Studies of Johns Hopkins University in 1945 and his Ph.D. from Columbia University in 1954. Formerly Chairman of the Political Science Department and Director of the East Asian Institute of Columbia University, he specializes in Japanese foreign policy and international relations in the Asia-Pacific region. His recent publications include, as co-author and editor, *Driven by Growth: Political Change in the Asia-Pacific Region* (1993) and as editor, *The Final Confrontation: Japan's Negotiations with the United States, 1941* (1994).

Masashi Nishihara is Professor of International Relations at the National Defense Academy of Japan. From 1970 to 1972 he was affiliated with Kyoto University's Center for Southeast Asian Studies in Jakarta; he then taught at Kyoto Sangyo University from 1973 to 1977. He was a Rockefeller Foundation Visiting Fellow in New York from 1981 to 1982. Professor

Nishihara is on the Council of the International Institute for Strategic Studies in London and is a member of the Trilateral Commission, as well as a member of the Japanese Committee for the Pacific Economic Cooperation Conference (PECC) and of the Japanese Committee for the Council for Security Cooperation in the Asia Pacific (CSCAP). Professor Nishihara graduated in Law from Kyoto University and earned both his M.A. and Ph.D. in political science from the University of Michigan. His recent publications include *New Roles for the Japan-U.S. Security Treaty* (1991) and *Northeast Asia and Japanese Security* (1993).

Tatsumi Okabe is Professor of International Relations at Tokyo Metropolitan University. He was a staff member of NHK (Japan Broadcasting Corporation) before working as a research fellow at the International Christian University. He was also Senior Researcher at the Japanese Embassy in Beijing from 1979 to 1980. Professor Okabe served as President of the Japan Association of Asian Political and Economic Studies from 1987 to 1989. He received his M.A. and Ph.D. in international relations from the University of Tokyo and studied at the University of Washington as a Fulbright scholar from 1960 to 1961. His recent publications include *Modernizing the Middle Kingdom* (in Japanese, 1989), *Twenty Years of ASEAN* (in Japanese, 1988; in English, 1989), *China During the Reform and Open-Door* (in Japanese, co-editor with Professor Mouri, 1991), and *International Politics, a Framework for Analysis* (in Japanese, 1992).

Yoshihide Soeya is Associate Professor of International Relations at Keio University. Before joining Keio University in 1988, he served as Academic Assistant at the Institute for International Relations of Japan's Sophia University and Researcher at the Research Institute for Peace and Security in Tokyo. Professor Soeya earned his B.A. and M.A. in international relations from Sophia University and his Ph.D. in political science from the University of Michigan. His recent publications include *Japanese Diplomacy and China 1945–1972* (in Japanese, forthcoming), "The Evolution of Japanese Thinking and Policies on Cooperative Security in the 1980s and 1990s" (in English, 1994), "Japan's Policy Toward Southeast Asia: Anatomy of 'Autonomous Diplomacy' and the American Factor" (in English, 1993), and "The Asia-Pacific and Japanese Diplomacy in the Post-Cold War Era" (in Japanese, 1993).

Seki Tomoda is Professor of International Relations at the Institute for Asian Studies of Asia University in Tokyo. Before joining the Institute, he was Professor at Sanyo Gakuen Junior College. He graduated from Waseda

University and worked as a staff writer on international affairs for the *Tokyo Shimbun* until 1962. He then joined the *Sankei Shimbun,* for which he served as correspondent in Saigon and Phnom Penh from 1967 to 1969 and in Paris in the late 1970s and later as an editorial writer. Professor Tomoda studied at the University of Montpelier and the University of Paris on a scholarship from the *Sankei Shimbun.* His major Japanese publications include *Betrayed Revolution of Vietnam* (1981), *Introduction to Contemporary Japanese Diplomacy* (1988), *New Currents in France* (co-author, 1988), and Japan's Search for a Political Role in Asia: The Cambodian Peace Settlement" (*Japan Review of International Affairs,* Spring 1992).

Donald S. Zagoria is Professor of Government at Hunter College and the Graduate Center of the City University of New York and Fellow at the East Asian Institute, Columbia University. He has for 35 years been a student of international politics, with a particular focus on Russia, China, and American policy in the Pacific region. Professor Zagoria studied at the Russian Institute of Columbia University when that institute first opened in the late 1940s. He gained his Ph.D. at Columbia in 1963. He is an Adjunct Professor of Government at Columbia. He is the author of *The Sino-Soviet Conflict* (1962) and *Soviet Triangle* (1969), and editor of *Soviet Policy in East Asia* (1982). He has also written more than three hundred articles.

List of Tables, Figures, and Maps

Overview

Vietnam Joins the World

James W. Morley and Masashi Nishihara

One of the most dramatic developments in Asia today is the reemergence of Vietnam—not as the belligerent champion of a militant ideology, but in the guise of a pragmatic, open, friendly country seeking a respected place in the world community. This is no small matter. With an energetic population of over 70 million, Vietnam is larger than any other nation in Southeast Asia except Indonesia. Its resources are rich and virtually untapped. Its location on the southern border of China and alongside the sea-lanes that link East and West gives it unique strategic leverage.

The Failure of Socialism

Vietnam, of course, is an ancient land, but it has rarely been able to be itself. Coveted by great powers throughout most of its known history, it was sequestered for centuries by the Chinese, then in the late nineteenth and early twentieth centuries by the French, and briefly during the Pacific War by the Japanese. It is hardly surprising, therefore, that when Ho Chi Minh and his comrades moved into Hanoi in 1945, their immediate agenda was to unite the country and liberate it from foreign control. The opposition of the French and the competition from the rival, non-Communist leadership, supported by the United States and others, was severe; but, after thirty years of nearly continuous war, success was attained. In 1975 Vietnam emerged, united and independent.

Nationalism, however, was not the Communist Party's only agenda. The party also was dedicated to realizing the dream of Marx and Lenin. It looked on itself as part of the world communist movement. It was convinced that the road to prosperity and a good life for the Vietnamese people lay through socialism. In the North in the 1950s and early 1960s the party had collectivized agriculture. Industrial production also, such as it was, became a state monopoly. But the requirements of war had distorted all production and distribution systems, and in any event, the South had not been involved.

When, in 1975, the party finally established its control nationwide, therefore, it was eager to collectivize the South and at last to complete what it called the "transition to socialism." It was also eager to emerge from the isolation that the war had engendered; and it proclaimed Vietnam's readiness to join the world community as a peaceful, friendly state.

But the efforts to build a socialist Eden proved disastrous. While throughout the North and, indeed, in much of the South, most of the Vietnamese people felt a deep gratitude toward the party for uniting the country and establishing its independence, there was little sentiment for further socialization. Collectives were doing badly. The attempt to extend them to the rural South was resisted so violently that it had to be called off.

The truth was, the people were exhausted. Most families had lost fathers, sons, or brothers in the decades of fighting. Those individuals who survived were physically impoverished by the wars' demands and psychologically drained by the relentless drives for national mobilization. The entire productive system was breaking down. Accurate data are unavailable, but the per capita income in the late seventies could not have been more than U.S.$200 a year, probably less. Absolute poverty was widespread.

Unfortunately for the regime, the state was incapable of responding. It had, in fact, under the relentless pressures of war, almost ceased to exist. The elective organs had atrophied. The executive agencies had become virtually crushed by the encircling vine of the party. Corruption was rampant.

The contrast with Vietnam's neighbors could not have been starker. The economies of Japan and the four tigers—Korea, Taiwan, Hong Kong, and Singapore—had long since left Vietnam behind. Those of Malaysia, Thailand, and Indonesia were taking off. Everywhere, central planning seemed to be failing. The engine of growth seemed to be private enterprises linked to the global market.

The efforts to emerge on the world scene also were frustrated by the regime's decision in 1978 to plunge back into war, this time in Cambodia. The purpose, it said, was to drive out the rogue Khmer Rouge, who had violated the Vietnam border, and to save the Khmer people from destruction. But the noncommunist world saw the Vietnamese move as an attempted land grab, designed to extend Vietnamese control over the entire Indochina peninsula. International support was extended to the opposition factions, even including the Khmer Rouge. In early 1979 the Chinese went so far as to invade the northern provinces, thereby pinning down a large portion of the Vietnamese forces at some distance from the Cambodian front.

The New Departure

In the succeeding years, the party's sense of crisis grew, climaxing in December 1986 at the Sixth National Party Congress. The death of Le Duan, its secretary general for the previous 26 years, permitted the completion of a nearly clean sweep of the old revolutionaries from the Political Bureau and the selection of a new leadership, under Secretary General Nguyen Van Linh, a reformer from the South. And with the old leaders went the old policies, which seemed to many of the party members to lead only to perpetual war and perpetual depression.

The decision for fundamental renovation, known as *doi moi,* was taken. Henceforth, all efforts were to be concentrated on economic growth; and since collectivization and central planning had failed to produce that result, socialization was to be slowed. State ownership and central planning were not to be wholly abandoned. Instead, alongside them was to be encouraged a supplementary economy of private enterprise, free markets, and global engagement. Ideology was stretched to accommodate.

To be effective, it was recognized, such a policy required a heavy infusion of capital, technology, and managerial skills from abroad. Accordingly, in May 1988 the party announced the adoption of a foreign policy less tied to the Soviet bloc. It rejuvenated its efforts to persuade the United States to normalize relations and Japan to resume economic assistance. It also began a campaign to feel out its neighbors in the Association of Southeast Asian Nations (ASEAN).

The building of a relationship with the noncommunist world, of course, required an end to Vietnam's invasion of Cambodia. Exactly when the decision was made to withdraw is not known, but the orders were clearly given in 1987. It was a painful decision—as painful, one might observe, as the withdrawal earlier of the American forces from Vietnam itself. The Vietnamese, after all, were exceedingly fearful of the return of the Khmer Rouge, who were seen as dangerous in themselves and also as the instruments of the even more dangerous anti-Vietnamese strategy of the Chinese. A policy of Cambodianization of the conflict was adopted, that is, of turning over responsibility to the government and forces of their protege, the People's Republic of Kampuchea, as a step-by-step withdrawal of Vietnamese troops was undertaken.

The operation was not completed until September 1989; and, in fact, the reality and permanence of the evacuation was not believed by most countries, at least those outside the Soviet Union and Eastern Europe, until October 1991, when Vietnam acceded to the international convention known as the Comprehensive Political Settlement of the Cambodian Problem, which set in motion the United Nations peace plan in that country.

By this time the Vietnamese situation was even more desperate. Over the years the budget of the country had become heavily dependent on Soviet subsidies. With the collapse of the Soviet Union in 1989, these subsidies had come to an end, confirming the necessity of Vietnam's withdrawal from Cambodia and making it more urgent to settle with China and widen the opening to its neighbors and the West.

Fortunately for Vietnam, China too, by the mid-1980s, had begun to think a rapprochement to be more and more desirable—as a condition for improving relations with the USSR, as a way to offset the relative isolation imposed on it by major Western powers following the Tiananmen incident, and later as an ideological tie that might strengthen its own internal cohesion in the face of the collapse of communism in Eastern Europe and the Soviet Union. In early September 1990 a secret summit meeting was held in Chengdu, China. There an understanding was reached on Cambodia; and in November 1991 Secretary General Do Muoi and Prime Minister Vo Van Kiet returned from Beijing to announce that China-Vietnam relations had been normalized, presumably on a pragmatic rather than a "comradely" basis as before.

The land border between China and Vietnam remains undetermined, and claims to the Spratly Islands are still contested. Both issues feed Vietnam's deep, historical concerns about possible Chinese designs on Vietnam and, indeed, on all of Southeast Asia. Nevertheless, Vietnam's trade with China is now flourishing, particularly with the neighboring Chinese provinces of Guangxi and Yunnan.

With most of its other adjacent neighbors, the six states grouped in ASEAN, Vietnam had long ago established diplomatic relations. The problem with these countries was to persuade them to relax such embargoes as they had imposed, following Vietnam's invasion of Cambodia. Vietnam's withdrawal from Cambodia and its signing of the 1991 peace accords opened ASEAN's doors.

Common economic interests in trade, investment, and growth are drawing these countries together. So is a common strategic suspicion of great powers, particularly China. Especially warm ties have developed with Indonesia and Singapore, but all of the ASEAN states have welcomed Vietnam back into the Southeast Asian fold, admitting Vietnam in 1993 to membership in ASEAN itself. Similar common interests have also drawn Taiwan into a warm relationship with Vietnam, resulting in Taiwan's business persons becoming the largest foreign direct investors in the country. Most of the Western powers also have responded eagerly. Diplomatic missions have been reinvigorated. Investments are picking up, trade is going forward, and aid money is flowing. The United States has been the major holdout, nursing its wounds from its disastrous war in Vietnam and refusing to recognize the change in direction that has taken place there. Even conversations with that regime were not resumed until July 1990, when Foreign Minister Nguyen Co Thach visited Washington and for the first time learned its terms: negotiations for normalization could not begin until a comprehensive settlement was reached in Cambodia. And even then, it was soon made clear, they could not go forward until there had been secured as complete an accounting as possible of all American prisoners of war and missing in action in the Vietnam War.

Over the past five years negotiations have continued on these issues. Gradually, following Vietnam's agreement to the Comprehensive Settlement in Cambodia and as it has showed increasing cooperation in settling the POW/MIA problem, the United States relaxed its position, ending the embargo on U.S. firms doing business and unblocking the international financial institutions, such as the World Bank and the International Monetary Fund, from responding to Vietnam's needs. Finally on July 11, 1995, President Bill Clinton announced his intention to establish full diplomatic relations, and the deed was done on August 5. More steps need to be taken before relations can be said to be normal, but the United States is no longer odd man out.

The American position had a serious impact on Vietnam, not only because of the potential in the bilateral relationship itself, but also because of the obstacle the United States posed for so long to Vietnam's access to the international financial institutions. It also deterred Japan from resuming as quickly as it would have preferred its large-scale aid program, which it suspended during Vietnam's war in Cambodia and which, together with trade and investment, it restrained for some time thereafter in deference to the wishes of its American ally.

But the American embargo did not prevent Vietnam's economic reform program from achieving some remarkable successes—more, most observers believe, than have most other socialist regimes attempting similar transformations. The reasons are no doubt multiple. The discipline of the Vietnamese work force is often cited. It may also be relevant to note that Vietnam has a smaller state sector and a smaller industrial sector than the other socialist countries, and the exposure of the whole country to central planning has been shorter—only since 1975 in the South.

But substantial credit must also go to the economic reforms it has adopted, particularly since 1989. The money supply has been brought under control. Government expenditures have been reduced. Land-use rights have been returned to peasant households. Prices and exchange rates have been freed. Banking reforms have been introduced. The number of state enterprises has been reduced, and private enterprise has been encouraged.

Vietnam's policy of opening its economy to the outside has been equally impressive. Since 1988 exports have increased by more than 30 percent per year. Commodities and official development aid have poured in, and foreign direct investment has begun.

The result is that from 1992 Vietnam seems to have entered a period of high growth. In that year the country's real GDP growth rate hit 8.6 percent. In 1993 it registered 8.1 percent. In 1994 the party's Central Committee was so encouraged that it raised the target still higher for the next six years. The average annual growth rate goal is now set at 9.55 percent, with the ambition of doubling the 1990 per capita income by the year 2000.

Problems Ahead

This is not to say that Vietnam faces only fair weather ahead. There are still serious obstacles to growth that must be overcome. A tangle of regulations and corruption still needs to be cleared away. State enterprises still need to be rationalized. Rural access to credit still needs to be unblocked. Ways to bring indigenous capital into play still need to be found. Further progress in building a legal system that supports the market structure and encourages both local and foreign investors is still required.

Even more serious is the continuing plight of the Vietnamese people. The benefits of the economic growth that has so far been achieved have not trickled down to the vast majority. The per capita GDP is still less than U.S.$200 per year. The demobilization of part of the armed forces and the downsizing of the civil bureaucracy and state enterprises have added to urban unemployment. The stimulus given to agricultural production by returning the land to household use in April 1988 has been salutary, but rural poverty remains the number-one social problem. Nearly all sectors of the population have suffered from a general decline in health and education as a result of the disruption of social services. The plague of corruption continues to spread.

So far the party seems to feel confident that it can manage the situation. Its prestige from having unified the country and won its independence remains strong, especially among the older generation, and the economic reforms have generated a feeling of hope. Moreover, the population has never known anything but autocratic rule, and, in any event, with all organized opposition having been liquidated, there is no alternative to the party—for the time being.

It is hardly surprising, therefore, that the reforms initiated in the 1980s and carried through in the 1990s have been limited in large part to the economic sphere. There have been some political changes, of course. Communications abroad have been opened up, for example. Intellectuals are encouraged to seek information and ideas wherever they can be found, provided they do not publish material critical of the party, its leaders, or socialism. The elected bodies, particularly the National Assembly, as well as the executive organs of the state, have been given clearer definition and greater powers. But, as reaffirmed in the new Constitution of 1992, the party is still the leading force in the society; it sets all policy, and it brooks no opposition.

Unfortunately for the party, it is not as unified as it once was. The economic policy advice being given by the World Bank and other external agencies is welcomed by the technocrats in Hanoi and Ho Chi Minh City, but major decisions must still be filtered through the party, and there the ideological lens has been fractured. "New thinking," dedicated to the new line of economic reform, and "old thinking," nostalgic for the old line of transition to socialism, clash on many issues. What are the appropriate roles of the state and the private sector, for example? How much foreign direct investment is advisable? Is it desirable that a capitalist middle class should be forming? What should be the objectives of development and industrial policy?

And what should be done about the pressures for greater participation in public affairs? As the "new thinking" and the economic reforms spread throughout the country, the solidarity of the population is being shaken by the reappearance of long-suppressed group identities. The peasants are asserting themselves against local "mandarins"; labor strikes are being reported; religious groups are demanding more autonomy; a veterans' movement has been co-opted by the party-state, but the veterans' restlessness with their impoverished condition persists; the Chinese feel deprived; and the hill tribes are protesting against the traditional discrimination.

The economy is still too undeveloped to have produced a sizable middle class, but one is clearly forming. One can only expect that, if the economy continues to grow over the next several decades and the lines of international communication remain open, such a middle class will become a formidable political force and will demand that the party-state abandon its monopoly of power. Will the transition be peaceful or violent? The issue has not yet been posed, but it is clearly on the horizon.

The Challenge for Japan and the United States

The reemergence of Vietnam in this new, dynamic form presents a serious challenge to the United States and Japan. As two of the most influential countries in the Asia-Pacific region, how we respond will have a major influence on the success of the reforms now under way. Our responses will also have a major impact on the development of the Asia-Pacific community that both of us are championing. And the degree to which our responses can be harmonized will have a direct bearing on the future viability of their own partnership. It is urgent, therefore, that we think through what kind of Vietnam we should like to see arise.

The authors believe that, fortunately, the same kind of Vietnam is in the interests of both Japan and the United States. It is one that is market oriented, democratically inclined, and militarily secure:

- market-oriented, because such a Vietnam provides more opportunities for our own business people; it becomes a more useful partner to the other countries in the region; and the social changes that economic growth produces will help propel Vietnam in a more liberal political direction;
- democratically inclined—a Vietnam that grows increasingly respectful of human rights and increasing liberal in its political system—because in the long run only such a Vietnam can satisfy its people and advance without cataclysmic disruption; and
- militarily secure, because only then can it continue to concentrate its energies on peaceful development; only then is it likely to cooperate fully in efforts for arms control and military transparency in the region; and only then, should an emergency arise in the region, will it be able to make a constructive contribution.

It would seem incumbent on us both, Japan and the United States, therefore, to explore ways to work together to bring this kind of Vietnam about. What can we do? The authors make the following recommendations:

- We should open our own markets, facilitate our own bilateral trade, investment, and technology transfers, and extend aid. At the same time we should support the full engagement of Vietnam in ASEAN, the Asia Pacific Economic Cooperation forum (APEC) and other regional economic structures.
- We should urge Vietnam to reduce its armed forces to a size that is economically sustainable and commensurate with its needs, while at

the same time offering what assistance we can to help professionalize those forces and involving them in regional security discussions.

- We should make our own values clear, support those in Vietnam that share them, and offer our assistance in building the legal and other infrastructures that the observance of human rights requires.
- We should launch vigorous programs of cultural exchange, offering to help improve Vietnam's educational system and including projects for bringing Vietnamese students to study in our countries and for improving our own study of Vietnam.
- Finally, we should encourage our nongovernmental organizations to develop active programs of their own in Vietnam.

Are we up to the challenge?

Reform at Home

1

Politics in Transition

James W. Morley

Vietnam, like China, is conducting a political experiment of historic proportions, testing whether a communist party-state can liberalize its economic
system without weakening the dictatorship of the party.

Since the late 1970s, when the Vietnamese leadership first began to
accept the fact that the dream of the revolutionary generation had failed,
Vietnam has come a long way, thanks particularly to the economic reform
program inaugurated at the Communist Party's Sixth Party Congress in
December 1986. It was then, following years of experimentation with new
models, that the party decided to deconstruct its Soviet-style command
economy.

On that occasion the party recognized also that the political system was
not in good shape. Over some forty years of nearly constant warfare, decay
had set in. As described in the *Political Report* adopted by the congress, the
leadership had failed to renew itself.[1] The organs of the state as well as the
party had been allowed to grow "too big" and "overlapping." Cadres had
become dissolute. "Social justice" was being denied. Corruption and the
abuse of power were flagrant. As a result, the party had not adapted itself to
changing circumstances as rapidly as it should have, and "the confidence of
the masses in the party leadership and the functioning of state organs" was
weakening.

There was no sense that the system itself was at fault. The leadership was
convinced that the party's control was still secure. The former military
officers and civilian officials of the defeated southern regime had been
safely put away in reeducation camps, and among the remaining population,
in spite of a growing sense of frustration, there had been no riots or strikes,
or even demonstrations. In any event, the delegates knew that it was the
party that had led the country to victory in the war for independence and

unification, and they were convinced now that it was only the party that could bring victory in the struggle for economic reform.

No, it was not the Leninist model of the party-state that was at fault. Rather, it was the abuses to which it had been subjected. The call for reform of the polity, therefore, was not for transformation of the system as in the economy, but for the tightening of the "proletarian dictatorship" and for a rectification of the party's "shortcomings" in ideological and organizational activity and in its cadre work: in short, a return to first principles.

Whether such a "renovated" Leninist system can long endure is a question. For there are reasons to believe that the anomalous attempt to graft the mixed capitalist economy, now being experimented with, on a Leninist political system, even one rectified as envisaged by the Sixth Party Congress, is bound to fail. Already social changes are eating at the system. Eventually more fundamental political changes would seem to be required. The question is: what form will these changes take, and when and how will they come about?

Doi Moi: Reform within Limits

When the delegates to the Sixth National Party Congress met in December 1986, their first imperative was to rejuvenate the leadership. Ho Chi Minh had passed from the scene in 1969, but many of his old revolutionary comrades had continued in power long after. Le Duan, for example, who had been elected secretary general in 1960, was still in office 26 years later. Others had continued even longer, exercising power from within the Central Committee and the Political Bureau (Politburo), the party's ultimate seat of power. They found it difficult to adjust to new circumstances, yet they were reluctant to go, and the party was reluctant to force them out. Factional fights and coups were not in the party style.

Nevertheless, there could be no renovation without new faces. In fact, the effort to rejuvenate the Political Bureau had already begun. In 1976, several new members had been added, including the conservative Vo Chi Cong, a leader in the effort to socialize the South, and the reform-minded Nguyen Van Linh and Do Muoi, each later to hold the post of secretary general. In 1982, the retirement of six of the old comrades from the Politburo had brought in additional new blood and at the same time had opened the way for a second generation of leaders to move into responsible party and state positions. Among the new Politburo members and alternate members, for example, Nguyen Co Thach, a reforming technocrat, was named foreign minister; Nguyen Duc Tam was made chief of the party's Organization Department; General Van Tien Dung became minister of national defense; and Vo Van Kiet, another economic reformer, was given the office of vice premier.[2] But several key elders hung on.

It was the death of Le Duan six months before the Party Congress in 1986 that finally enabled the party to complete the transition. All but one of the remaining first-generation seniors were finally eased out of the bureau. Nguyen Van Linh, a southerner and an economic reformer, was given the supreme post, that of secretary general. At the same time, the membership in the Central Committee was expanded from 152 to 173. In the process, representation from the military and from central state and party offices was reduced. Administrators and technicians from the provinces now held the plurality.[3]

The surviving elders were not rusticated. The first-generation leaders retiring from the Politburo were made "advisers" to the Central Committee. The premiership, technically a position determined by election by the National Assembly, but actually like all important posts decided by the Politburo acting through party members in the assembly, was left for another year in the hands of Pham Van Dong, who had held the post for the past 32 years. The following year it was transferred to Pham Hung, the last of the early revolutionaries still in the Politburo. It was not until 1988, when Pham Hung died, that the premiership passed out of the hands of the first generation, going briefly to Vo Van Kiet, then later to a co-member of the Politburo class of 1976, Do Muoi.

It would be difficult to exaggerate the importance of this generational transition. Its peaceful accomplishment greatly strengthened the belief of the party in itself at a very critical time, and while individuals in the new leadership cohort have changed offices from time to time, the cohort itself has proved to be remarkably durable.

Having resolved the leadership question and having enjoined the cadres —once again—to observe strict party discipline, the delegates turned their attention to what the *Political Report* called the party's "shortcomings." These were acknowledged to be primarily in the areas of ideology and organization.

Not that there was any inclination to challenge the "truth" of "Marxism-Leninism and the Thought of Ho Chi Minh." After all, that doctrine provided the fundamental rationale for the party's monopoly of power. Nor was there any inclination to challenge the doctrine's overarching programmatic conception that the nation's fundamental task was to complete the "transition to socialism." But the delegates were acutely aware that the "transition" had been taking an intolerably long time and that efforts to speed it up, most recently the frantic effort to collectivize the South following the end of the war, had brought not the increased productivity expected, but an intensification of poverty. How was this to be explained without vitiating the underlying theory?

The party's first attempt had been to lower expectations. At the Fifth National Congress four years earlier it was suggested that the party's understanding of the Vietnamese reality had been incorrect and therefore its application of theory had been faulty.[4] The party had tried to move too rapidly. It had been wrong in pushing so hard so early for collectivization and heavy industrialization. The further pursuit of these tasks—though ultimately required—would have to be deferred to a later time. Vietnam had been and still was simply too weighted with an impoverished rural population for the fruits of socialism to be within grasp. Regrettably, said the Central Committee, the party had to recognize that the country was still only in the "first stage" of the transition to socialism and that compromises with the old order were still unavoidable.

By the time of the Sixth Congress in 1986, it had become much clearer that a simple slowing of the pace of collectivization and heavy industrialization was not going to be sufficient to get the economy going. The rapid advance of Asia's newly industrializing economies—South Korea, Taiwan, Hong Kong, and Singapore, together with the success of various local experiments, offered convincing evidence that private entrepreneurship was a more powerful engine of growth than the state enterprises that the party had been favoring. In accord with this pragmatic understanding, the "general line" was adopted to reopen the economy nationally to the forces of the market and the enterprise of private individuals.

How to explain this ideologically? Taking a leaf from the new line adopted by the Soviet Communist Party at its Twenty-Seventh Congress earlier that year, the party decided to give the "first stage" conception more positive content. Vietnam's economic problems had arisen, the *Political Report* contended, from misapplying the Marxist theory of the necessary stages of development, namely, that the transition to socialism could not be successfully undertaken until capitalism had done its essential work. In its enthusiasm, the party had tried to skip the capitalist stage and construct socialism in an economy that was not ready for it. The correct line now, therefore, was to go back, to acknowledge the positive role that private entrepreneurship had yet to play, and to accept the new task for the present stage, not of intensifying socialist construction, but rather of building a mixed economy, embracing alongside the socialist sectors a powerful non-socialist sector that would be integrated in the world economy.

For this task to be accomplished, the country would need to overhaul the institutional structure, open the doors to "new thinking," and elicit more active public participation. In the early years of the republic before the party's exclusive control was established, people's councils had been set up locally and a National Assembly had been instituted centrally. These bodies had been heralded as elected organs of the new state. Mass organizations, such as the unions for youths, women, peasants, and others, also had been established in the early years, essentially to secure the people's active participation in the implementation of the party's decisions. It was not long, however, under the exigencies of war, before the elected bodies withered. Elections became sporadic. Nominees became limited to individuals vetted by the party. Whatever real power these bodies had had in the beginning or had been expected to have was soon taken over by individuals and administrative instruments appointed directly by the party. The councils and the National Assembly became essentially rubber stamps and the mass organizations largely conveyor belts for party directives and requisitions.

Again as in the case of the ideology, the fault was found not in the original principles. The basic model of the party as commander, the state as executor, and the people as supporter was not questioned. The fault was found rather in failing to articulate each of these roles correctly and to establish effective institutions to coordinate them.

The party needed to retain its role as the authoritative leader, deciding the "general line," setting forth the tasks to be accomplished, and checking to see that the work was done. To do this, it needed to reinvigorate its allegiance to the principles of democratic centralism, collective leadership, individual responsibility, and submission by the minority to the majority, by the lower to the higher echelons, and by the whole party to the Central Committee.[5]

But it needed also to get out of direct administration. That was the job of the state, and to carry out that job effectively the various organs of the state needed to be respected and strengthened. At the time, the peak of state authority was ostensibly the Council of State, often referred to as the "collective chairman."[6] It served as the National Assembly's standing committee and had the power to interpret the constitution and to annul or modify decrees of the Council of Ministers. It also supervised the work of the Supreme People's Court and the Supreme People's Procurate; its chairman also served, ex officio, as commander in chief of the armed forces and chairman of the National Defense Council. A second organ, the Council of Ministers, was charged with making day-to-day administrative decisions and supervising the work of the state bureaucracy. Over the years both of these bodies had been chaired by senior Politburo members and run by cadres under party discipline. They had become virtual appendages of the party. Now, it was felt, their structures needed to be streamlined, their duties defined, and a "direct expert-type work style" adopted.

In addition, both the party and the state needed to secure more effectively the participation of the people in the implementation of their programs. "Elected" bodies needed to be given serious legislative responsibilities. The people's councils at all levels needed to be freed from the domination of the appointed administrative committees. Members to all these representational bodies needed to be less forcibly recruited, and in general the people needed to be listened to more carefully.

Finally, "socialist legality" needed to be observed. The arbitrary exercise of power by the party-state and its organs and the protection of such behavior by the security apparatus had to cease. If the party and the state were to retain the support of the people and become efficient organs of economic development, they needed to shift to a rule of law. All organs of the state needed to be organized and operated "in accordance with the law," all cadres needed to live and work "in strict compliance with the law," and all citizens needed to be recognized as being "equal before the law."

By such reforms it was hoped that the political system could be made more efficient and more responsive—without changing its Leninist character. Modest though the political reforms were, their success, like the success of the economic reforms then being inaugurated, obviously required the restoration of peace. Except for the brief period between the end of the war for unification in 1975 and the beginning of operations in Cambodia in 1979, the making of war had been the central preoccupation of the party and the state. As the Sixth National Party Congress met, more than one million regulars were under arms. Several millions more were serving in the militia, self-defense, and local back-up forces. Expeditionary units were fighting the Khmer Rouge in Cambodia, while the main units were crouching in readiness to defend the northern border against China.

With victory nowhere in sight, Vietnam impoverished, and Soviet support weakening, a drastic decision was called for. The assumption of withdrawal was therefore part and parcel of the renovation decision. Sometime between April and June 1987 the Politburo issued a secret directive, referred to thereafter as Politburo Resolution 2, that set forth a wholly new national defense policy. It called for systematic withdrawal from Cambodia, the reduction in force of the Vietnam People's Army (VPA), the creation of a "ready reserve" of the demobilized soldiers, and changes in force, structure, and assignments, the latter stressing expanded responsibilities for local defense and economic reconstruction.[7] Especially important was the renewed emphasis on economic reconstruction, a task that the VPA had been given at the end of the war for unification but that had had to be deemphasized during the Cambodian war.

The Struggle to Implement the Line

In the years that have followed, strenuous efforts have been made to implement the line enunciated in 1986. It has been an experimental process, characterized by advance, retreat, and consolidation.

The state has been restructured and given a far more important role than ever before. Under the new Constitution, adopted in 1992, the elected National Assembly has been elevated as "the highest representative organ of the people and the highest organ of state power."[8] It has been entrusted with most of the oversight functions formerly exercised by the Council of State, which has been abolished. In addition, the assembly is empowered to elect the newly revived president, who serves as chief of state, commander of the armed forces, and chairman of the National Defense and Security Council. It is also empowered to elect other high central officials, including the chairman of the National Assembly, the prime minister, cabinet ministers, the president of the Supreme People's Court, and the head of the Supreme People's Office of Supervision and Control.

The oversight and control functions, of course, are additional to the assembly's legislative function. This too has been strengthened, the government now being specifically obligated to submit to the assembly the plan for socioeconomic development, the national budget, and all national financial and monetary policies.

The assembly has undoubtedly acquired a new assertiveness. Officials are interpellated and criticized. More and more bills are being submitted to it, and they are often vigorously debated. In 1993, nearly three dozen pieces of legislation were drafted, including a significant new Land Law.[9] Additional laws were debated and passed at the June 1994 session, including ones giving the people's councils more authority and labor unions a limited right to strike.

The National Assembly's enhanced role reflects the party's search for ways not only to increase the efficiency of the system, but also to "democratize" it, in the "socialist" sense—that is, to open the system to constructive public criticism and to secure greater popular participation in implementing the system's decisions. Electoral practices were closely examined. New election laws were passed. To bring the electors closer to the candidates and give the electors a sense of choice, National Assembly election districts have been reduced in size, independent candidates have been permitted to run, efforts have been made to increase the number of candidates per seat, and at campaign time more open debate has been encouraged.

Between the elected bodies and the people, indeed between the party-state and the people, stretched the vast, decaying mass organizations: the

Vietnam Fatherland Front and its components, including principally the Vietnam Women's Union, the Ho Chi Minh Communist Youth Union, the Vietnam Peasants' Union, and the Vietnam Confederation of Workers.[10] Since the Sixth Party Congress, the effort has been made to revive them. Ostensibly they have been given extraordinarily wide, quasi-governmental powers. According to the Constitution of 1992,

> The front promotes the tradition of national solidarity, strengthens the people's unity of mind in political and spiritual matters, participates in the building and consolidation of people's power, works together with the state for the care and protection of the people's legitimate interests, encourages the people to exercise their right to mastery, ensures the strict observance of the Constitution and the law, and supervises the activity of state organs, elected representatives, and state official and employees.[11]

Modest reforms have been instituted. The Peasants' Union, for example, has opened its membership to all farmers, not just to members of cooperatives.[12] Labor unions, which function much as mass organizations, have opened their committee elections to self-nominated candidates. The party has enjoined party committees to respect the organizational independence of all these organizations.[13] And countless public meetings have been held to sound reactions to changes that are contemplated.

In addition, the party has not failed to recognize that the creation and management of a mixed economy, linked to the world system, is as impossible a dream as communism unless the requisite technical experts can be trained and recruited. Accordingly, the party's traditional hostility to "the intelligentsia" has been scrapped. Under the Constitution of 1992 for the first time the educated elite have been admitted into the alliance of the working class and the peasantry, on which all state power is theoretically based. The educated elite are now eagerly encouraged to enter the party and to accept state offices. Their colleagues in the higher research institutions have been freed to pursue their research wherever it leads: to secure all the information they can from the outside, to travel abroad, to exchange views with experts of all ideological persuasions, and to feed their observations and proposals into party central.

The public too has been urged to turn a critical eye on the behavior of officials. In May 1987, shortly after the end of the Sixth Party Congress, the new secretary general, Nguyen Van Linh, began publishing a column in the party newspaper, *Nhan Dan,* under his own initials criticizing various officials for corruption and malfeasance. In 1987 the party announced that every citizen had the same right.[14] By early 1988 *Nhan Dan* was receiving almost 300 complaint letters a day.

In the early years of the new line, state subsidies to the publishing houses were reduced, forcing editors to enliven their appeal to readers and advertisers. The embargo on foreign news, television programs, and films from nonsocialist countries was lifted. Licensing requirements went unenforced. Prepublication censorship was dropped. The party seems to have had in mind that such a loosening of publication controls would enliven the people's cultural life and particularly encourage the intelligentsia to offer their "new thinking" for renovating the economy. What it got when the lid was lifted was an outburst of not only "new" thinking, but unacceptable thinking.

There was the desired cultural flowering. Pre-1975 works were republished, and new novels, plays, and films appeared. The video cassette industry blossomed. But in the popular press there appeared also articles on drug addiction, prostitution, draft evasion, and other topics formerly prohibited.[15] In the official press articles appeared not only criticizing the implementation of the party line, but revealing that the consensus reached at the Sixth Party Congress was more fragile than had been supposed.

A group of southern veterans within the party had already given some evidence of that. Led by General Tran Van Tra, a former zone commander in the South and military governor of Saigon immediately after the victory, they had organized an unauthorized "Club of Former Resistance Fighters" and published their own newspaper. They seemed to have ambitions of becoming a kind of intraparty bargaining group, pressing its own program and candidates on the party.[16] In 1988 they went so far as to champion Vo Van Kiet for premier against the chosen candidate of the Politburo.

Later that year a prominent party intellectual, writing in the official trade union press, challenged the party's relationship with the working class and called for a much greater freedom of opinion.[17] The next year several even more radical articles appeared in the party's own theoretical journal. One writer questioned whether Marxism-Leninism, the doctrinal basis on which the party's monopoly of power rested, was a suitable guide for Vietnam in its present stage of development. What the country needed with its multisector economy, he felt, was a multiparty political system, the "pluralism in political parties and ideology" that was practiced in bourgeois states.[18]

With views such as these swelling up within the party, the Central Committee decided that enough was enough. At its Sixth Plenum on March 20–29, 1989, it denounced political pluralism and ordered a reverse course.[19] Regulations on the media were strengthened, and eight journals were banned.[20] In August the Central Committee declared a proscription of what might be called the three "no's": no calling into question the leadership of the Communist Party, no calling into question the one-party state, and no pluralism, or multiparty democracy.[21]

Secretary General Nguyen Van Linh, the leader of the reform, sensitive to the reaction that was building, had discontinued his column months before. Now in a speech on September 1 he made the argument for reaction.[22] No new multiparty ideology was needed, he maintained, because, even at the present stage when a multisector economy was being constructed, all sectors were being "transformed by the state in the direction of socialism." Moreover, there being no conflict of interest between classes, the nonsocialist sectors did not need to be represented in the political system. On September 30 he came down harder, declaring in a statement reminiscent of an earlier one by Mao Zedong, that between "capitalist dictatorship" (the party's orthodox characterization of liberal democracy) and "proletarian dictatorship" there was no "middle path."[23]

Controls over the press were tightened. In October Prime Minister Do Muoi admonished journalists that, "generally speaking, the press in our country is the voice of the party" and "should reflect the party's viewpoint and stance."[24] Shortly thereafter some of the more prominent deviationists were purged. Tran Xuan Bach, a pluralistically inclined member of the Politburo, was ousted from that body in March 1990.[25] The writer Duong Thu Huong and Bui Tin, former deputy editor of the party paper, *Nhan Dan,* and the officer who had taken the surrender of South Vietnamese forces in 1975, were expelled from the party. The chairman and vice chairman of the Club of Former Resistance Fighters were forced to resign. The organization itself was restructured as an officially authorized mass organization, known now as the Vietnam Veterans Association, and brought under the umbrella of the Vietnam Fatherland Front.[26] Countless, nameless other individuals deemed to be counterrevolutionary were sent to the "reeducation" camps.

At the Seventh National Party Congress June 24–27, 1991, a new Central Committee was elected that in turn put a new Politburo in place, one that dropped the three most senior members, including the reform-leading secretary general Nguyen Van Linh; brought in eight new members; and raised to the top three positions Do Muoi as number one, General Le Duc Anh, as number two, and Vo Van Kiet as number three.[27] Do Muoi, known as a skilled political manager, came from the North; he was elected the party's new secretary general. Le Duc Anh, the army's most prestigious general, came from the middle of the country; then minister of defense, he was shortly named president of the republic. Vo Van Kiet, with a solid reputation as an economic reformer, came from the South; he replaced Do Muoi as premier.[28]

Symbolizing in themselves the regime's tripod of power—the party, the army, and the state—these three were designed not to stop the reform—all believed in the reform—but to stabilize the regime in the face of the arguments that the reform had been generating and to reaffirm the party's control of the political pace.

An attempt was made at this time to reclarify the degree of autonomy to be accorded the state and its organs. But the result was muddied. The party, declared the new secretary general, should of course "refrain from making decisions on behalf of state organs"—a conception presumably implemented in part by reducing the number of Central Committee departments and forbidding them to approach state organs directly. But, Do Muoi emphasized, the party must set forth its "concepts, orientations, and principles" and offer "guidance" to all. The fundamental proposition, he said, is that the party "is to rule over the state and not to act according to the state's orders."[29]

So far, most of the key decisions dismantling the command structure of economic management have been made by the Politburo and the Central Committee.[30] Moreover, the National Assembly still meets for only a few weeks annually. It has little expertise of its own. Its membership, like those of the people's councils, is still dominated by party members whom the party recommends for election and who are habituated to taking their "guidance" from the party central.[31] High party officials still head these organizations, and the Fatherland Front still drafts the slate of candidates for all elected bodies—under party direction. Independents may now run, and a few have tried, but none have been elected.

The new constitution adopted in 1992 puts the matter succinctly and unequivocally. The Communist Party of Vietnam is still "the vanguard of the working class."[32] It is still "the force leading the state and society." It still acts on "the Marxist-Leninist doctrine and Ho Chi Minh's thought."[33] Its decisions continue to be made according to the principle of "democratic centralism."[34]

The VPA's withdrawal from Cambodia was completed in 1989 and the downsizing of the forces seems to have proceeded pretty much as envisaged, with about one-half having been returned to civilian life[35] and more and more units having been assigned under the army's Economic General Department to duties in agriculture, industry, transport, communications, and capital construction, profits being divided between the unit and the Ministry of Defense.

These changes have obviously been disruptive. Moreover, the flowering of many voices in the first years of the reform, the emergence of General Tran Van Tra's independent veterans' movement in the South, and particularly the collapse of the USSR and the fraternal East European regimes in 1989 sent a real chill through the leadership. After all, the Vietnam People's

Army and the supporting forces reached into nearly every family in Vietnam. They have been a principal recruiting ground for the party. They have been also a principal support of the party's hold on power and a principal executor of the party's will. Most of their officers have been party members. Senior officers have been prominent in the highest organs of the party and the state. The loyalty of the troops is absolutely essential to the survival of the regime.

The reaction to discontent in the armed forces, therefore, has been swift. To the campaign against multipartyism was added a campaign against the so-called depoliticization of the army. At the Fifth All-Army Party Organization Congress in April 1991 the call went out for the armed forces "to have 'absolute faith' in the leadership of the Vietnam Communist Party and to become an 'active arm' of its politics." The congress also reaffirmed the VPA's determination to "defend the party and the socialist regime."[36] At the Seventh National Party Congress in June 1991, even stronger language was used, asserting the party's "absolute, direct control." In August 1992 the Central Committee restored political officers and party committees in each unit—the traditional mechanism of party control that had been abolished ten years earlier. And in October, General Le Duc Anh was elected president of the republic.

How Has Stability Been Maintained?

So far, the strategy adopted in 1986 and pursued thereafter has been remarkably successful. As the mixed economy comes slowly into being, trade is expanding, the gross national product is rising, and the world is welcoming Vietnam into the fold. Moreover, in spite of the disruptions caused by changing economic policies, the party has maintained its control. Dissent has been managed. Powerful opposition forces have not emerged as in the Soviet Union and Eastern Europe, nor have there been any Tiananmens, as in China. Why should this be so?

History may provide a partial explanation. The Vietnamese population has long accustomed itself to autocratic rule. In one form or another, from the days of the early kingdoms to the adoption of the Chinese imperial model in the fifteenth century and on to the imposition of French colonial administration in the late nineteenth and early twentieth centuries, Vietnam has always been ruled by arbitrary governments over which the common people have had little or no influence.[37] When the Communists followed suit, they were seen by most Vietnamese as simply following a long tradition to which they had become inured.

To be sure, an autocratic past does not make Vietnam unique. Most states in the world have autocratic pasts. But, in many of these states, as economic development has taken place and contacts with the outside have increased, society has been transformed. The hold of traditional autocratic values has weakened and more liberal, more participatory values have come to the fore. Vietnam under the French had a brief foretaste of that experience in the late nineteenth and early twentieth centuries. As business flourished, the cities, particularly Hanoi and Saigon, began to grow. A group of wealthy merchants began to form. Other Vietnamese became doctors, lawyers, and civil servants. A few others became writers. Newspapers and magazines flourished. But through the end of the French period, this incipient middle class remained small and relatively isolated. Its hunger for Western life styles had little influence on the mass of the people, from whom it was largely alienated. When the Communists first took over, therefore, they faced a largely preindustrial society, a nation essentially of poor farmers, toiling in the fields with traditional methods, and looking for guidance in the wearying round of their lives to the authoritarian, family-centered, village-circumscribed values of their ancestors. And so, in large part, they do today.

But at least by the older generation and particularly in the North, the party today is more than tolerated. Most visitors in recent years have come away with the impression that there is genuine support for the party. When older Vietnamese are asked why, in view of the wringer through which so many of them have been put and the catastrophic failures of so many of the economic policies the party has pursued, they frequently answer to the effect: "But, don't you see? we didn't support the party in the beginning because of its communist program, and we don't fault it now for the failures of that program. We joined it, we fought for it, and many of us died for it because it led us to victory in the struggle to free the nation and to unify it, and we shall always be grateful." Then, after a pause, comes an additional reason: "In any event, there is no alternative." That at the moment also seems to be part of the explanation of Vietnam's political stability. So also is the attitude of the younger generation, one less of positive support than apathy.

It is also important to note that the gutting of such representative institutions as had been established in the early years has given little opportunity even to those elements that have been most cooperative with the regime to learn the art of politics outside the party. As for those elements that opposed the party, most have been destroyed. During the thirty years from 1945 to 1975 when the party was fighting what it calls "the people's national democratic revolution," it built a powerful security force. Comprising of the people's army, the people's police, and the people's courts, that apparatus effectively eliminated individual "enemies," punished landlords, crushed the anticommunist parties, and intimidated the religious sects.[38] Following the fall of the southern regime in 1975, the South's former civilian officials, military officers, and intellectual supporters were targeted, some for execution, most for incarceration in the so-called reeducation camps. Since the beginning of the national economic reform program in 1986, this particular group of "counterrevolutionaries" has finally been released, but the party has not slackened its vigilance. All individuals and groups suspected of disloyalty to the party have been and are systematically ferreted out, constrained, executed, or driven abroad.

The party of course gives a different answer, crediting a large part of its success to its strategy: on the one hand, recognizing earlier than the Soviet and Eastern European communist leaders that the economy needed a radical overhaul, and on the other, rejecting the notion that became popular in the Western communist systems that effective economic reform required the dismantling of the Leninist party-state dictatorship. Certain it is that the party had caught some of its mistakes before they proved fatal.

But the future may not be so kind.

The Challenges Ahead

The party has shown that it is capable of making wrenching decisions. It has been able to change its historic priorities from the making of war to the promotion of economic development, and it has shown that it is prepared to scrap its long-held devotion to collectivization—at least for the immediate future—if that is what economic growth requires. It has restored the peasant-farmer's right to use the land, recognized the worker's right to bargain collectively and in some cases to strike, and eased discrimination against the private business person. It has also invited foreign investment, pushed foreign trade, and begun to build the institutional structure needed for the market to operate. And yet, much remains to be done if the mixed economic system is to succeed. The massive state-run enterprises have yet to be privatized. The legal and financial systems have yet to be perfected. The physical infrastructure has yet to be built. The education system has yet to be involved. Private investment by the Vietnamese themselves has yet to be released. And no one can say when these changes are made where they will lead, whether the present concept of a unique multisectoral economy is achievable or whether the private sector will eventually take over, or indeed whether progress will continue to be made at all. Nor can one say whether the party will have the courage and the expertise to meet the economic requirements of growth wherever they may lead and whether it will have the acumen to bridge the fissures that are now opening up—between the

North and the South, the cities and the countryside, the old and the young, and the rich and the poor.

What one can say, however, is that the party has not yet accepted the likely social and political consequences of its actions, both for itself and for the nation. It is deeply aware that its strength is eroding. Despite the good intentions proclaimed at the party congress in 1986 and the calls for party reform repeated by party leaders many times ever since, morale is declining. Stories appear frequently in the press of arbitrary actions taken by local cadres quite out of line with directives from party central. Corruption is widespread. According to a party study in 1989, less than one-third of the party's members retain their "revolutionary" zeal.[39] "The police are drunk," one official recently complained, "the party bosses in the countryside are trying to accumulate land, and the sons of the bosses are running private companies. The party has lost its heroic past."

The party is also losing its relevance. The war for national unification is long since over. The war in Cambodia also has been brought to a close. The people, who have been asked to sacrifice so much for so long, are exhausted. A political apathy grips the nation. Old members are quitting the party, and the recruitment of new members is down, from 100,000 in 1987 to 66,000 in 1989, to 36,000 in 1991.[40] By 1991 party membership had fallen to some two million (roughly 3 percent of the population nationwide and only 1 percent in the south).

The vast majority of the people want nothing so much as to get their lands and shops back, restore their family ties, and get on with their private lives. The younger generation, on the other hand, scenting a new freedom in the air, are eager to strike out on their own—for themselves. It is not party membership, but the prospect of going into business for oneself that puts sparkle in the eye.

The trend toward privatization is being fed also by the reforms themselves. Economic "renovation" is breaking the state's domination of the economy, and the opening to the outside is destroying the party's monopoly of information. Older special interests are reasserting themselves. New and varied ideas are circulating, and new interest groups are forming. A process of social differentiation is taking place that is eating away at the party's control.[41]

Among the older groups, the clergy have become most active. Whether Buddhist, Christian, Cao Dai or Hua Hoa, they have always been rivals of the state and the party for leadership in Vietnamese society. On occasion they have played powerful political roles. The Christians, for example, supported the southern regime in the 1950s and 1960s. The Cao Dai and the Hua Hoa opposed it. The Buddhists helped to bring it down. That is a history the Communists remember well, and while always proclaiming freedom of belief, they have sought determinedly to destroy the autonomy of church organizations.[42] In the past the party shut down the schools, hospitals, and orphanages run by the various religious establishments. It closed the seminaries. It asserted its authority over the ordination, selection, and transfer of religious leaders and imprisoned the recalcitrants. In the aftermath of the 1986 reform decision, most clergy were released from prison, a few seminaries were allowed to reopen, and limited social work has been allowed to resume. Attendance at churches and pagodas is up.

But the struggle between the clergy and the party has not been resolved. The Catholic Church is still fighting the regime's insistence on approving Vatican appointments and its efforts to draw priests into the National Assembly and the mass organizations. The Buddhist clergy also has been active in trying to prevent the co-optation of its leaders. The effort to replace the more autonomous Unified Buddhist Church (UBC) organization by a new Vietnam Buddhist Church that is under political supervision is being met with resistance. UBC Secretary General Thich Quang Do and Executive Director Thich Huyen Quang have been outspoken. Both have been removed and exiled to other pagodas. But the mass demonstrations that greeted the speech of Quang at the funeral of Thich Don Hau, another critic of the party, demonstrates the continuing strength of autonomous Buddhist sentiment.

Even more direct political action has been taken by a newer group, the war veterans. The formation of the Club of Former Resistance Fighters in the 1980s and its championing of greater reforms than the party was ready for reveals that among the war veterans, numbering in a 1991 estimate some four million,[43] there is also a sense of identity and interest separate from the party's. "Most soldiers thought they were struggling for social equality, democracy, liberty and national reconstruction," says Bao Ninh, a veteran and author of *The Sorrow of War,* one of Vietnam's most popular novels of 1991. "But after 16 years few things in this beautiful picture have been realized . . . most real soldiers are unhappy and disappointed."[44] Many have found it difficult to get employment.

But the intellectuals have been the most consistently outspoken. The measures taken in 1989 and after to reinforce the limits on public discussion have been relatively successful. Generally speaking, there are no longer public speeches or publicly published and circulated articles attacking the leadership of the party or the legitimacy of the one-party state. The infrequent violators are jailed. But intellectuals—students, professors, scientists, writers, think tankers, and technocrats in state and party service—evince little hesitation in reading the literature and listening to the tapes and radio and television broadcasts they prefer. Nor do they appear to be constrained in following their thoughts where they will and expressing their views privately. One, the mathematician Phan Dinh Dieu, went so far in 1991 as to recommend liberal democracy to the party's secretary general.[45] Publicly the lid is on, but privately the cauldron is bubbling.

Other sectors—peasant farmers, industrial workers, private entrepreneurs, and ethnic minorities—also are showing an increasing awareness of their autonomous interests. Collectivization of agriculture was never popular. It was accomplished in the North in the late 1950s only with violence. The drive in the South, following unification, was likewise met with resistance and finally had to be called off. The reforms that have now restored the land to private use, if not ownership, have eased the tension. But disputes over land ownership, frequently with corrupt party officials who are attacked locally as "mandarins," continue to trouble the countryside.[46]

Locally, too, private entrepreneurs, particularly the petty business people dispersed widely throughout the country, also can hardly be said to be under close party control.[47] Despite past efforts of the party to close them down, they have proved to be amazingly resilient. The so-called black market probably supplies more of the everyday needs of the population than the state-run distribution system, and now that the free market is acquiring legitimacy, the native entrepreneurs, like the Chinese business people, are not waiting for party authorization to expand their activities.

The Chinese, of course, have always been a community apart.[48] Historically, despite the fact that they contributed skilled workers and dominated Vietnam's trade, manufacturing, and banking sectors, they kept largely to themselves along the Chinese border or in the Cholon quarter of Saigon. They took little part in politics and remained socially isolated, speaking their own language, providing their own education, and caring for their own in need. The community was devastated by the party's action in 1975 to close all remaining private companies and all private schools and hospitals. A further assault came in 1979 in the wake of the Peoples Republic of China's invasion of the North when the country was swept by an anti-Chinese hysteria. Nearly half of Vietnam's Chinese population fled the country, leaving only one million today. Those remaining have been recovering gradually. The free market reforms have restored some of their economic opportunities and the party has taken measures to try to reduce anti-Chinese discrimination. But historic experience has bred a hesitancy to trust the regime, and extensive family ties with Chinese abroad give this community a channel to the outside that the party both values and worries about.

The other ethnic minorities, of which there are 52 and who number roughly seven million (about 10 percent of the country's population), live mostly in the mountains and central highlands in a state of deprivation and poverty even more severe that of the ethnic Vietnamese population.[49] Isolated for many centuries, they are becoming more and more engaged with the Vietnamese lowlanders as the strategic importance and economic value of the borderland they occupy has been recognized. The only armed resistance to the Vietnamese regime seems to be what is left of the United Front for the Struggle of Oppressed Races (FULRO), the alliance of four minorities in the central highlands that was once supported by the French and the Americans to fight the Communists during the war. But inequalities are rankling, land disputes are growing, and the Vietnamese government is too poor to be able to respond effectively.

The party recognizes this situation but so far has been inclined to see it as aberrant behavior that can be corrected along the general line of limited reform that was formulated at the party congress in 1986. To those hungering for a new vision it offers only the stale old concept of the "transition to socialism." The attempts of the ideologists to save it by defining the current era of economic liberalization as the "first stage" of that long-anticipated transition have offered little substance. For the economic task at hand, the orthodox ideology is becoming more a mantra of party loyalty than a guide to action. Party members who believe are becoming hopelessly out of sync with the public they claim to lead, and those who have lost their belief are seeking answers in the "new thinking," which is an undigested melange of state-led and market-led economics and of authoritarian and democratic political thought. The result is a loss of consensus on where Vietnam is heading. Clearly the country is in transition, but transition to what? There is, one official admits, an "ideological vacuum."[50]

There is also, it would appear, a growing policy vacuum. Some Central Committee members, particularly among the younger and newer additions, advocate opening the country wider, privatizing the economy faster, and getting on with the process of liberalizing the political system. Others, particularly among the older members, think things have gone too far. They are frustrated by the ideological confusion, shocked by the corruption, and fearful of the foreign influences.

The result is an eroding concensus as to where Vietnam is or should be heading. At the Eighth Party Congress in June–July 1996, while reaffirming the basic line of economic reform, the delegates found little agreement on how to advance it safely.[51] They could think of little better to do than to stand pat on the economic reform program, reaffirming the general line, but giving it no new thrust; reelect the septuagenarian troika of Muoi, Anh, and Kiet, to their posts as general secretary, president, and prime minister, respectively; and strengthen the party's control mechanisms, adding two security specialists, General Le Kha Phieu, head of the Army's political department, and Nguyen Tan Dung, a vice minister of interior, to the troika at the center of power as members of the new, five-member Standing Board of the Politburo.

This is not to suggest that the party is in any imminent danger. As already pointed out, the mass of the people is still politically apathetic. A civil society is still only nascent. The private interests that Vietnamese are gradually becoming conscious of are still by and large politically unformed. Organized opposition does not now exist.

The armed forces are the one element in Vietnamese society today with the physical strength and organization to disrupt. To be sure, there is evidence of growing dissatisfaction there.[52] With the withdrawal from Cambodia in 1989, the army's numbers have been cut in half. Its share of the national budget has been reduced. This plus the loss of Soviet aid has resulted in a deterioration of its equipment and, according to official reports, a shortage of food, housing, medicine, and uniforms for soldiers. In the spring of 1991 a military commander who was also a member of the party's Central Committee reported that "the living standard of our soldiers everywhere in Vietnam is too bad, too terrible, and has produced a negative impact on their work, study, training and combat preparedness."[53] Failures of discipline, declining morale, draft dodging, and desertion are regularly complained of.[54] Smuggling by units along the border is reported. From time to time officers have expressed their fears that national security is being endangered.

On the other hand, there is no evidence of insubordination. The VPA is thoroughly politicized. The overwhelming majority of the officer corps as well as a sizable minority of the troops continue to be party members. A military block occupies seats in the National Assembly. Generals on active duty continue to serve on the party's Politburo and Central Committee. There seems to be no quarrel with the traditional view, as reasserted by Secretary General Linh in December 1990, that the army's duty is to protect "the party, the socialist state, and national independence."

Transition to What?

But the present situation is unlikely to last. One has only to look around at the experience of other states championing economic development to realize that the present weakness of Vietnam's civil society and the political apathy of its general population are transient. As the economy advances— and advance it must if the party is to hang on at all—the civil groups that are now so nascent seem destined to grow in both economic strength and self-consciousness. And as they do, there is every reason to believe that they will demand an increasing share of political power, as they are clearly doing in Vietnam's more economically advanced neighbors in Southeast Asia.[55]

Will the party be able to meet this ultimate challenge? Will it be able to recast its self-image as manager of the transition, not only to a more mixed economy, but also eventually to a pluralistic democracy, as radicals have advocated? It may be this, of course, that some party leaders have in mind when they insist that *doi moi* is a concept of comprehensive reform. It seems more likely, however, as the political reaction of the past five years suggests, that a direct challenge to the party's power—at least for the foreseeable future—will be met with a firm "no."

If the way it has taken up economic reform is any guide, the party will probably avoid reformulating its vision. As political pressures grow, ideology will be likely to atrophy further. The party will also avoid sudden political changes but prefer to experiment locally with various politically liberalizing reforms until their effect on political stability can be judged. National political reforms will have to come gradually, possibly waiting until a new generation with newer thinking occupies the party leadership. From time to time violent confrontations will probably not be avoidable. Corrections will be demanded when things seem to be moving too fast for the party's old-timers. But as Lenin once advised with a far different objective in mind, two steps forward will have to be taken for every one back if the party is to meet this most fundamental challenge.

Can it do so? Can it come to accept the idea that its economic and informational reforms require it to manage a very different political transition than it has had in mind, a transition not to a consolidated party-state under its control, but to a softer authoritarianism in which pressures will eventually force a further transformation to democracy? Perhaps, but it may not be irrelevant to note that the only party even quasi-Leninist to have accomplished such a peaceful transformation is the Kuomintang on Taiwan, and that party from the beginning held up democracy as its goal.

Notes

1. Communist Party of Vietnam. 1986. *Political Report of the Central Committee to the Sixth National Party Congress,* December 15. English translation in FBIS, Hanoi Domestic Service in Vietnam, December 17, 1986.

2. Gareth Porter, *Vietnam: The Politics of Bureaucratic Socialism* (Ithaca: Cornell University Press, 1993), p. 107.

3. Carlyle A. Thayer, "The Regularization of Politics: Continuity and Change in the Party's Central Committee, 1951–1986," in *Postwar Vietnam: Dilemmas in Socialist Development,* edited by David G. Marr and Christine P. White (Ithaca: Southeast Asian

Program, Cornell University Press, 1988), ch. 11.

4. Motoo Furuta, "The Sixth Congress of the Communist Party of Vietnam: A Turning Point in the History of the Vietnamese Communists," in *Indochina in Transition: Confrontation or Co-prosperity,* edited by Mio Tadashi (Tokyo: Japan Institute of International Affairs, 1989).

5. Communist Party of Vietnam, *Political Report,* pp. 3–16.

6. Porter, *Vietnam: The Politics of Bureaucratic Socialism,* p. 77.

7. Carlyle A. Thayer, *The Vietnam People's Army under Doi Moi* (Singapore: Institute of Southeast Asian Studies, 1994), pp. 14–15.

8. Socialist Republic of Vietnam, *The Constitution of 1992* (Hanoi: The GIOI Publishers, 1993).

9. Douglas Pike, "Vietnam in 1993," *Asian Survey,* 34, no. 1 (January, 1994), p. 67.

10. Porter, *Vietnam: The Politics of Bureaucratic Socialism,* pp. 87–96.

11. Socialist Republic of Vietnam, *The Constitution of 1992.*

12. Porter, *Vietnam: The Politics of Bureaucratic Socialism,* pp. 92–93.

13. Communist Party of Vietnam, *Political Report.*

14. Porter, *Vietnam: The Politics of Bureaucratic Socialism,* pp. 160–170.

15. Carlyle Thayer, "Political Reform in Vietnam: Doi Moi and the Emergence of Civil Society," in *The Development of Civil Society in Communist Systems,* edited by Robert F. Miller (Sydney: Allen and Unwin, 1992), p. 119.

16. Ibid., pp. 123–125.

17. Tran Bach Dang, "Gia Cap Cong Nhan va Doi Moi" (The Working Class and Renovation), *Lao Dong,* special Tet issue, 1988, quoted in Porter, *Vietnam: The Politics of Bureaucratic Socialism,* p. 97.

18. Nguyen Ngoc Long, "Contradictions between the Economic Bases and the Political Institutions—'The Key Link' of the Current Process of Social Renovation in Our Country," *Tap Chi Cong San,* March 1989, FBIS *East Asia Daily Report,* pp. 54–55, quoted in Porter, *Vietnam: The Politics of Bureaucratic Socialism,* p. 97.

19. Thayer, *The Vietnam People's Army under Doi Moi,* p. 57.

20. Tsuyoshi Hasegawa, "The Connection between Political and Economic Reform in Communist Regimes," in *Dismantling Communism: Common Causes and Regional Variations,* edited by Gilbert Rozman (Baltimore: The Johns Hopkins University Press, 1992), p. 228.

21. Thayer, "Political Reform in Vietnam," p. 127.

22. Porter, *Vietnam: The Politics of Bureaucratic Socialism,* p. 99.

23. Ibid., pp. 99–100.

24. Ibid., p. 169.

25. Ibid., p. 100.

26. Michael Leifer and John Phipps, *Vietnam and Doi Moi: Domestic and International Dimensions of Reform* (London: Royal Institute of International Affairs, 1991), p. 11.

27. Lewis M. Stern, *Renovating the Vietnamese Communist Party* (Singapore: Institute of Southeast Asian Studies, 1993), pp. 145–157.

28. Carlyle Thayer, "Recent Political Developments: Constitutional Change and the 1992 Elections," in *Vietnam and the Rule of Law,* edited by Carlyle A. Thayer and David G. Marr (Canberra: Department of Political and Social Change, Research School of Pacific Studies, Australian National University, 1993), p. 75.

29. Hanoi Radio, December 8, 1991, cited in William S. Turley, "Party, State, and People: Political Structure and Economic Prospects" in *Reinventing Vietnamese Socialism,* edited by William S. Turley and Mark Selden (Boulder, CO: Westview Press, 1993), p. 269.

30. Porter, *Vietnam: The Politics of Bureaucratic Socialism,* ch. 5.

31. Ibid., pp. 155–156.
32. Socialist Republic of Vietnam, *The Constitution of 1992,* Article IV.
33. Ibid., Article IV.
34. Ibid., Article VI.
35. Thayer, *The Vietnam People's Army under Doi Moi,* pp. 14, 24–25.
36. Ibid., pp. 60–63.
37. Porter, *Vietnam: The Politics of Bureaucratic Socialism,* pp. 1–11.
38. Ibid., pp. 11–30.
39. Murray Hiebert, *Vietnam Notebook* (Hong Kong: Review Publishing Company Limited, 1993), pp. 192–193.
40. Ibid., p. 194.
41. Carlyle Thayer, "Political Reform in Vietnam: Doi Moi and the Emergence of Civil Society." Paper presented at the Vietnam Update 1994 Conference: Doi Moi, The State and Civil Society, November 10–11 (Canberra: Australian National University, 1994).
42. Hiebert, *Vietnam Notebook,* pp. 81–87.
43. Thayer, *The Vietnam People's Army under Doi Moi,* p. 26.
44. Hiebert, *Vietnam Notebook,* p. 98.
45. Ibid., p. 175.
46. Thayer, "Political Reform in Vietnam," pp. 125–127.
47. *Loc. cit.*
48. Hiebert, *Vietnam Notebook,* pp. 120–125.
49. Porter, *Vietnam: The Politics of Bureaucratic Socialism,* pp. 34–35; and Hiebert, *Vietnam Notebook,* pp. 53–65.
50. Hiebert, *Vietnam Notebook,* p. 192.
51. Adam Schwarz, "Vietnam: Safety First" in *Far Eastern Economic Review,* July 11, 1996, pp. 14–16.
52. Hiebert, *Vietnam Notebook,* pp. 22–36.
53. Ibid., p. 26.
54. Thayer, *The Vietnam People's Army under Doi Moi,* pp. 23–41.
55. Harold Crouch and James W. Morley, "The Dynamics of Political Change," in *Driven by Growth: Political Change in the Asia-Pacific Region,* edited by James W. Morley (Armonk, NY: M.E. Sharpe, 1992), pp. 277–309.

2

The Economic Take-off

Masahiko Ebashi

Following the unification of the country in October 1976, the Vietnamese leadership looked forward at last to achieving the transition to prosperity that had been socialism's promise, only to be frustrated by the renewed demands of war, this time in Cambodia, and the disastrous effects of the centrally planned economy they attempted to enforce. The need for fundamental rethinking became apparent. After several experiments with liberalization, a thoroughgoing reform policy called *doi moi* was inaugurated in 1986. *Doi moi* represents a basic change from the economic policy of the past: it reduces the role of the state in the economy; it respects the market, favors private enterprise, and welcomes global traders and investors. The problems in executing such a policy have been legion, but the successes are dramatic, and now Vietnam seems well launched on a path of high growth and international economic cooperation.

Early Efforts at Reform

The first efforts at rehabilitation and reconstruction were embodied in the Second Five-Year Plan (1976–80). The results were miserable. The plan set a target of 13–14 percent growth of the national income annually; however, it achieved only 0.4 percent annual growth during the period, far below its population growth.[1] Food production in 1980 reached only 14 million tons, which was lower than the plan target by 7 million tons. People's living standards deteriorated sharply during the period and famine was experienced in several provinces in 1978, when a number of natural disasters hit Vietnam over two successive years.

The principal causes for the failure of the Second Five-Year Plan can be summarized as follows:

1. The enforcement of the socialist reform of the economy in the South by collectivization of agricultural farms and nationalization of trade and industry completely damaged the people's incentives for production in the South.
2. Excessive bureaucracy, distorted prices, and the incentive system, and the wrong industrialization strategy[2]—all the products of a central command economy—greatly hindered its economic efficiency.
3. Vietnamese intervention in Cambodia since the end of 1978 had not only invited the China-Vietnam War but also resulted in diplomatic and economic isolation of the country, which further strained its resources.

The serious economic crisis and increased conscription for wars in Cambodia and on the Chinese border invited strong criticism by the people. Sensing the danger to its existence, the party decided to try overcoming the economic crisis by launching a New Economic Policy (NEP). The Sixth Plenum of the Central Committee in September 1979 called for encouraging production by the nonstate sector and relaxing the operation of distribution checkpoints. In 1981 the "contractual farming system"[3] was introduced, with higher prices for agricultural goods, and greater freedom of management was assured for state-owned enterprises.

Economic liberalization brought economic recovery, with an average 7 percent gross domestic product (GDP) growth during 1981–84 (see Figure 2.1). However, this partial relaxation of the economic management system and partial adjustment of the pricing system[4] not only brought about a huge budget deficit and high inflation, but also was accompanied by damaging side effects, such as income disparity and graft and corruption among party cadres.

Consequently, conservatives who advocated the revival of an orthodox command economic system grasped power at the Fifth Party Congress in March 1982. The collectivization of agriculture was restarted, management of state enterprises was again centralized, private trade and services were restricted, and overseas remittances were severely checked. But the reintroduction of a command economic system once again started to bring stagnation of agricultural production, while on the other hand inflation continued unchecked.

The struggle between the reformists, who emphasized drastic reform with an open policy and transformation of the economic management system from central planning to a market mechanism, and the conservatives intensified. The reformists gradually began to gain a stronger position in the party from around the end of 1984. Nguyen Van Linh was restored to the

Figure 2.1 **Vietnam: Trends of Economic Growth Rate (1980–94)**

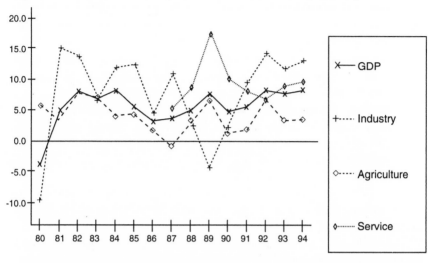

Source: 1980–86—IMF, *Vietnam: Recent Economic Development, 1985–90;* 1987–89—*Vietnam: A Development Perspective,* Hanoi, September 1993; 1990–1993—World Bank, *Vietnam: Public Sector Management and Private Secctor Incentives,* September 6, 1994; 1994—*Vietnam Investment Review,* April 3–9, 1995.

Politburo, and a drastic reform of "prices, wages, and currency" was adopted at the Eighth Plenum of the Central Committee in June 1985.

This reform, implemented in September 1985, was a kind of shock therapy that aimed at stabilization of the currency, reduction of the budget deficit, and control of inflation at the same time. Instead, it brought explosive inflation and economic disorder.[5] The struggle between reformists and conservatives was again intensified, each blaming the other for responsibility for the economic disorder. However, the option of returning to the orthodox Soviet model was no longer persuasive.

Due to the 1985 crisis, the Vietnamese government came to the view that the market-oriented economic reforms would need to be a long and continuous process. Truong Chinh, who succeeded Le Duan as general secretary of the party, strongly supported the reformists by sharply criticizing the old socialist model.

The Adoption of the *Doi Moi* Policy

In December 1986, the Sixth Party Congress elected reformist Nguyen Van Linh as general secretary of the party and adopted the policy of *doi moi.*

Although its main thrust was economic, *doi moi* also had political, social, and cultural objectives. In the economic field, the key elements of the *doi moi* policy were:

1. abandonment of the old central-planning economic model by transforming Vietnam's economic management system into a market-oriented one,
2. adoption of an outward-looking policy in external economic relations,
3. encouragement of the nonstate sector as the engine of economic growth, and
4. revision of the orientation of its industrial policy away from heavy industry.

In these ways, the policy of *doi moi* was quite different from the New Economic Policy, which had been a partial reform within the existing system.

The Vietnamese government decided to adopt *doi moi* apparently for the following reasons:

1. the reduced credibility of the party because it could not solve the economic crisis,
2. the increased economic and technological gap between Vietnam and its neighbors,
3. the rapid progress of China's economic reform and its economic development, and
4. the indication of a reduction in Soviet aid, as implied in its "New Thinking on Diplomacy," which forced Vietnam to seek a new development strategy without Soviet assistance.

In spite of the basic policy of *doi moi,* the actual pace of the transition to a market economy was slow, because the party leaders had chosen a gradual reform process following the bitter experience of the 1985 "shock therapy." The party focused its efforts on increased production of food and foodstuffs, consumer goods, and exports. At the same time it introduced a gradual reform of the prices of agricultural goods and of the agricultural production system and encouraged private-sector activities.

But with this gradualist approach to reform, the government could not check inflation, and economic activities were weaker than anticipated. In 1987, a mini-economic crisis developed, mainly caused by poor food production. This economic crisis again brought famine in some central provinces. And the crisis again strengthened the position of the reformists, enabling the introduction of more drastic reform measures.

In 1988 the government enacted the Foreign Direct Investment Law and granted autonomy to state enterprises in exchange for cutting financial support from the national budget. By issuing Politburo Resolution 10, the party instituted a family-based agricultural production system with land tenure rights and also allowed farmers to engage freely in the exchange of goods, both in their outputs and inputs. In addition, the party permitted private ownership of assets, including the means of production.

In March 1989 more epoch-making reforms were implemented. In accordance with the policy package recommended by the International Monetary Fund, the following measures were implemented:

1. total price liberalization, except for a few items such as electricity, oil, cement, steel, and transportation,
2. unification of the foreign exchange rate after a significant devaluation of the *dong,*
3. adoption of very tight fiscal and monetary policies to control excessive demand,
4. trade liberalization,
5. curtailment of all kinds of state subsidies, and
6. reorganization of the banking system.

This series of reform measures, administered as shock therapy over a short period, successfully and quickly curbed inflation and rectified the distorted price and incentive structure, thereby reviving agriculture, exports, and the service industries. The increased food production raised Vietnam to the position of third-largest rice exporter in the world. Thanks to its oil and rice exports, Vietnam's total exports in 1989 increased about 2.8 times over the previous year.

However, Vietnam's state-owned industries suffered greatly from the introduction of these reforms. Most state-owned enterprises, obliged to look after themselves without state subsidies and faced with the problem of obtaining essential capital and raw materials, had to decrease production and start to lay off workers. In addition, the political and economic chaos in the former Soviet Union and Eastern European countries after 1989 severely affected the Vietnamese economy.

Economic aid from former Council for Mutual Economic Assistance or CMEA countries started to decline in 1989. Vietnam was obliged to seek alternative sources of oil, chemical fertilizers, iron and steel, and cotton, which had been supplied mostly from the former Soviet Union. Furthermore, the Gulf War brought higher prices for oil and chemical fertilizers in the summer of 1990.

Since 1991 all transactions with former CMEA countries have been done on a hard-currency basis at international prices, and all economic aid from these countries has virtually stopped. The collapse of the CMEA and the economic disorder in these countries greatly damaged Vietnam's exports.

In addition to a lack of operating capital, state-owned enterprises lost access to cheap raw materials from the former Soviet Union, which forced many of the enterprises to close down. Anticipating possible high unemployment and economic dislocation, the Vietnamese government started once more to extend low-interest loans and introduce special tax treatment to state-owned enterprises. But this practice brought the reemergence of inflation in 1991–92.

The years 1990 and 1991 were critical for Vietnam. Agricultural production stagnated because of bad weather and the unemployment situation became serious, with mass layoffs in state-owned enterprises, a drastic reduction of personnel in the military forces, and the return of overseas workers from the former CMEA countries and Iraq.

In spite of these difficulties, Vietnam's economy continued to grow, with a moderate increase in the GDP growth rate, due to a great extent to the successful mobilization of the potential of the agricultural, private enterprise, and household sectors, as well as a large unofficial sector,[6] as a result of the earlier reform efforts. In fact, improved capital and labor efficiency and the expanded service sector were the keys to economic growth during these difficult years.

Unlike most of the CMEA countries, including the Eastern European states, the former Soviet Union, and Mongolia, all of which have experienced continuous contraction of production and hyperinflation, Vietnam has at no time experienced negative economic growth since the transition period began in late 1988. Besides, it has been able to keep inflation at a manageable level. In spite of very difficult conditions, such as a lack of access to economic assistance for reform, curtailment of aid from the former Soviet Union, and the loss of traditional export markets, why was Vietnam able to shift its economic system towards a market economy comparatively smoothly?

The initial conditions for reform and the sequence of the reform process seem to be the keys to Vietnam's success. In contrast to the initial conditions for reform in most of the former socialist countries, Vietnam was endowed with a small state sector, providing only 30 percent of national income in 1986 and employing only 14 percent of the work force in 1988; a small industrial sector, accounting for only 28 percent of national production; and a shorter exposure to central planning for the whole country, with the South enjoying a market economy until 1975.

Because of these factors, the impact of price distortion, the lack of an incentive structure, and bureaucratic practice under the socialist system have been relatively mild, while the entrepreneurial spirit has remained largely intact. This suggests that Vietnam was able to implement its reforms at a rather small adjustment cost compared with other CMEA countries, and it was able to obtain a rather quick market response from its farmers, private individuals, and enterprises.

As for the international environment, although Vietnam's economy depended upon CMEA countries for 50–60 percent of its trade in 1988, Vietnam's favorable geographical location in the center of a dynamically growing Asia offered it access to these Asian countries. This enabled Vietnam to quickly shift its trade partners from the CMEA countries to its Asian neighbors. In addition, Vietnam was fortunate to be able to export oil and rice when aid from the former Soviet Union started to be curtailed. In fact, export earnings from oil and rice alone almost compensated for the value of Soviet aid cut since 1989.

There are different opinions as to whether the Vietnamese reform approach should be called one of a shock therapy or gradualism. According to the World Bank *Annual Report* for 1991, shock therapy is the type of approach used to implement drastic reform measures such as price reform, privatization, trade liberalization, and very tight demand control measures in less than two years. On the other hand, gradualism is the approach adopted to introduce reform while minimizing the cost of adjustment by implementing the same reform measures gradually over a longer period. As we have seen, Vietnam has implemented most of these measures within a short time. This is quite different from China's gradualist approach and thus may reasonably be classified as shock therapy.

However, there are many who classify Vietnam's reforms as gradualist. Those people look at Vietnam's reform process in a longer and broader sense. They consider that Vietnam's reforms started in 1979 with its New Economic Policy (NEP), which was a kind of reform within the socialist system. They also emphasize that Vietnam's initial reform of the agricultural production system began in 1981 and that Vietnam did not accelerate the privatization of state-owned enterprises, unlike other CMEA countries.

In any case, the following sequence of reform measures that Vietnam has taken seems to be another key factor in the initial success of Vietnamese reform.

1. Before the application of shock therapy in 1989, Vietnam had already revitalized agriculture and raised farmers' income through the reform of agricultural prices and production.

2. Vietnam's approach to reform of state-owned enterprises was on a gradual, step-by-step basis. Since 1981 Vietnam tried to give more autonomy to state enterprises, thereby giving them time to get accustomed to "hard budget constraints" rather than facing them with rapid and drastic reform, such as privatization.
3. Before total price liberalization in 1989, Vietnam had already started partial price reform on a trial-and-error basis.
4. Only after these steps were taken was the above-mentioned "shock therapy" implemented.

Because these prereform measures were introduced before the shock therapy, farmers and state-owned enterprises were able to prepare to respond to the new market environment. This avoided supplyside contraction, which would have led to inflation through shortage of supply.

It cannot be denied that the Vietnamese government may have learned from the experience of China, which had started its reforms in agriculture. It also must be mentioned that the shock therapy, which forced enormous hardship on people at one time, could be implemented without much trouble thanks to the stable political situation provided by strong party leadership.

The Beginning of High Growth

After overcoming the critical years, Vietnam seems to have entered a high-growth era in 1992 (see Table 2.1 for major economic indicators). The Vietnamese economy registered an 8.6 percent GDP growth rate and achieved macroeconomic balance in 1992. Vietnam enjoyed a trade surplus for the first time in its history in 1992. Revenue against GDP increased from 14.7 percent in 1991 to 19 percent in 1992,[7] which enabled Vietnam to increase its current expenditure and capital investment in infrastructure for the first time since 1989, when tight fiscal policy was introduced.

The industrial sector, which suffered most from the reforms and was forced to lay off many workers, quickly recovered starting in the latter part of 1991 and has become a leading sector of economic growth, along with the construction industry. In spite of the very low level of investment, Vietnam's economy grew at a satisfactory rate thanks to the improvement in capital and labor efficiency.

Vietnam's GDP continued to increase by 8.1 percent in 1993 and 8.8 percent in 1994, led by industry and the construction sector. Gross fixed investment, which had been severely constrained in previous years, grew about 20 percent in 1993. Foreign direct investment accounted for about a third of Vietnam's gross fixed investment.

Table 2.1.

Vietnam: Major Economic Indicators (1990–94)

Items	1990	1991	1992	1993	1994
1. Real GDP growth rate (%)	5.0	6.0	8.6	8.1	8.8
Industry	2.5	9.9	14.6	12.1	12.9
Agriculture	1.5	2.2	7.1	3.8	3.9
Service	10.3	8.3	7.0	9.2	10.2
2. Inflation rate (%)	67.5	67.5	17.6	5.2	14.4
3. Food production (000 tons)	21,490	21,990	24,200	25,500	26,200
4. Per capita food production (Kg)	324	325	349	359	359
5. Trade balance (U.S.$ million)	−348	−251	40	−939	−1,400
Export	2,404	2,087	2,580	2,985	3,600
Imports	2,752	2,338	2,540	3,924	5,000
6. Oil export (000 tons)	2,617	3,917	5,446	6,153	6,942
7. Rice export (000 tons)	1,624	1,033	1,946	1,722	1,950
8. Current account balance (% to GDP)	−4.2	−1.9	−0.7	−8.3	−4.9
9. Statistic to investment ratio (% to GDP)	11.7	15.1	17	19.4	19.9
10. Investment by domestic saving (%)		65.8	75.8	57.2	65.4
11. Gross national saving (% to GDP)	7.4	13.1	16.3	11.2	15
12. Revenue against GDP (%)	14.7	13.5	19	22.3	25.4
13. Budget deficit (% to GDP)	−5.9	−1.5	−1.7	−4.7	−1.9

Source: 1–7: *Statistical Yearbook 1994,* Statistical Publishing House, Hanoi, 1995. 10: *Vietnam Investment Review,* January 208, 1995. 8–9, 11–13: World Bank, *Vietnam Financial Sector Review,* March 1, 1995.

However, the twin budget and current account deficit widened, and higher inflation reemerged in 1994. The budget deficit ballooned from 1.7 percent of GDP in 1991 to about 5 percent in 1993.[8] Higher salaries for government employees and increased spending on infrastructure and social services were the main reasons. The higher inflation rate from the latter part of 1994 was due to the expansionary monetary policy introduced in 1994 and to higher food prices, caused mainly by flooding in the two major rice-producing areas.

The trade deficit registered U.S.$939 million in 1993 and U.S.$1.4 bil-

Table 2.2

Vietnam: Upward Revision of Growth Target and Investment

	Original (June 1991)	Revised Target (July 1994)
Growth target	Double the 1990 GDP by the year 2000	Double the 1990 per capita GDP by the year 2000
Average growth rate (%)	0.072	0.095
Investment requirement (U.S.$ billion)	Cover period (1991–2000)	Cover period (1994–2000)
ODA	7–8	10
FDI	12–13	18–20
Domestic capital	20	20
Total	40 (4/Year)	48–50 (6.9–7.1/Year)

Source: State Planning Committee, *Report of the Government of the SRV to the Consultative Group Meeting,* November 15–16, 1994.

lion in 1994. While Vietnam's exports stagnated because of lower prices for primary export commodities, imports jumped greatly. The sudden import growth reflected increased demand for inputs and raw materials, as well as the relaxation of trade restrictions and import quotas. Vietnam's GDP in 1995 is expected to grow faster; however, it is likely to be accompanied by higher inflation and a bigger current account deficit. As a heavily indebted low-income country, Vietnam will continue to be faced with this dilemma between high economic growth and macroeconomic imbalance.

In July 1994 the Central Committee of the party decided to raise the economic growth target and accelerate industrialization. The original growth target set for the year 2000 by the Seventh Party Congress in 1991 was to double the 1990 GDP by the year 2000. This target was revised to double the 1990 per capita GDP by the year 2000. This means raising the average annual growth target from 7.2 percent to about 9.5 percent (see Table 2.2). In order to achieve this goal, the investment requirement was revised upward from U.S.$40 billion over ten years (U.S.$4 billion per year) to U.S.$48–50 billion over seven years (U.S.$6.9–8.1 billion per year).

The reasons for this upward revision of the target seem to be the assessment by the Vietnamese Party leaders that:

1. A higher rate of economic growth is necessary for Vietnam to catch up with other Asian neighbors, who have been developing at high speed; otherwise, Vietnam would not be able to keep pace with other ASEAN countries, even after becoming a member of the organization; and

2. Vietnam will be able to obtain more aid and foreign direct investment (FDI) in the new and increasingly favorable international environment, characterized by the lifting of the U.S. embargo and the resumption of aid from Japan and international financial institutions, opportunities that did not exist when the original target was set in 1991.

It will not be easy for Vietnam to achieve this ambitious new plan. As for FDI, it is said that Vietnam must attract U.S.$33–35 billion on an approval basis in order to reach the target amount of actual FDI inflow during these seven years. To attract approved FDI of U.S.$4.7–5 billion per year would seem to be a difficult task unless Vietnam takes bold steps to rectify the current bottleneck in investment promotion, an issue that will be discussed later.

Regarding economic aid from different sources, Vietnam obtained U.S.$1.86 billion of aid commitment at the donors' meeting in Paris in November 1993. The new commitment at the Consultative Group meeting in November 1994 was U.S.$2 billion. The aid commitment to Vietnam is expected to increase in the near future. The problem seems to be Vietnam's aid absorption capacity, rather than the size of the commitment. Vietnam's capability to identify projects, undertake feasibility studies, and administer aid should be raised quickly. Whether Vietnam will be able to collect enough counterpart funds for project implementation is another key issue.

The mobilization of domestic capital seems to be a more difficult task. In addition to tax reform, Vietnam must build an effective tax collection system. State-owned enterprise reform leading to improved management is also essential if domestic capital is to be mobilized.

The government has great difficulty attracting savings deposits from households and business enterprises. In spite of the relatively high savings deposit rate, which is currently about 10 percent in real terms, the government still cannot attract unutilized private capital, which is estimated to be U.S.$2–3 billion. Since the people have had bitter experience with their bank savings in the past, it may take a longer time for the government to obtain the people's confidence in the banking system unless it offers greater incentives to save, such as favorable tax treatment and welfare pension insurance.

In spite of continuous government efforts to mobilize domestic capital, including the introduction of a Popular Credit Fund and creation of a stable and attractive capital market, there is a strong possibility that Vietnam will not be able to attract the full amount of targeted investment capital during 1994–2000. However, if it can persevere in stable macroeconomic policies and open and competitive trade and industrial policies, Vietnam should be able to attain an annual economic growth rate of about 9 percent toward the year 2000, since there is much scope for Vietnam to raise its capital efficiency further by improving its soft and hard infrastructure, modernizing its plant and equipment, and improving the management of its state-owned enterprises. Besides, a significant amount of unofficial investment can be expected during this period.

The Opening to the Outside

There has been a major change in Vietnam's external economic relations since the end of the 1980s, when its reform and open door policy became fully effective. The favorable turn in the international environment for Vietnam since the withdrawal of Vietnamese troops from Cambodia in September 1989 was the key factor in this change. In addition, the change was accelerated by the economic difficulties within the CMEA countries and curtailment of their trade and aid to Vietnam; the development of new exports from Vietnam, such as rice and oil; the increased inflow of aid and foreign direct investment from capitalist countries.

Drastic changes in Vietnam's trading partners were seen during this transition period (see Figures 2.2 and 2.3). The share of the former Soviet Union in Vietnam's total trade has sharply dropped since 1991. This share, which constituted 34 percent of Vietnam's exports and 63 percent of its imports in 1989, dropped to only 10 percent and 13 percent respectively in 1991.[9] Asian countries, including Japan, the newly industrialized economies (NIEs), and the ASEAN states, have taken over the former Soviet Union's share of Vietnam's trade since then. Singapore consolidated its position as a major supplier of oil products, which used to come from the Soviet Union. South Korea became a major supplier of steel and chemical fertilizers, while Indonesia became a major supplier of urea, formerly provided by the Soviet Union. Neighboring Asian countries, which include Japan, China, the NIEs, and the ASEAN countries, provided 82 percent of Vietnam's imports and took 60 percent of its exports in 1993.

The rapid expansion of exports since 1987 was also a significant development in Vietnam's trade patterns. Vietnam's exports jumped 3.4 times, from U.S.$653 million in 1986 to U.S.$2,234 million in 1990. In 1991, after Vietnam's exports to the former Soviet Union and East European countries

Figure 2.2 **Vietnam's Exports by Region, 1986–93** (in %)

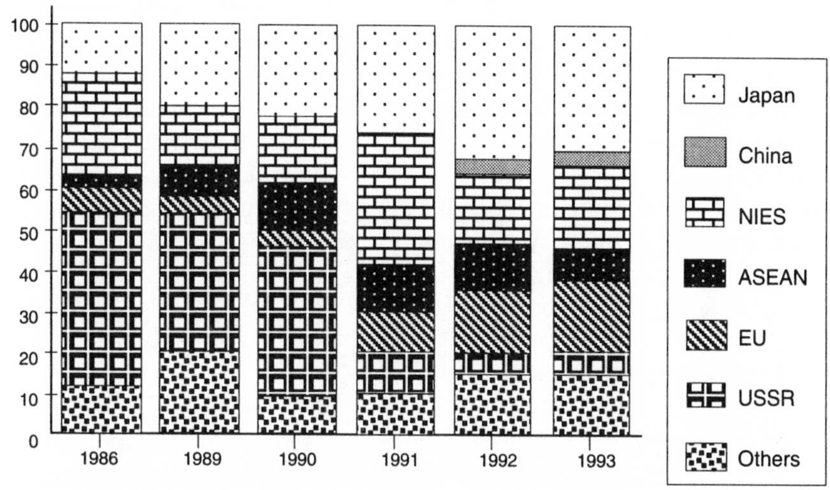

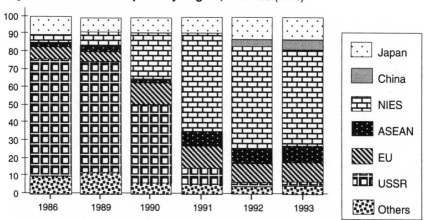

Source: IMF, *Direction of Trade* and other national statistical yearbooks.

Figure 2.3 **Vietnam's Imports by Region, 1986–93** (in %)

Source: IMF, *Direction of Trade* and other national statistical yearbooks.

dropped sharply, Vietnam's total exports decreased slightly. However, in 1992 its exports recovered and already surpassed the peak level reached in 1991. In addition to oil and rice, the export of other primary commodities such as coffee, rubber, tin, and shrimps and of light industrial goods like clothes and footwear to nonsocialist countries has grown significantly because of trade liberalization and foreign exchange rate adjustment since 1989.

Figure 2.4 **Two Different Vietnam Trade Figures** (U.S.$ million)

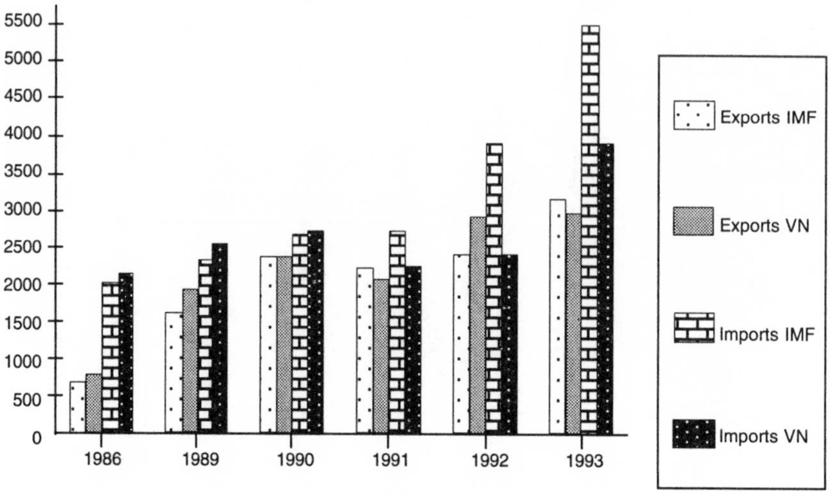

Source: *Vietnam Trade Statistics* and IMF, *Direction of Trade.*

In contrast to the significant changes in its trading partners, Vietnam's trade commodity structure did not change so much. About 86 percent of Vietnam's imports were production materials. Between 1986 and 1990, 52 percent of imports were fuel and raw materials and 34 percent machinery and parts, while on average only 14 percent were consumer goods.[10] The structure of import commodities has shown little change since then. As for exports, though there was a shift among primary commodities because of the emergence of oil as a new major export item, the existing structure has not changed, with about 70 percent of total exports being primary commodities.

It also should be noted, however, that there are significant differences between official Vietnamese import figures and the figures collected from Vietnam's trade partners. These differences have increased since 1991, reaching U.S.$488 million in 1991, U.S.$1,470 million in 1992, and U.S.$1,595 million in 1993. The gaps were 22 percent over the official figure for 1991, 61 percent for 1992, and 41 percent for 1993 (see Figure 2.4).

According to a Vietnamese expert on trade statistics, these differences are caused by two main factors. The first is the undervaluation of imports to avoid tariffs, and the second is that the government has been excluding capital goods imports relating to foreign direct investment projects. If these differences are taken into account, probably a higher proportion of consumer goods will be reflected in Vietnam's import commodity structure.

Vietnam's imports can be expected to grow faster than its exports for some time. Import demand for capital goods and consumer durable goods will remain high. FDI- and official development assistance (ODA)-related capital goods will continue to increase. This will lead to a further deterioration of the current account in the near future. Though the current account deficit will increase, it should be easily financed by the inflow of official and private capital, including foreign direct investment. However, unless Vietnam expands its exports significantly, it will soon accumulate foreign debt and will further undermine its financial credibility.

Vietnam's future exports will depend mostly on the growth of exports of labor-intensive manufactured goods, though it hopes to increase the export of primary commodities, such as oil, coffee, bananas, tea, rubber, and shrimps. There is a concern that the Vietnamese dong in real terms has appreciated against the U.S. dollar in the past few years. This is due to the increased foreign capital inflow and government policy to keep the exchange rate stable in order to control imported inflation and to restore the people's confidence in the currency. However, if this practice continues, it may hinder Vietnam's export development.

The Vietnamese government still does not have a strong and unified export promotion policy incorporating policies on foreign exchange rates, import tariffs for raw material, fiscal incentives, and foreign direct investment. Vietnam should appreciate the importance of exports for its economy more and learn from the export promotion policies of Korea and Taiwan of the 1960s and 1970s.

Foreign direct investment in Vietnam has been increasing at a faster rate since 1991 (see Figure 2.5). Investment approvals reached about U.S.$3.7 billion in 1994. Total approvals since 1988 reached about U.S.$11 billion as of the end of 1994. Accumulated actual FDI inflow reached U.S.$3.5 billion by the end of 1994, of which U.S.$1.5 billion was realized in 1994.

The top three investors as of 1994 were Taiwan, Hong Kong, and Singapore, followed by Korea, Japan, Australia, and Malaysia. Ethnic Chinese capital is a dominant element in investment in Vietnam.

The oil and gas industry took a major share in value terms in the early years, but recently the share of industrial, hotel, and infrastructure projects has been increasing.

In the early years, most of the FDI went to the South, mainly to Ho Chi Minh City and its suburbs; however, the North is attracting more FDI lately. The value of FDI approvals for Hanoi and Haiphong was only 3 percent of the total approvals in 1988–91. But this share increased to 28 percent between 1992 and June 1994. With improving soft and hard infrastructure in the North, investors are now starting to appreciate such factors as cheaper labor and land, access to government deci-

Figure 2.5 **FDI Flow into Vietnam, 1988–94** (U.S.$ million)

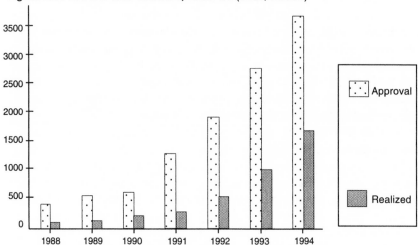

Source: Vietnam, The State Committee for Cooperation and Investment.

sion makers, and the availability of suitable partners and engineers in the North.

The factors that attract foreign investors to Vietnam are its low-cost and hard-working labor force, its fast-growing potential market of 71 million people, its relatively abundant natural resources, such as oil, gas, and coal, its favorable geographical location, and its stable political and civil order.

Taiwan has been the number-one investor in Vietnam since 1990. Taiwan's positive investment activities in Vietnam can be explained by:[11]

1. the traditional cultural affinity between the two societies,
2. the existence of ethnic Chinese in both economies who speak the same language,
3. geographical proximity,
4. the Taiwanese government's policy of encouraging investment in Southeast Asia, and especially Vietnam, and
5. the existence of a broad range of industries in Taiwan that are suitable for transfer to Vietnam.

In addition, Taiwanese investors feel confident about the successful development of Vietnam in the future. They believe the situation in Vietnam is similar to that in Taiwan about twenty years ago.

Japan still ranked as the number five investor in Vietnam as of the end of

1994. Japanese investment projects in Vietnam are in general on a small scale. Except for ten big projects with an average level of investment in excess of U.S.$20 million, such as oil development, car manufacturing, steel manufacturing, and industrial estate development projects, the average value of all the other projects was only U.S.$1.3 million. Import substitution projects that target the Vietnamese domestic market are increasing lately. Steel, cement, automobiles, motorcycles, electric appliances, pvc, plastics, and sugar are the key projects of this type. Unlike recent Japanese investment in ASEAN countries, there are few Japanese investments in modern-oriented industries.

Slow Japanese investment activity in Vietnam can be explained as follows:

1. Because of the deteriorating financial situation in Japan caused by the long recession, most Japanese firms have become conservative in investing abroad, especially in countries where the investment risk is uncertain.
2. Most Japanese firms have already completed a round of relocation of their labor-intensive production facilities to NIE or ASEAN countries since the Plaza Accord of 1985. It is still too early for these firms to shift to establish new production bases in other countries.
3. For those firms that have been losing international competitiveness as a result of the recent appreciation of the yen, ASEAN countries are preferred as relocation sites because these countries have better hard and soft infrastructure, administrative services, and supporting industries than Vietnam, at least at this time.

However, it is a fact that many Japanese firms are interested in investing in Vietnam in the future. A survey undertaken among Japanese firms by the Export-Import Bank of Japan in October 1994 ranked Vietnam as a number-two prospective investment market after China.[12]

In spite of this response to the survey, it is likely that a few more years will be required before the large, modern export industries such as electrical appliances, electronics, and automobile parts manufacturers that have moved to the NIEs, Thailand, and Malaysia will choose Vietnam as an export base. As for manufacturing industry, when we consider the current level of development of Vietnamese industry and the cheap and abundant labor, the NIEs and some countries in ASEAN that have appropriate industries to transfer to Vietnam will continue to be major investors.

In spite of the government's intention to attract further FDI, Vietnam still has many hurdles slowing foreign investment. FDI inflow to Vietnam will stagnate sooner or later unless the following major obstacles can be removed;

1. the lack of necessary laws and regulations and the lack of transparency in application of laws,
2. lengthy investment application procedures and bureaucratic red tape,
3. difficulty in securing industrial land and the high rental costs for land and offices,
4. limited freedom to choose partners and the lack of suitable partners with appropriate management experience,
5. inadequate infrastructure such as electricity, transport, communications, and accommodations,
6. a dual pricing system for public utility fees, which imposes higher prices on foreigners,
7. unresolved debt to the foreign private sector, which is limiting the availability of investment finance from foreign commercial banks,
8. the lack of a long-term industrial policy vision and uncertain investment policy,
9. the lack of necessary information and statistics for project feasibility studies, and
10. the requirement to keep a foreign exchange balance in each foreign firm.

Perplexing Issues of the Transition

In addition to the common problems that most developing countries face, Vietnam faces certain special problems arising out of its effort to transform its central command economy to a market economy. Four are particularly perplexing: redefining the role of the state, devising appropriate industrial policy, restructuring agriculture, and reforming state enterprises.

What Role Should the State Play?

Vietnam has officially adopted a "multicomponent commodity economy functioning in accordance with market mechanisms under state management and following a socialist orientation" (1992 Constitution) as its new economic structure and abandoned the former centrally planned economic system. However, what a "socialist-oriented market economy" means to Vietnam's leaders and economists is not at all clear.

The author's interviews with Vietnamese economists and party leaders in August 1994 in Hanoi revealed that most of them conceive of a "socialist society" as one whose goal is to achieve a "wealthy, strong and equal, highly civilized society." The problem is how to achieve this goal. The former socialist countries had tried to achieve this goal through a centralized planning command system. They failed not only to achieve efficient resource allocation but also to make a free and equal society. Against this background, Vietnam now is trying to achieve the same goal through market mechanisms instead of central planning. However, the market economy that Vietnam is now pursuing seems not to be the same as that of developed capitalist countries, but a "market economy under state management." Moreover, "the state is led by the Communist Party."

China also adopted a "socialist market economy" at the Fourteenth Communist Party Congress in 1992. According to its theory of the socialist market economy as defined by the Development Research Center of the State Council and the Chinese Academy of Social Sciences,[13] the "market economy is not the landmark that divides socialism or capitalism. Since the market economy is based on [the] market mechanism, socialism could be developed under the market economy." The research center defines socialism as a system in which "public ownership plays the central role in the economy, and the Communist Party leads politics." At the same time, socialism carries the social goal of "co-prosperity among the people."

The Chinese theory explains that such a system recognizes the "superiority of publicly owned enterprises in efficiency and vitality over the private enterprises" and offers a "favorable condition for rational allocation of national resources and orderly market management." It further claims that "the socialist nature of the regime led by the Communist Party will be better in pursing its social policy to secure social justice and to alleviate poverty."

Since the theory neglects the facts that state-owned enterprises have been generally more inefficient than private enterprises and that the former socialist countries were unable to solve the problem of alleviating poverty and achieving social justice, it can hardly be said to be a persuasive theory.

Compared with the Chinese socialist market economy, Vietnam's concept of "socialist-oriented market economy" seems more flexible. The Vietnamese do not state explicitly that the public-owned sector is the center of their economy. The problem remains, however, to define what role the state should play and how big that role should be in managing the market economy.

That the state's role will be large seems clear. Since the private sector and the market system are not yet well developed, the ideal allocation of resources can hardly be achieved simply by eliminating various past control measures and thereby transforming the formerly centrally planned economic system to a market economic system. The state would seem to be called on to play a large role in formulating public rules in such matters as contracts and the protection of private property, in building physical and institutional infrastructure, and at the same time in developing skilled managers and workers so that the market can function well. In addition, it seems reasonable also to expect that the state will be called on from time to time to intervene in the market to prevent speculation arising from supply shortages and to prevent "market failure." It would also seem to follow that the state will need to direct the allocation of saving and investment capital by formulating an industrial policy appropriate to the economy's level of development and the availability of resources.

For the Vietnamese state to play such a role effectively, it will require extraordinary resources and a strong budgetary base, both of which are currently lacking. For the moment, the debates over strategy focus on broad questions such as these:

1. What policy should be adopted toward state enterprises and what regulations should be imposed on private enterprises?
2. To what extent should foreign enterprises be allowed to invest directly?
3. Should a capitalist and a middle class be allowed to develop?
4. Should industrial development policy be primarily export oriented or import substitution?
5. Which industries should be supported?

The preoccupation with such large questions and the difficulty in arriving at a consensus as to the answers seem to be core factors in slowing down the decision-making process and thereby compounding the problem of bureaucratic red tape in the approval of FDI projects and in undertaking the required action.

Behind this policy debate, there appears to be a power struggle between so-called conservatives and reformists. Conservatives seem to be basically reluctant to undertake reform; they still adhere to the orthodox Marxist-Leninist ideology and the Stalinist model. They support emotional, nationalistic thinking on self-reliance rather than economic rationalism and adhere to traditional Vietnamese values and customs. They worry that the reform has not only widened the income gap between the rich and the poor and caused the emergence of class distinctions, materialism, graft, corruption, and other crimes, but also has weakened the foundations of the party, which, they argue, will invite political instability and economic disorder in the near future.

So far, political stability has been maintained in Vietnam by way of "compromise politics" between conservatives and reformists, with policy generally following a reformist direction. However, because of the existence of these influential conservatives within the party, there is always a risk that excessive intervention by the state in the economy may distort the market and hinder market dynamics. The history of the recent reform process in Vietnam teaches that the conservatives have reluctantly made concessions to the reformists only when Vietnam has faced economic crisis.

Industrial Policy: Export Led or Import Substitution?

Vietnam seems to have been pursuing an industrial development strategy that is a mixture of export orientation and import substitution. However, since the policies of export expansion and import substitution often contradict each other, it is difficult to achieve both targets at the same time.

The export-oriented industrial development strategy requires a flexible foreign exchange rate policy, low, effective protection rates, minimal direct import-control measures, strong incentives for export-oriented industries, including foreign-affiliated companies, and efficient export and import procedures. On the other hand, the industrial development strategy for import substitution requires market protection through import restrictions, high tariffs, overvalued currency, and special incentives for target industries, with easy access to the foreign exchange quota and to low-interest financing.

With its weak industrial base, current strong demand for imports, and the future potential size of the domestic market for cement, iron and steel, chemical fertilizer, sugar, textile, oil products, petrochemicals, electric appliances, and automobiles, etc., Vietnam's desire to achieve import substitution on these products as soon as possible is understandable. Also, Vietnam may consider it necessary to own these industries and strengthen their competitiveness before the ASEAN Free Trade Area (AFTA) liberalization is in full swing.

However, considering the fact that Vietnam has been faced with serious problems of widespread poverty, high unemployment, strong pressure for employment from new entrants to the labor market, a heavy debt burden, and a chronic current account deficit, plus low saving and a weak financial base, the top-priority target of economic policy should be placed on employment generation and the expansion of exports, at least for a certain period. The extension of employment to the people will not only alleviate poverty through transfer of wealth, but also will extend education through the job, which is very important to raise the potential of the country.

In order to achieve the twin targets of generating employment and expanding exports at the same time, it is essential to adopt an industrial development strategy that sets priority on developing labor-intensive export industries where Vietnam has a comparative advantage. At the same time, small and medium enterprises and rural industries for exports and domestic supply should be strongly promoted. Then, import substitution of raw materials for the export industries should be pursued in accordance with the development of its exports. This kind of phased industrial development policy would be most appropriate for Vietnam.

However, there seems to be a tendency for Vietnam to be moving rather toward a more import-substitution type of industrialization. Most of the large FDI projects approved in the manufacturing industry so far are import-substitution projects, such as automobiles, motorcycles, electric appliances, cement, chemical fertilizers, iron and steel, plastics, etc. And the import tariffs on these commodities have been raised to encourage FDI in such areas. Since most of these import-substitution projects are joint ventures with state enterprises, there is a danger that those import-substitution industry groups will act as a powerful lobby to maintain an overvalued dong.

Because of the influence of traditional socialist thinking in Vietnam, there are still many nationalists in the party who put self-reliance in industrial goods as a higher priority than division of labor, despite the cost. The huge flow of Chinese goods into Vietnam through the border may also be influencing Vietnamese leaders to expedite self-sufficiency in industrial goods. Because of these factors, there is always a tendency for Vietnam to choose an import-substitution type of industrialization. In fact, Vietnam's profit tax structure for domestic firms favors heavy industry, which has the lowest tax rate, at 25 percent; light industry is taxed at 35 percent and service industry at 45 percent.

It seems wise for Vietnam to avoid building new high-cost import-substitution heavy industry unless the environment for such industries is very favorable. If Vietnam is to build such industries, the priority should be given to the following industries: (1) an industry whose productivity increase through technological innovation and mass production is predicted to be large and whose acquisition of international competitiveness should come early; (2) a "growth industry" that has high income elasticity and whose set-up cost for creation of the industry is low; and (3) an industry with a low degree of imports used directly or indirectly. It is also essential to limit the time for market protection and encourage competition even within the protected period.

How to Improve Agriculture?

The successful development of agriculture, which currently absorbs more than 70 percent of total employment, is the key issue for the future Vietnamese economy. However, the initial condition of Vietnam's agriculture is not favorable. Per capita cultivated land is only 0.1 hectare, which is about one-third of that of Thailand. Basic agricultural infrastructure has deteriorated during the long period of war. Population increase also has forced the farmers' income down to a subsistence level in many regions. The pricing system and the agricultural management system, which were originally designed to boost agricultural savings for investment in state industries in an organized manner, discouraged farmers and brought a long period of stagnation in agriculture in Vietnam.

The New Economic Policy applied to agriculture after 1979 checked this stagnation. Finally, Politburo Resolution 10 in 1988 established the position of the peasant household as an autonomous economic unit. Price and foreign exchange liberalization, implemented in 1989, raised the relative prices of agricultural commodities against industrial goods. All this has provided incentives for peasants willingly to invest more labor and capital in order to improve production. The area of cultivated land has expanded and the rice yield per hectare increased from 2.78 tons in 1985 to 3.43 tons in 1993. Total food production increased by 37 percent during 1985–93, which enabled Vietnam to export 1.5 million tons of rice per year between 1989 and 1993. Export items such as coffee, rubber, coconuts, tea, and animal products likewise increased.

The rise in agricultural production and higher relative prices improved farmers' income greatly, which brought a housing construction boom in some rural areas from around 1989. However, this phenomenon did not last long. Food prices declined because of increased supply, while the price of agricultural inputs, such as chemical fertilizer, pesticide, and oil, increased in line with higher international prices. Farmers' income started to decline from the latter part of 1991.

In order to protect farmers from price fluctuations in agricultural commodities and agricultural inputs, the government established the Price Stabilization Fund in April 1993. However, the government's indirect intervention in food prices to improve farmers' income and the serious flooding in two major rice-producing areas caused sharp increases in the prices of food and foodstuffs. This was the major cause for the revival of inflation from the latter part of 1994.

One of the difficult tasks for Vietnam's agricultural policy is to solve the dilemma of two contradictory targets under current poor fiscal conditions: on the one hand, to keep food prices at a low level to stabilize the macroeconomy and support industrialization, and on the other hand, to keep food prices at a level sufficient to ensure an adequate income for farmers. The Price Stabilization Fund has been introduced to solve this dilemma; however, because of its small financial size, the adjustment capability of the fund is limited, as its income depends only on the differential between the international and the domestic price of the targeted commodities.

Furthermore, it is questionable whether Vietnam can continue to increase its food production. In the past, agricultural production in Vietnam has been influenced greatly by weather. If it is again hit by large floods, as it was in 1994, export potential will drop and cause high food prices. In addition, there is the possibility that Vietnam may face the same problem of stagnation of agricultural production that China has been facing. China's food production increased greatly following the introduction of a new farm management system in 1981, but it has been stagnating since 1985. This is believed to have been caused by the reduced state investment in agriculture; the reduced area of cultivated land, because of land being turned over to industry and housing; the decreased collective labor investment in construction of agricultural infrastructure such as irrigation and land development in off-farming periods because of the virtual dissolution of the people's communes; and the decreased farmers' investment in their own land because of better returns from nonagricultural activities.[14]

Since China's agricultural pricing system has been under greater state control than Vietnam's, we cannot generalize. However, a decrease in the area of land under cultivation and a decline in collective labor for construction of infrastructure are already apparent in Vietnam. In fact, the Vietnamese government prohibited the conversion of rice land to other usage in March 1995.

The options open to Vietnam to tackle the above-mentioned problems in agriculture appear to be: (1) diversification of agriculture, by shifting from rice to other commodities with higher price elasticity; (2) attainment of higher productivity by increased input of chemical fertilizer, capital, and technology; and (3) improvement of basic agricultural infrastructure, such as irrigation, drainage, road, electricity, and social infrastructure, such as education, health, and medical services.

In order to achieve these goals, it will be necessary to improve access to rural financing and extension services and to raise nonagricultural income by promoting rural industry and increased fiscal investment in infrastructure. To do so, it seems essential to utilize foreign aid and FDI effectively in the agricultural field at least for the time being. It is also important to tackle major pending problems in the agricultural field. The first need is for the government to speed up the clarification of farmers' land-use titles by promoting mapping and issuing land-use certificates. The second need is for the government to help organize farmers' cooperatives that are suitable to the new environment under the market economy. In addition, the government should further liberalize domestic trade and the pricing of agricultural products and their inputs to increase farmers' incentives.

How to Reform State Enterprises?

The state enterprise sector in Vietnam is small compared to most socialist economies. This may be a reflection of its slow industrialization, which was disturbed by a long war, and by incomplete socialist transformation of the South, which was under the capitalist system until 1975. The share of the state enterprise sector of GDP was 23.7 percent in 1989, and its share of total employment was only 5.3 percent in 1993.

However, the state enterprise sector contributed about 70 percent of the industrial production in 1993. In addition, because of the development of the state-owned oil industry and recent progress in industrialization, the share of the state enterprise sector has been increasing. This is a phenomenon seen only in Vietnam among countries undergoing transformation to a market economy. For example, in China the share of the state enterprise sector in industry decreased from 78 percent in 1978 to 48 percent in 1992.[15] It could be said that, unlike in China, the part played by the private sector in industry in Vietnam has not been growing satisfactorily.

The problem of state enterprises for Vietnam is their inefficiency. Income from state enterprises contributed about 50 percent of national revenue in 1993; however, if the contribution from the oil industry is excluded, the share of the state enterprises was only 30 percent of national revenue. Furthermore, it is estimated that the net contribution of the state enterprises is minor, if credit subsidies, investment grants, retained depreciation, and amortization by the government are taken into account.[16] It will be a big problem for the future economic development of Vietnam if the current situation continues, since state enterprises absorb about 70 percent of aggregated capital and material, produce only about 30 percent of GDP, employ only 5 percent of the employed labor force, and make only a minimal net contribution to the budget.

Vietnam recognizes this problem and has taken some measures to overcome it. Since 1987, the government has introduced an initial set of measures to harden budget constraints on state enterprises. In 1989, the government eliminated subsidies from the budget and undertook interest reform that reduced implicit subsidies through the banking system. It then applied the principle of equal taxation to all enterprises, both state and private.

From 1991 to 1993, the government reduced the number of nonviable enterprises. The total number of state enterprises decreased from 12,084 in January 1990 to about 7,000 in October 1993. It is said that with this reform, the number of loss-making state enterprises decreased from 40 percent of total in 1990 to 15–20 percent by the end of 1994.[17]

The government's basic policies for state enterprise reform were reaffirmed during the midterm National Conference of the party in January 1994.[18] They are:

1. The number of enterprises will be reduced [and] financial management and control need to be improved.
2. State enterprises should be concentrated in key sectors such as socioeconomic infrastructure, the financial-banking system, insurance and a number of key production and service enterprises.
3. It is necessary to carry out equitization to sell a portion of shares to local workers and employees [and] trial sales must be conducted of the stocks and shares of state enterprises to outside organization and individuals.
4. Board of Directors should be set up, on a share-holding basis, composed of members representing ownership by the state, local workers and others.
5. Forms of contractual work in state-run enterprises should be perfected and applied on a broader basis.
6. The system of ministries and administrative levels that own and manage enterprises and the distinction between centrally and locally run enterprises must be gradually abolished.

Based on these policy guidelines, a reduction in the number of state enterprises and their reorganization, strengthened financial management control, and a pilot equitization program are being implemented. However, the actual reform process seems slow. The process in the trial equitization program that started in 1992 is especially disappointing. So far only three out of nineteen pilot firms completed equitization by the beginning of 1995.

In order to promote equitization, Vietnam needs to tackle the following pending issues:

1. the lack of a state business law that defines the owner, the role and responsibility of management, the rights and duties of the workers, etc.;
2. the lack of a level playing field between public and private enterprises;
3. the lack of clarification of the strategic industries that will be retained by the state;
4. the lack of capital and property markets; and
5. the lack of a highly professional organization that implements equitization and privatization.

The solution of these problems will not be easy for Vietnam. The major reason for the slow progress of state enterprise reform seems to be the lack of agreement on the future vision for state enterprises, though the official policy line was reaffirmed, as mentioned above. Everybody now agrees on the necessity of state enterprise reform to increase efficiency. But in terms of equitization and privatization, there is no consensus. Conservatives still believe that the state sector should play a leading role in the national economy. They oppose equitization and privatization of state enterprises. They also strongly oppose foreign participation in the management of existing state enterprises from a nationalist point of view. They especially seem to have strong reservations against Chinese capital. In addition, the conservatives' attitude is supported by interest groups such as administering government agencies and managers and workers of the enterprises, who do not want to equitize the state enterprises.

On the other hand, reformists favor limiting state enterprises to the socio-economic infrastructure and to a few key industries and others, releasing the rest for equitization and future privatization. They consider competition to be the key to efficiency and argue that the private sector should play a leading role in the national economy in the future.

Because of these differences of opinion among the leaders, and because of the immaturity of conditions for equitization and privatization, the process of state enterprise reform may well be a gradual one. It should be reemphasized that since Vietnam's state sector in comparative terms has not been large, most state enterprises are small and regionally dispersed, making the adjustment cost of state enterprise reform not large compared to China. On the other hand, the necessity for reform is more acute because of Vietnam's low saving and poor financial base.

The Prospects

Until recently, Vietnam has not been able to make full use of its economic potential, despite its large and industrious work force imbued with strong entrepreneurial spirit, its relatively rich natural resources, and to favorable geographical location. In the past, socialist ideology and the international environment did not allow Vietnam to develop such potential. However, since the introduction of *doi moi*, Vietnam has been liberated from the custody of ideology and has begun the transformation of its economic system to a market economy. Furthermore, thanks to the end of the Cold War regime, the international environment has turned favorable for Vietnam. Now, Vietnam seems well launched on a path of high growth through the realization of the potential of its innovative farmers and private sector, aided by international cooperation.

Of course, the problems that Vietnam continues to face are legion. Among them, the lack of human resources essential for managing the market economy is the most urgent issue to be tackled. Moreover, due to the short history of the market economy in Vietnam and the continued, if diminishing, influence of socialist doctrine and the one-party system, the government, economy, and society in Vietnam are still not open enough when compared to other ASEAN countries. In addition, real conciliation between the North and the South has yet to be achieved.

However, Vietnamese leaders and technocrats are rapidly developing an understanding of international society and the market economy. They appear to be highly motivated to learn from abroad, especially the key factors that have brought socioeconomic development in neighboring countries. But rather than accepting wholesale the lesson from foreign countries, they are adapting them to suit Vietnam's culture and circumstances.

If this flexible and practical attitude to learn from its neighbors and adjust its policies and institutions is maintained, Vietnam may emerge as another dragon in the Asia-Pacific region in the future. The further development of the market economy, increasing economic interdependence with neighboring countries, and expanding economic cooperation with international financial institutions and other donor countries should help to maintain the high-growth trajectory on which Vietnam is now launched.

Notes

1. Tetsusaburo Kimura, "Economic Reform of Soviet Style Socialist Countries" (Tokyo: Institute of Developing Economies, February 1988), p. 47; and *Tap Chi Cong San,* August 1986, pp. 14–15.

2. The industrialization strategy of Vietnam's Second Five-Year Plan was characterized by its "inward-looking" nature, consisting of a set of policies aiming at achieving self-sufficiency of industrial goods production. Such measures included a policy of import substitution that was heavily biased toward heavy industry, strong market protection, and an overvalued national currency.

3. This was a system of two-way contracts whereby the farmer enters into a contract with the cooperative to cultivate a given plot of land by using agricultural inputs provided by the government, and in return he supplies the cooperative with a set quantity of products at fixed prices. The farmer is also given the freedom to sell above-quota production on the free market.

4. By maintaining subsidies for state enterprises and a dual price structure with fixed and market prices, Vietnam tried to adjust official prices and wages to match free market conditions. The subsequent large budget deficits associated with the loose credit policy and easy monetary policy caused high inflation.

5. The adjustment of prices and wages in 1985 was more comprehensive and was also accompanied by a 92 percent devaluation. But no measures were taken to control credit expansion, and the practice of budget subsidies to cover enterprise losses was retained. In addition, advance public knowledge of the proposed devaluation led to a rush for goods and foreign exchange.

6. As a developing economy in transition to a market economy and lacking a reliable statistical system, it is not surprising that the size of the unofficial sector in Vietnam is significant. It includes: (1) the unreported income from the fast-growing private sector and the undervalued profits of state enterprises, (2) unreported family income, especially income from nonfarm self-employment, which accounts for 37 percent of the average household income (UNDP and State Planning Committee, *The Reports on Income, Savings and Credit for 1994 in Vietnam,* Hanoi, 1994), and (3) the large quantity of gold and U.S. dollars kept unofficially in the private sector, which is roughly estimated at about U.S.$2–3 billion. The Vietnamese government's official estimate of per capita GDP in 1994 is U.S.$289 (*Vietnam Investment Review,* January 2–8, 1995). This is about 42 percent higher than the per capita GDP figure of U.S.$204 computed from official GDP figures based on the official exchange rate. The difference may indicate the size of the current Vietnamese government estimates of the unofficial sector.

7. World Bank, *Vietnam Public Sector Management and Private Sector Incentives,* September 26, 1994, p. 123.

8. Budget deficit in cash basis. Ibid., p. 123.

9. Based on the IMF, *Direction of Trade,* and other trade data of Vietnamese trading partners.

10. Mya Than and Joseph L.H. Tan, *Vietnam's Dilemmas and Options* (Singapore: Institute of Southeast Asian Studies, 1993), p. 224.

11. Author's interview at CETRA, Ho Chi Minh Office, August 1994.

12. Naoki Tejima,"Questionnaire Survey Result on Japan's FDI in 1994," *Journal of Research* (Institute for International Investment and Development), 21, no. 1, January 1995, p. 36.

13. Development Research Center of the State Council and Chinese Academy of Social Sciences, *What the Socialist Market Economy Is* (Beijing: China Development Publishing House, 1993).

14. To Shin, "Rural Reform and Agricultural Issue in China," *Asian Economy* (Tokyo: Institute of Developing Economies, January 1991), p. 22.

15. Sumio Kuribayashi, "Issue on Privatization of State Enterprises in China," *Japan Review of International Affairs* (Japan Institute of International Affairs), January 1994, p. 38.

16. World Bank, *Vietnam: Restructuring Public Finance and Public Enterprises,* April 15, 1992, p. 90.

17. *Vietnam Investment Review,* March 27–April 2, 1995.

18. Raymond Mallon, *Overview of Recent Developments in State Enterprise Reform in Vietnam,* Project Working Paper Series, State Enterprise Reform Program, April 1994.

3

A Society Emerging from Crisis

John Bresnan

The crisis that has shaken Vietnam has profound social dimensions. Poverty is the country's most serious social problem, stemming from a long history of political conflict and failed economic policies. Recent economic reforms, on the other hand, create a host of new social problems, including official corruption, urban unemployment, and declining medical and educational services. Still other social issues that have their roots in the politics of the past remain to be resolved, including relations with the ethnic Chinese minority, with upland tribal minorities, and with Buddhists and Catholics. Vietnamese authorities have indicated some degree of concern about most of these matters, although adequate policy responses in some cases may be some time in coming. Foreign assistance could help speed the resolution of some issues and improve the environment for attention to others.

The Crisis Defined

Vietnamese society has experienced many traumatic events in recent decades. They have included: nationalist resistance to the return of the French beginning at the end of 1946; the division of the country by the Geneva Conference in 1954; subsequent mass migration from North to South out of fear of religious persecution; a violent process of land reform in the North in 1954–56; armed conflict between the North and the South, involving the armed forces of the United States on a large scale between 1965 and 1973, including the aerial bombing of both North and South by U.S. forces from 1968 on; the deaths of 3 million Vietnamese in that conflict; mass relocations of populations in the course of the conflict, involving at one time or another half the entire population in the South; the imprisonment of tens of thousands of civil officials and military officers of the defeated government of the South; the attempted collectivization of land and the nationalization of all private business in the South after 1975; involuntary relocation of several millions from urban to rural areas after 1975; the invasion of Cambodia by Vietnamese forces in late 1978; the subsequent invasion of the northern border provinces of Vietnam by Chinese forces; and the flight of some 1.5 million refugees by land and sea from both the North and the South of Vietnam that has only recently ended.

To these events that have been primarily political in origin must be added other developments that have been principally economic in nature. Do Muoi, the Communist Party general secretary, said at the January 1994 national party conference that the socioeconomic crisis "emerged in the late 1970s and early 1980s, has lasted for over a dozen years and became most acute in the years 1986–88, when inflation was skyrocketing, and again in 1991."[1] The general secretary indicated that the crisis included, in addition to inflation, widespread unemployment, poverty, shortages of food, unmet needs of war invalids and the families of fallen soldiers, and a high incidence of school dropouts among the children of the poor.[2]

Thus Vietnamese society experienced a prolonged political and economic crisis that has had profound consequences for the country's population. The human cost of the violence between 1965 and 1975 is incalculable; to the millions killed must be added the widows, orphans, and disabled left in large numbers to be cared for by the impoverished and divided society that survived. Even had Vietnam in 1975 entered a period of healing and reconstruction, the society would today still be experiencing a level of material and social welfare that suffered by comparison with other Southeast Asian societies. As it was, however, Vietnamese society was reduced to still lower levels of income and welfare after 1975, especially in the South, over the space of another decade, leaving the population impoverished and resistant, even hostile, to government policies.

Public policy changes since 1986 have begun to repair the damage. As the reader will have seen in the previous chapter, economic recovery is well under way. Social recovery, on the evidence of the available data, has been slower in coming. And the new economic pragmatism has brought its own problems, some of them undoubtedly transitional, some perhaps more durable in nature.

The Demographic Situation

The population of Vietnam was estimated in mid-1992 to number 69.3 million, which makes it the twelfth largest national population in the world.

Table 3.1.

Southeast Asian Countries: Population

Country	Population (millions) mid-1992
Brunei	0.27
Cambodia	9.0
Indonesia	184.3
Laos	4.4
Malaysia	18.6
Myanmar	43.7
Philippines	64.3
Singapore	2.8
Thailand	58.0
Vietnam	69.3

Source: World Bank, *World Development Report 1994,* Table 1, pp. 162–163 and Table 1a, p. 228.

In the subregion of Southeast Asia, it is much smaller than the population of Indonesia and somewhat larger than the populations of either the Philippines or Thailand (see Table 3.1).

This population is settled on a land area of 331,690 square kilometers and thus had a density in mid-1992 of 204.3 people per square kilometer. This compared with densities of 95.2 for Indonesia, 111.4 for Thailand, and 101.8 for East Asia and the Pacific as a whole. Among the larger Southeast Asian states, only the Philippines had a density of population approximating that of Vietnam (see Table 3.2).

The comparative situation is even more disadvantageous to Vietnam than these data suggest. The population of Vietnam is more heavily rural than most others in the region—80 percent compared with an East Asian average of 70 percent. And the land area of Vietnam is less well suited for agriculture—only 20 percent is agricultural land, compared with an East Asian average of 44 percent. So Vietnam suffers a serious comparative disadvantage as an agriculture-based economy.[3]

The population and arable land of Vietnam are concentrated in a narrow strip of land that runs the length of the country along its eastern coast, reaching inland at the deltas of the Red River in the north and the Mekong River in the south and extending to the urban centers of Hanoi and Ho Chi Minh City (formerly Saigon). The ethnic Viet (or Kinh) people, who constitute 88 percent of the population, are concentrated in this densely populated coastal, deltaic, and urban zone.[4]

Ethnic minorities fall into two significant groups, along lines common to

Table 3.2.

Southeast Asian Countries: Population Density

Country	Land Area (thousand km^2)	Density (pop. per km^2, most recent estimates) 1987–92
Brunei	5.77	45.9
Cambodia	181.04	48.8
Indonesia	1,904.57	95.2
Laos	236.80	18.0
Malaysia	329.75	55.1
Myanmar	676.55	63.2
Philippines	300.00	209.6
Singapore	0.62	4,456.5
Thailand	513.12	111.4
Vietnam	331.69	204.3
East Asia	16,367.18	101.8

Source: World Bank, *Social Indicators of Development 1994,* relevant country tables.

other countries of mainland Southeast Asia. Ethnic Chinese, who have migrated into what is now Vietnam over two millennia, are concentrated in the northern provinces along the Chinese border and in larger numbers in urban areas of the South, particularly Ho Chi Minh City. Of 1.7 million Chinese resident in the country in 1977, some 700,000 left Vietnam between 1978 and 1982. Another 6 million people are members of 52 smaller ethnic groups, who live in the forested and thinly populated mountains bordering China, Laos, and Cambodia. These minority peoples share the cultures and lifestyles of groups in these neighboring countries, and thus have long been of strategic interest out of all proportion to their numbers.[5]

Decades of armed conflict have given the population of Vietnam additional characteristics that are more or less unique in Southeast Asia, although some are shared with Cambodia. A marked imbalance of the sexes has existed in Vietnamese society ever since the anti-French resistance period and was exacerbated by the war with the United States, creating a significant deficit of males between the ages of 16 and 64 as of the 1979 census.[6] The mobilization of 1.2 million males into the armed forces after 1975 left civil society still further dependent on female labor in the 1980s; the agricultural labor force in the North became 80 to 90 percent female, and females dominated all other fields of work with the sole exception of heavy industry. Similarly, the years of fighting and the subsequent demobilization following the withdrawal from Cambodia in 1989 have given Vietnamese society a very large number of male veterans who are claimants on public offices and public services in the 1990s.[7]

The population of Vietnam also is growing rapidly in comparison with many of its neighbors. The growth rate was 2.2 percent in 1992, compared with 1.6 for Indonesia, 1.5 for Thailand, and 1.4 for East Asia as a whole. Again the Philippines matched Vietnam with a population growth rate of 2.2 percent.[8]

These demographic characteristics have several implications for Vietnam's economic and political development. The limited access to arable land by the heavily rural population has helped to make land issues prominent in the nation's politics and also means that how these issues are resolved has enormous consequences for the welfare of the bulk of the population. Moreover, because the rapidity of population increase is consuming a significant share of every increase in production, the distribution of per capita incomes is a source of public concern as well. The imbalance between the sexes that has arisen as a result of the fighting has added implications for participation in economic and political life that challenge traditional assumptions of male and female roles.

Measures of Poverty

Vietnamese intellectuals have found many ways of describing the poverty of their nation and the consequences for the people. Pham Xuan Nam has written that the socioeconomic situation had sunk "nearly to the 'bottom' " in 1986. "Agricultural production stagnated. Food shortage dragged on. . . . The market was in a terrible turmoil. Inflation reached a galloping rate . . . of 774.7 percent. . . . The monthly wages of workers and employees . . . were just enough for 10 to 15 days' subsistence. In the countryside, prior to harvest time, food shortage was widespread. . . . The majority of the masses found life unbearable."[9]

Le Van Toan and others have estimated average annual per capita income in 1990 at 576,535 Vietnamese dong and, depending on the rate of exchange used, at U.S.$98 to U.S.$202 (see Table 3.3). Based on the Vietnam Living Standards Survey of 1992–93, the World Bank put per capita consumption at 1.4 million dong, or the rough equivalent of U.S.$140.[10] All these estimates put average Vietnamese income at extremely low levels by world standards (see Table 3.4). The World Bank put the GNP per capita of all low-income countries in 1990 at $350, including India at $350 and China at $370.[11]

Income levels in Vietnam also vary markedly from the national average, depending on location within the country. The General Statistical Office has reported that the average income per capita of the families of workers and

Table 3.3.

Vietnam: GDP Per Capita

In dong at current prices in 1990	576,535
In U.S. dollars at exchange rate of state bank in 1989 (U.S.$1.00 = VN dong 3438)	98
In U.S. dollars at FOB export exchange rate in 1989 (U.S.$1.00 = VN dong 1912)	202

Source: Le Van Toan, ed., *Vietnam Economy: 1986–1991* (Hanoi: Statistical Publishing House, 1992), Table 4, p. 69.

Table 3.4.

Southeast Asian Countries: Real GDP Per Capita

Country	Purchasing Power Parities (international $*) 1985–88
Brunei	14,590
Cambodia	1,000
Indonesia	1,820
Laos	1,000
Malaysia	5,070
Myanmar	660
Philippines	2,170
Singapore	10,540
Thailand	3,280
Vietnam	1,000

Source: United Nations Development Programme, *Human Development Report 1991*, Table 1, pp. 119–120.
*International dollars, not to be confused with U.S. dollars, are notional units of currency that embody an average of the price structures of different countries.

officials, which is to say urban people, in 1990 was 48,084 dong, with very significant differences between the northern and southern parts of the country: 37,639 dong in the North, and 58,955 dong in the South.[12] Moreover, the same source reported average monthly income per capita of the families of farmers in the North in the same year at 32,248 dong. The World Bank found this picture confirmed by the Vietnam Living Standards Survey:

> Looking at differences in real consumption . . . shows a fairly large disparity between the 80 percent of the population that live in rural areas and the 20 percent that live in urban areas. Real per capita consumption expenditures are almost twice as high in urban areas, and caloric consumption levels

are also higher. There are also major disparities among the different regions. In general, the southern regions are better off than those in the North and the two southernmost regions are noticeably better off both in terms of per capita consumption expenditures and calories per capita. By all accounts the best-off region is the Southeast, which includes Ho Chi Minh City.[13]

A group of Vietnamese government analysts in May 1993 put the level of "absolute poverty" at an income valued in food at 15 kilograms of rice per person per month or valued in money at 30,000 Vietnamese dong (equivalent to U.S.$3 per person per month). This was the level of income necessary to supply 10.5 kilograms of rice per person per month, which was the minimum judged necessary for subsistence given a structure of consumption in which 70 percent of total family spending went for food. The Vietnamese analysts estimated that 13.8 million people, in 2.847 million households, or nearly 30 percent of the total number of rural households, were living at this level of "absolute poverty."[14] Using the number of calories deemed necessary per day in the international biomedical literature, and based on actual consumption patterns, the World Bank has classified about 51 percent of the Vietnamese population as poor. It also has estimated that "25 percent of the population . . . are food-poor in the sense that they cannot meet their daily basic caloric requirement, even if they were to spend *all* of their money on the basic food basket."[15]

Vietnam is thus an extremely poor country by world standards, and dealing with this condition must be given the highest priority in any program for the nation's development. The extent of absolute poverty and caloric deficiency is so widespread that not much can be done without a major increase in rural productivity. Such an increase will hinge on a number of factors, of course, including appropriate government policies and programs. Underlying these will be, as it has been for some years now, the issue of how best to engage the productive capacities of Vietnam's rural society.

Rice-Farming Families of the Deltas

One of the striking features of rural society in Vietnam, not only between the Kinh people of the lowlands and the minority peoples of the hills, but also between the North and South, and in particular between the Red River delta of the North and the Mekong River delta of the South, is the variability of community structure. The Red River delta is particularly subject to periodic floods as a result of deforestation of the surrounding hills, and communities here depend on flood control by a complex system of major embankments. The population is very dense, numbering more than 1,000 persons per square kilometer, and villages are nucleated for communal help and located where there is some security against the risk of floods. The Mekong River delta is by comparison a region of (usually) gentle floodwaters, needs little irrigation, and has a density of only 384 persons per square kilometer. Human settlements line the Mekong River banks much as in lower Cambodia and Thailand.[16]

These ecological differences are reflected in the social and political structure of Vietnamese rural society, in the view of many students of the subject. James Scott, for example, in his study of subsistence and rebellion in rural Southeast Asia, is highly attentive to the relationship between ecology and society.[17] Even before the arrival of the French, Scott writes, Cochinchina (the southern third of Vietnam, and the most recent to be settled by the Vietnamese) was "the domain of the large landowner and the landless peasant."[18] Such "frontier" areas across Southeast Asia "produced a fluid social structure with high rates of mobility, scattered rather than nucleated settlement patterns, low social cohesion, and not a little anarchy and disorder."[19] The problem in Cochinchina was "not so much poverty per se as economic insecurity and the absence of a protective social fabric."[20] By comparison, Tonkin and Annam (the northern and central thirds of Vietnam) "remained the strongholds of the small holding peasant. Most of those without land were sharecroppers with security of tenure who cultivated land owned by village-based landowners rather than outsiders."[21] Here "local authority and popular norms were stronger; landlords themselves did not have the vast domains their counterparts ruled in the south."[22] In short, the South of Vietnam had a peasantry with weak communal traditions and sharp class divisions, while the North and Central parts of the country had peasantries with strong communal traditions and few sharp internal class divisions.[23]

It was against such varied ecological and historical backgrounds that land reform was pressed in independent Vietnam. In the North, between 1954 and 1956, poor peasants were mobilized to accuse landlords of crimes, several thousand landlords or alleged landlords were executed, the economic base of the landlord class, never large, was eliminated, and the structure of land ownership was leveled.[24] In the South, the pattern of land ownership was transformed by pressure from the revolutionary Viet Minh on the one hand and U.S. intervention on the other. By the early 1970s the system of landlords and tenants was turned into one in which family farmers were the dominant socioeconomic stratum.[25]

Land redistribution was followed by programs of land collectivization in both the North and the South, although the efforts in the North preceded those in the South by some 15 years and were markedly more successful, at least at first. Beginning in 1961, farmers in the North were organized into hamlet-level cooperatives, generally four or five to a village. (It would be more accurate to call these new institutions collectives, because the land was managed as a unit and members were paid according to the number of days worked. But we follow the usage common in Vietnamese writing on the subject.) Thus the historic relationship between access to land and the structure of rural society was broken. Production increased significantly at first, and the availability of rice reached its highest level in 30 years. With the entry of the United States into the war in 1965, the economy of the North was put on a tighter reign, and the existing cooperatives were merged into "high-level cooperatives"—ones that included entire villages and even groups of villages. Production in the North decreased drastically in the years that followed this step.

Buoyed by their victory in 1975, party leaders pushed for the creation of still larger agrarian units in the interest of large-scale socialist production. Now, not only land, but draft animals and all the other means of production were collectivized. Able-bodied males were organized into specialized brigades, and women and children into basic production brigades. The availability of rice decreased precipitously in the North in the late 1970s in the wake of these actions. A survey of cooperatives in the Red River delta in 1979 found a direct correlation: the larger the cooperative, the less productive it was and the less income its members earned.[26]

While poor management undoubtedly contributed to the decline in production on these new state farms, more than poor management was involved. Gareth Porter has written that, where rural society had once been organized hierarchically on the basis of access to land, the society was now "restratified primarily on the basis of access to position in the economic management and political-administrative bureaucracy." In the new system, "the wealthiest families in northern villages . . . are usually those with members who have positions of authority in the village or the cooperative— both the party committee members and those who have economic functions, such as cooperative directors, accountants, unit heads . . . the leading party or state cadres."[27] A similar view emerged from surveys carried out by Vietnamese scholars in 1990 in the northern highlands, Red River delta, and central coast. Most peasants expressed disapproval of the behavior of village and cooperative officials in such matters as land distribution and tax collection. In areas where cooperatives still existed and local officials still played a dominant role, the Vietnamese researchers reported:

> Democratic freedoms are not being guaranteed, a plague of "new local despotisms" has appeared in many areas, law and order are almost non-exis-

tent, social and moral dislocations have increased, unemployment is widespread, the peasants are uncomfortable in expressing themselves and feel repressed, and village solidarity has decreased.[28]

It seems reasonable to conclude that the increasing intrusion of state and party agents and their increasing exactions in terms of rice deliveries and taxes were causally related to the decline in reported production.

In the South, and particularly in the Mekong delta, collectivization never reached this point. As late as 1988, whereas cooperatives were said to constitute from 90 to 99.6 percent of rural households in the northern and central provinces, they constituted only 6.9 percent in the Mekong delta. Half of the cooperatives here were in a single, relatively poor province. The prosperous provinces of the Mekong delta had only a handful of cooperatives each, involving no more than 2–3 percent of their households.[29] Moreover, households in the Mekong delta had long been resisting state policy in other respects as well, producing for their own subsistence, and holding their produce back from the overly regulated market.[30] Total area sown to rice throughout Vietnam declined in 1986 and again in 1987, yields per hectare also fell in 1987, and total rice production fell in the same year, triggering the food shortage referred to by the party general secretary starting in 1987–88.[31]

In these circumstances, on April 5, 1988, the Politburo of the Communist Party of Vietnam reversed the course of more than three decades of agrarian policy. In a resolution thenceforth known as Resolution 10, the party leadership announced a return to the rural household as the principal unit of rural production. A key provision was the leasing of rice fields to individual farming families for fifteen years. The impact was immediate. Rice production rebounded in 1989, and the country exported rice for the first time since independence. Rural communities in all parts of Vietnam had acted promptly to allot the bulk of collective land to individual households. Many rural families, especially in the Mekong delta, began investing in tractors, trucks, plows, pumps, threshers, hullers, and livestock. Some families in the South and in the central highlands even began to hire extra labor. Many cooperatives were left uncertain of their function, and budgets and staff were cut significantly while leaders tried to sort out what to do next.[32]

It remains to be seen how these extraordinary events will be interpreted in Vietnam over time. It is possible that the view of many economists, agriculturists, and other intellectuals that collectivization failed and that private ownership is the key to further development will prevail. But that is not assured. The view of provincial party leaders, as expressed in the lead-up to the Seventh Party Congress in 1991, that rural inequalities are increasing might block any further movement. Certainly the debate between these two perspectives proved contentious in the drafting of the constitution that was ratified in 1992; the convoluted final wording reflects the lack of consensus. The new multisector economy is to allow private ownership, but the foundation for this is "ownership by the entire people and collective ownership" (Article 15). In regard to land, the state "maintains unified management" but may hand land over to individuals for long-term use, and individuals may "transfer and inherit the use rights according to the stipulations of the law" (Article 18). Finally, "the development of the household economy is encouraged" (Article 21). Such language falls short of long-term guarantees; the 15 years for which the rights of use were initially granted are already half gone.

Resolution 10 will nevertheless stand as a major signpost in the history of reform in Vietnam. It marks not only the abandonment of a significant political program by the ruling party, but also the beginning of upward movement in gross national product, food availability, and the material welfare of rural people. The process of improvement has only begun, however. The production of a rice surplus has occurred principally in the Mekong delta and to a lesser extent in the Red River delta. It is believed that the improvement of living conditions in both regions has been fairly widespread. Much of the rest of rural Vietnam has yet to experience increased productivity, however, and bringing growth to the rest of the countryside, while sustaining it in the deltas, will require multifaceted action.

Among changes that will be required are: diversification of crops away from the single-minded focus on rice of the past and in the direction of a varied pattern of subsistence and cash crops that is suited to conditions outside the deltas; improvement of physical and social infrastructure to bring the farmers of poor areas into closer contact with urban suppliers and markets; increased availability of rural credit, including credit for nonagricultural production; improvement in the quality of primary education as an element of the antipoverty program, with special attention to the needs of ethnic minorities in the hills; and increased rural-urban migration as the share of agricultural production in gross national product declines to regional levels.[33] All this will require time and will occur more speedily with international assistance.

The New Urban Rich

As serious as the problem of absolute poverty in Vietnam is, concern also is rising over the growth of relative poverty and relative wealth. Many observers have noted that the difference in income between rich and poor is becoming particularly conspicuous in urban areas. At a conference on the socioeconomic impact of reform held in Haiphong in December 1993, concern over the growing gap between rich and poor was a prominent theme of the papers presented by Vietnamese scholars.[34]

In the words of Trinh Duy Luan:

> An important social corollary . . . of economic reform is social . . . stratification, the polarization between rich and poor in the urban population. In the transitional conditions from the centrally planned economy to the market one, the phenomenon of social stratification has often [been seen in] sudden development outbreaks, sometimes even "exorbitant ones," due to innumerable slits [or] defaults in the economic and social management field, due to "twilight" areas for manipulating laws. In the big cities, such as the capital Ha Noi and Ho Chi Minh City, because of the complicated and dynamic character of the urban life, [and] because of the diversity in the social and professional structure of the population, . . . the polarization between rich and poor has increased significantly.[35]

Data for earlier periods are not available to make possible any measurement of income distribution in Vietnam over time. In the terms in which international comparisons are commonly made, income distribution in Vietnam has not been highly unequal in recent years. Data collected by the Living Standards Survey in 1992–93 showed that the wealthiest 20 percent of the population had a real per capita consumption level that was five times higher than the poorest 20 percent. The World Bank found that this put Vietnam among the relatively good performers in terms of the degree of inequality.[36]

The social critics are not concerned about inequality in these terms, however; they are concerned about the wealth of a small group at the very top of the income scale. Consumption studies usually fail to capture data on the income of the top 1 or 2 percent of a population. They also fail to identify who these wealthiest individuals are. And they fail to explain how these individuals acquired their wealth.

Who are the new rich of Vietnam? According to Trinh Duy Luan, they are the members of three advantaged groups: people in positions of administrative power, people who control economic capital, and people with prestige, experience, and employable skills. Those getting rich most quickly are in positions that enjoy a monopoly in some sector of the economy. They include people engaged in foreign affairs, foreign trade, customs collection, real estate, major engineering projects, aviation, and shipping.[37]

Anecdotal evidence abounds that links such people with financial corruption. In 1993 the heads of the customs and housing departments in Ho

Chi Minh City and the chiefs of Hanoi's commercial-crime division and traffic police were purged for corruption. In 1994 the director and deputy director of Legamex, a textile firm that was to be the flagship of the country's privatization program, were dismissed on charges of using company funds to help the businesses of their friends and of steering allocations of company shares to their relations. The head and deputy head of the people's committee that governs Danang, Vietnam's fourth largest city, were dismissed for allegedly allocating land to their relatives.[38]

In December 1993 Prime Minister Vo Van Kiet, in an address to the National Assembly, called for a nationwide campaign to curb smuggling and corruption. Earlier in the month, Interior Minister Bui Thien Ngo had reported to the assembly that trafficking in illicit goods, including weapons, explosives, opium, and foreign-made cigarettes, was on the increase. He said that more than 900 cases of corruption were uncovered in the previous year, in which customs officers, police officials, and tax collectors, among others, were implicated. The interior minister reported that more than 2,600 officials had been disciplined for taking bribes and more than 2,000 people, including a former cabinet minister, already faced legal proceedings.[39]

The problem of corruption, like the problem of income distribution, is not necessarily worse in Vietnam than elsewhere in Southeast Asia. Nor is it necessarily worse in the South of Vietnam today than it was under previous regimes there. But it may be especially difficult to control in the North of Vietnam for several reasons. The state and the party have long been pervasive in the economy of the North, as in China, with the result that state and party officials have come to command much larger economic resources there. The shift toward a market economy has opened up innumerable opportunities for these officials to divert some of these public resources to private gain. And party discipline is no longer sufficient to control cadre behavior. This last may prove to be the most troubling dimension of the problem over the longer term.

The Urban Unemployed

Since 1988, the government of Vietnam has actively worked to reduce the level of public employment as a necessary part of its cost-containment strategy. Military personnel were reduced by about 50 percent from an estimated 1.0–1.2 million to an estimated 500,000 to 600,000 following the withdrawal from Cambodia in 1989. Civil service employment, principally in public service institutions such as schools and hospitals, was reduced from a high of 1.2 million by 136,000, or a little more than 10 percent, by the end of 1992; a further reduction of 100,000 was planned for 1993 and

Table 3.5.

Hanoi: Major Indicators

	1989	1990	1991	1992
Average size of population (000s)	1,987.5	2,052.3	2,070.0	2,099.6
Labor force (000s)	904.8	935.6	957.7	1,003.9
Labor force in state sector (000s)	501.2	457.8	498.6	510.2
Labor in industry (000s)	234.4	210.2	146.1	140.3
State sector	139.7	122.4	101.1	94.9
Nonstate sector	95.5	87.8	45.0	45.4
Gross product of industry (constant 1989 prices; million dongs)	1,055,842	1,060,042	1,046,379	1,168,162

Source: General Statistical Office, *Economy and Finance of Vietnam: 1986–1992* (Hanoi: Statistical Publishing House, 1994), Table 86, p. 158.

1994. The labor force of state-owned enterprises was reduced from a high of 3.1 million by 794,000, or 29 percent.[40] In short, something on the order of 1.5 million people were thrown on the labor market in a short period of time. Meanwhile a flood of people was flowing into the cities from the countryside in search of employment.

It has been estimated that private employment in trade and commerce meanwhile expanded over the 1988–91 period by a remarkable 22 percent per year. But most private sector activity is very small in scale. The largest private firm in the country has been reported as employing only 3,000.[41] More urban people are self-employed in some fashion than the number who earn wages.[42] So it is not as though the private sector has been able to provide wage-paying jobs to many of the newly unemployed.

The structure of employment also is such that the shift away from the command economy has inevitably been more costly in social terms in Hanoi than in Ho Chi Minh City. As Tables 3.5 and 3.6 show, the labor force in the state sector in Hanoi has remained in the vicinity of 500,000, while it was not half that size in Ho Chi Minh City in 1989 and has declined moderately since. More striking is the fact that the labor force in industry in Hanoi declined by 40 percent from 235,000 in 1989 to 140,000 in 1992, while that in Ho Chi Minh City remained more or less unchanged. Finally, gross production in industry remained largely unchanged in Hanoi, while it increased by almost two-thirds in Ho Chi Minh City.

Thus contrasting patterns of economic and social change have been occurring in Hanoi and Ho Chi Minh City. In Hanoi, employment in the state

Table 3.6.

Ho Chi Minh City: Major Indicators

	1989	1990	1991	1992
Average population (000s)	3,934.3	4,004.9	4,076.0	4,181.6
Labor force (000s)	1,698	1,735	1,773	1,785
Labor force in state sector (000s)	212	178	174	176
Labor in industry (000s)	281.5	266.6	283.8	288.4
State sector	131.7	122.6	127.5	128.7
Nonstate sector	149.8	144.0	156.3	159.7
Gross product of industry (constant 1989 prices, million dongs)	3,597,673	3,931,916	4,368,740	5,094,151

Source: General Statistical Office, *Economy and Finance of Vietnam: 1986–1992* (Hanoi: Statistical Publishing House, 1994), Table 110, p. 264.

sector has been relatively high and holding steady, industrial production has been stagnant, and industrial employment has declined dramatically. In Ho Chi Minh City, employment in the state sector has been relatively small and declining, employment in industry has remained more or less steady, and industrial production is booming.

A significant factor behind the decline in state industry production and employment in Hanoi has been the closure of state enterprises. Cabinet Minister Le Xuan Trinh announced in mid-1993 that reorganization would reduce the number of state enterprises from their then level of 12,000 to an eventual 6,000 or 7,000. It was reported at the time that the closure of state enterprises had already contributed to a significant increase in unemployment.[43]

Who are the victims of enterprise closures? One answer seems to be that most of them are female. Vietnam's female workers are engaged in the full spectrum of professions and occupations, unlike many other developing countries. But the majority of females in Vietnam nevertheless work in low-paying, menial jobs. Moreover, according to studies by the Institute for Female Studies and the Institute of Sociology, females have been disproportionately affected by the layoffs of tens of thousands of workers in the process of streamlining the state sector of the economy. Most women occupied positions considered expendable by the male-dominated corps of managers. Those who have survived so far now face a growing threat of unemployment and salary cuts. At the same time, many who have reentered the work force by setting up small businesses in their homes have not fared well. The average working day for women, including household activities, is 12–14 hours, or almost double the time put in by their husbands.[44]

The fate of those who have reentered the labor market by setting up small businesses in their homes is described with considerable poignancy in a small study conducted in Hanoi in May 1993. The majority of those found working out of their homes were middle-aged women, and almost all of them had previously had jobs in the state-run sector. A woman on maternity leave from a tile factory found there was no job for her when she was able to return to work; she tried making noodles to sell, then tried work as a hairdresser, but neither was profitable; now she and her husband are producing floor tiles on their own. An electrician in an electric motor plant was let go when Soviet support stopped and he received a one-time separation payment; now he produces meat paste and meat pies. Most of those studied were producing and selling food products. Most also were working much longer hours and earning much less than when they were paid employees.[45]

The loss of economic opportunities and status on the part of women appears to be well recognized officially in Vietnam. In July 1993, for example, the Politburo issued a resolution on women in the work force that said the country must "improve women's material and cultural life, raise their social status and establish equality between men and women." But the measures proposed fell far short of what is needed to rectify the situation.[46]

To the formerly employed must be added those who are seeking employment for the first time. This group is caught in the "twilight zone" of an economy that is no longer managed entirely by command but not yet managed entirely by market forces either. About a million young men and women reach working age in Vietnam each year, and the economy seems unable to provide jobs for more than a fraction of them. In 1993, Ho Chi Minh City was able to generate only 120,000 new jobs for the 300,000 individuals seeking them. Hanoi was able to provide employment for only 30,000 of the 180,000 seeking jobs there. The prospect of growing numbers of educated but unemployed youths is rightly a matter of urgent concern.

In sum, the population of Hanoi has suffered disproportionately from reductions in jobs and income as a result of reform, and the social costs have fallen disproportionately on women, the semi-skilled, and the young. One implication is that retraining is needed in urban areas of the North, serving especially women and directed toward self-employment opportunities in the private sector. Another implication is that the school system needs to be redirected, in urban areas of the South as well as the North, with a view to relating it more effectively to sectors of growth in the economy from place to place.

Social Services under Stress

The changing management of the economy of Vietnam is reflected in the society not only in widening differences in incomes and in transitional unemployment but also in stresses being placed upon social services, especially services to the most vulnerable members of society, the children and the poor. Where state-owned enterprises and cooperatives once sponsored health clinics, creches, and kindergartens and were responsible for supporting the elderly and disabled, these services have been seriously disrupted, and the society is now engaged in a search for viable alternatives.

One of the more problematic areas is health. Adam Fforde and Stefan de Vylder, writing in 1988 for the Swedish International Development Authority, drew a picture of a health system that had been under strong central administrative control, had been heavily dependent on state finance and foreign aid, and while better than most Third World systems in reaching rural areas, at least in the North, was nevertheless biased in favor of urban people. As state finance and foreign aid declined and inflation grew, the health bureaucracy fell back to the defense of its own high-technology institutions, such as hospitals and research centers. Local clinics came to depend on cash payments by the better off. Many people turned to the "parallel market" for drugs, without bothering to get a physician's prescription. Most health care professionals were forced to take additional jobs in order to make a living.[47]

The resulting health status of the population is difficult to assess. Vietnam has a significantly lower infant mortality rate and a significantly higher average expectancy of life, according to officially reported data, than its per capita GNP would lead one to expect. However, a World Bank report stresses that "health statistics published by the government and provided to international organizations must be viewed with caution. There is a great need to improve statistics in the health sector."[48]

At the same time, the Bank report has this to say about nutrition:

> Child malnutrition rates in Vietnam are very high in relation to the infant mortality rate. In fact, if the results from the 1987–89 General Nutrition Survey accurately represent the nutritional situation in the country, Vietnam has a higher proportion of underweight and stunted children than almost any other country in South and Southeast Asia, excepting Bangladesh and possibly Myanmar. Further, various household surveys undertaken over the last decade suggest that child malnutrition rates have not changed appreciably during the 1980s and may in fact have worsened in the latter part of the decade.[49]

Table 3.7.

Vietnam: Decrease in Education

Level of Education	1986–87	1989–90
Promotion rate from the primary to lower secondary level	92%	72%
Number of lower secondary students	3,273,000	2,758,870
Promotion rate from the lower to upper secondary level	45%	30%
Number of upper secondary students	922,000	691,300

Source: Pham Minh Hac, ed., *Education in Vietnam (1945–1991)* (Hanoi: Ministry of Education and Training, 1991), Table 6, p. 78.

The problem may reflect a lack of comparability of the data, but it also is possible that the economic crisis of 1984–88 contributed to a significant deterioration in nutritional status. If so, a rapid recovery is possible.

The educational status of the population seems relatively clear. Illiteracy is low in Vietnam. At latest count, only 12 percent of the population age 15 and above was illiterate in Vietnam, compared with an East Asia and Pacific average of 24 percent. Illiteracy is relatively low among females in Vietnam as well; only 16 percent of females age 15 and above were illiterate in Vietnam, compared with a regional average of 34 percent.[50]

Educational attainment suffers by comparison with the region, however. Vietnam had 64 percent of its children in the fourth-grade-age group actually in grade 4 in the most recent estimate, compared with a regional average of 89 percent. And Vietnam had 33 percent of its secondary-school-age youths in secondary school, compared with a regional average of 53 percent. Pupil-teacher ratios also were higher than regional averages.[51]

Moreover, the rate at which children are repeating a grade level or dropping out of school in the primary years has been high and rising. The number of children finishing the five years of primary school as a percentage of the number entering first grade was particularly low in mountain provinces and in the Mekong delta.[52]

The promotion rate from primary school to lower secondary school declined in the late 1980s, as did the promotion rate from lower secondary school to upper secondary school. This has led to an absolute decline in the number of secondary students at both levels (see Table 3.7). The pattern also applies to secondary technical schools and vocational training schools. The number of students in both types of institutions declined between

1986–87 and 1989–90. Even the number of technical and vocational schools themselves declined.[53]

Enrollment of full-time students in higher education dropped from 120,800 in 1980–81 to 85,700 in 1985–86, then recovered to 92,600 in 1989–90. Overall enrollment, including part-time and open-admission students, remained relatively stable throughout the decade. The most recent figure represents 20 students per 10,000 inhabitants, a very small proportion compared to some countries in the region (Thailand had 166 per 10,000 in 1987 and the Philippines had 266 in 1988).[54]

Several reasons have been advanced for the general educational decline. State subsidies are declining, and schools are forced to rely increasingly on parents' "contributions" for building repairs, classroom supplies, and informal payments to supplement teachers' state salaries. In cities like Hanoi, Haiphong, and Ho Chi Minh City, teachers now conduct "extra study" classes, for which parents must pay. As these contributions are more than some families can afford, children are dropping out of the system. Schools in the cities also are losing out because they are seen as unable to prepare students for the new work place. In rural areas the new climate of economic opportunity means that sending a child to school causes its labor on the family farm to be lost, and these days that means losing real money.[55]

A technical educator in Ho Chi Minh City, Nguyen Thien Tong, recently described higher education in Vietnam as in a state of "acute crisis." Heavy reliance on government financing at a time of tight budgets has resulted in a financial crisis. The liberalization of the labor market has revealed a large discrepancy between the skills of graduates trained for the command economy and those relevant to the emerging market economy. The quality of teaching and research has deteriorated "precipitously." An end result is growing graduate unemployment.[56]

Even official judgments of the educational system tend to be harsh. A joint evaluation by the Ministry of Education, the United Nations Economic and Social Council (UNESCO), and the United Nations Development Program (UNDP) summarizes its findings under such headings as: "decrease in quantity and deterioration of quality at all levels of general education"; "poor linkage between vocational/technical education and employment"; "weakness in and constraints upon teaching staff"; and "the irrelevance of education and training to society in transition."[57]

Reforms are beginning to take place in an effort to deal with the problems. In the case of higher education, there have been at least three significant policy initiatives. A system of fees was introduced in 1989, following the strategy adopted by other Southeast Asian countries, and causing private sources of funding to rise 22 percent by 1992—and as high as 40 percent in high-prestige institutions such as polytechnics and medical schools. The foundation of a private college of computer science in Hanoi in 1988 has been followed by the start of other private colleges. More recently, the government has begun acting on a decision reached in 1993 to restructure the current system of higher education, which has included 103 institutions, two-thirds of them with student bodies of under 1,000, many engaged in highly specialized studies.[58]

Academic staff in higher education present an acute problem. A 1991 survey found that doctorates had been completed by only 13 percent of the country's university teaching staff. Moreover, two-thirds of all those holding master's degrees and doctorates were over 50 years of age.[59]

One reason for the shortage of personnel is that Vietnam lost a large part of the educated elite of the South after 1975. Medical personnel left in such numbers that a severe shortage occurred, and medical doctors were temporarily recruited from Eastern Europe to provide medical services to the population. Universities in the South lost large proportions of their academic staff. As a result, the trained personnel of the North had to be spread more widely after 1975, and many positions in the South continue to be filled by them.[60]

Most master's degrees and doctorates held in Vietnam have been earned abroad. This is not unlike the rest of Southeast Asia a few decades ago; even today most doctorates in the region are still earned abroad. Vietnam has relied to an unusual degree on foreign training, however, and on training in the former Soviet Union and other socialist countries. These countries have produced for Vietnam a total of 30,000 university graduates, more than 4,500 associate doctors and doctors, more than 9,000 post-graduates, and 25,000 technical workers. Many have become scientists, high-ranking officials, and economic managers. They have been valued "for their high knowledge and skill as well as their good political viewpoint. Most of them have been highly recommended at the establishments they have worked for, and many of them hold high positions in the state and party bodies."[61]

The quality and relevance of these trained personnel in the new situation of Vietnam must be seriously questioned. The change from a command economy to a market economy involves a fundamental change in ways of thinking about products and productive processes, not to mention thinking about distribution and end uses. Some retraining is desirable in the short term, but new kinds of training are needed from the ground up. Economic managers are an obvious case in point. The market economies of Southeast Asia are managed by economists trained largely in the English-speaking world, particularly in the United States. They were trained in the 1950s and 1960s with the help of the Ford and Rockefeller foundations and subsequently with the help of their governments and families. It is urgent that Vietnam should begin promptly to narrow the gap of more than a generation that exists between it and its market-economy neighbors in the training of this crucial human resource. Only a small percentage of World Bank loan funds would be needed to begin a task that cannot be ignored.

Some Social Challenges Remaining

While the attention of Vietnamese policymakers and analysts has tended to focus on poverty, income distribution, employment, and medical and educational services, other social issues remain to be addressed that may be more resistant to resolution.

The Ethnic Chinese Minority

As the largest of Vietnam's minorities, the ethnic Chinese (usually referred to as *Hoa* in Vietnam) bulk large among the Vietnamese overseas community and among the population that remains. The border war with China in 1979 not only increased the flood of Hoa and other refugees from Vietnam; it also increased the mutual sense of alienation between the Vietnamese and the Hoa minority who stayed. The Hoa were seen largely as a "fifth column" in Vietnamese society; business in Cholon, the Chinese section of Ho Chi Minh City, was brought to a standstill. The severity of the economic crisis made obvious the need to bring the Hoa back into society. In 1987, the Council of Ministers issued a series of liberal decrees on the ethnic Chinese. The government allowed Chinese-language schools to reopen. Chinese were again admitted to Party ranks.[62]

Within the next few years, thousands of ethnic Chinese resumed trading activities and established small-scale industries processing food, producing textiles and shoes, or assembling electronic equipment, using funds made available from relatives abroad for the most part, as they had lost most of what they had owned themselves. In 1991 it was estimated that the ethnic Chinese, who made up 10 percent of the population of Ho Chi Minh City, accounted for one-third of the city's commerce and two-thirds of its small-scale industry. The same ethnic Chinese also have been credited with playing a major role in facilitating the flow of investment and trade from Singapore, Taiwan, and Hong Kong.[63]

The relationship between Vietnamese authorities and the ethnic Chinese minority will remain hostage to external events. Should sparring between Hanoi and Beijing over oil in the South China Sea erupt into violence, progress by the Hoa people of Vietnam might well be set back. But fear of domination of Vietnam's domestic economy by its resident Chinese, which is still encountered in Hanoi, is surely a misplaced concern. Especially now that the IMF and World Bank are on the scene, the government of Vietnam has every reason to be confident of its control over macroeconomic policy and every reason to continue to reduce state intervention in investment and trade. As such measures are taken, greater freedom will be provided to the ethnic Chinese minority as well as to the indigenous majority. And that should be to the benefit of both.

Highland Minorities

The most numerous group of non-Viet people is the more than seven million who live in the highlands of the country and who comprise 52 separate ethnic groups.

Possibly the most severely repressed of all these highland peoples during and since the war have been the native people of the central highlands of South Vietnam. Gerald Hickey estimates that 200,000 of these montagnards, or one-fifth of their total, died during the war, and that 85 percent of their villages were destroyed or abandoned.[64] Since 1975, the government has been moving the montagnards into fixed settlements and moving an estimated one million lowland Vietnamese into the highlands.

Murray Hiebert has reported that life for the highland peoples as a whole is harsh. Most groups face rice shortages for three to nine months each year. The literacy rate is only 10 percent, and only 12,000 out of 400,000 school-age children attend school. Diseases such as malaria and goiter are common. Opium production is increasing. Poverty condemns the highland peoples to the margins of society.[65] Nong Duc Manh, the first montagnard to become a member of the Politburo, told a party-sponsored conference in May 1992 that many montagnards "are still threatened by famine."[66]

Government efforts to cater to the needs of the montagnards have not been notably successful. Many studies of social services find the montagnards have been the victims of neglect. A harsh judgment was rendered by Hoang Dien, writing in the army newspaper in October 1992. Under the headline "Deplorable State of Affairs in the Mountain Regions," he described government programs as a "piecemeal, patchy, disjointed, short-lived, 'shower-like' effort."[67]

The government is aware of the need to improve the conditions of the highland peoples. Nam Duc Manh has been a forceful advocate of programs to improve their living standards while preserving their cultural identities. Ethnic minority people now number 70 members of the National Assembly (15 percent of the total). So political attention is being called to the problem. Resources remain a major constraint. But the rising global interest in minority peoples and the expanding presence of foreign aid agencies in Vietnam are sources of hope that resources too will soon be directed to the montagnards.

Religious Minorities

Religious affiliation continues to define significant cultural minorities in Vietnam, and their members continue to suffer restrictions on their religious practices. At the same time, there are signs that some in the Communist Party are beginning to take a more positive view.

The government banned the Unified Buddhist Church of Vietnam in 1981 and has tried to replace it with a government-sponsored body. The leader of the Unified Buddhist Church, the Venerable Thich Huyen Quang, has been under house arrest since 1982, and banished to Quang Tri province. Although he has been reported to be in poor health and deprived of proper medical care, Quang has continued to protest official religious policy in documents clandestinely disseminated within Vietnam and smuggled abroad. The government announced in August 1995, that Quang would be tried on criminal charges of "sabotaging religious solidarity." His chief deputy, who was found guilty of similar charges after a one-day trial, was sentenced to five years in prison.[68] Quang is in his late seventies, and emigres have discussed the possible need of establishing a new headquarters for the mother church in North America.

Other instances of church-state confrontation have centered on the Linh Mu pagoda in Hue. The funeral of a prominent monk in April 1992 led to arrests and demonstrations. These were followed in May 1993 by a self-immolation by fire at the pagoda.[69]

Buddhist intellectuals also have been prominent among those imprisoned for human rights activities. Perhaps the best known is Doan Viet Hoat, former vice rector of the Buddhist Van Kanh University in Saigon, who was imprisoned without trial from 1976 to 1988 and has been reimprisoned since 1990. His current imprisonment is for his involvement in the underground newsletter *Freedom Forum,* which called for major political changes in Vietnam.[70] The association of such Buddhist figures gives the human rights movement in Vietnam considerable stature among foreign observers. How widely the views of these activists are shared among their coreligionists within Vietnam itself is not known.

The government also exercises a number of controls over the Catholic Church and its ten million members in Vietnam. The government has been allowing seminaries to reopen and new churches to be built. Monsignor

Claudio Celli of the Vatican said during a visit in January 1992, that there were "signs of springtime."[71] But many restrictions continue. Australian Cardinal Edward Clancy visited Vietnam in September 1993 to raise concerns about imprisoned clergy and slow government approval for the ordination of priests and the installation of bishops; he was forbidden from saying mass at the Hanoi cathedral.[72]

Nevertheless, there are signs that the survival of religious attachments in spite of official efforts to wipe them out has begun to cause some rethinking to take place in Vietnam. In addition, the collapse of communism in the Soviet Union has led to rethinking about sources of modern intellectual movements other than Marxism. For example, Pham Minh Lang, writing in early 1994 in *Vietnam Social Sciences,* published by the National Center for Social Sciences and the Humanities in Hanoi, argues the need for adopting a scientific attitude toward philosophical trends outside Marxism. It is time that Vietnamese scholars acquire an understanding of Freudian psychology, American pragmatism, and existentialism by the direct study of work that stands in these traditions, and no longer just by reading articles about what is wrong with these schools of thought. ". . . Ancient Eastern philosophy has been attracting the attention of a lot of people," he writes, although "less [than] trustworthy explanations of Eastern philosophy are still rather widespread." There are important questions to be resolved concerning Taoism and Confucianism, and especially concerning Buddhism, which "it is impossible to ignore." And more broadly: "Religion has been one of man's forms of perception during innumerable generations. It has an important role in the spiritual life of a great number of nations. Nevertheless, in past years, religious problems have not been paid due attention." Lang calls for the development in Vietnam of programs of study of Eastern philosophy, Western philosophy, religion, and theology under the direction of "leaders and guides who have special knowledge and are enthusiastic, active and resourceful."[73]

Conclusions

Against the background of the many traumatic events that have been experienced by the people of Vietnam during the past four decades and the reforms that have been attempted particularly since 1986, it is not surprising that the principal social problem is poverty, especially in rural areas, or that the principal health problem is malnutrition. Thus increased rural productivity and improved food distribution must be central to any program for the improvement of the general welfare. This perspective is not yet as widely shared among economic policymakers and analysts in Hanoi as it might be.

There is still a pronounced tendency in these circles to think of development in terms of industry and foreign investment. The World Bank is playing a significant role in pressing the case for priority attention to poverty and malnutrition and can help the Vietnamese leadership to draw on the experience of other countries to design strategies to alleviate these very serious conditions.

Several large groups of people are clearly in need of considerable change in their economic circumstances: rural people outside the deltas, especially the ethnic minority people of the highlands; unemployed and underemployed workers in the cities, especially women and youths; and children of poor families, who appear to be suffering from serious deficiencies in their nutrition and education. Vietnam's leaders have yet to develop a framework for policy attention to these most needy of the country's citizens. Private efforts are being made on a small scale, and these may be significant over time in testing new approaches in the new environment; they should be encouraged. There is an opportunity here for members of Vietnam's elite and foreign donors to come together in efforts to seek new solutions to some of Vietnam's most complex social problems.

At the same time, not all social problems have an economic foundation. At least three large groups have been experiencing problems that are primarily political in origin: the ethnic Chinese minority in Vietnam and, among other religious groups, Buddhists and Catholics. There has been official recognition of the need to see the ethnic Chinese as resources that have much benefit to offer Vietnam, and some steps have been taken to reduce constraints on them. There also has been recognition by at least a few intellectuals that religion is here to stay and might even be of benefit to society.

Much remains to be done before such social problems can be resolved to any significant degree. The needed programs of action seem clear enough, but the time and resources they require might nevertheless prove waning. Hope seems to lie particularly in continuing improvements in Vietnam's international communications. The continued accessibility of Vietnam to foreign scholars and analysts, not only through travel and interviewing in Vietnam, but also through the publication of Vietnamese data and analysis, which recently has been much enhanced, is essential to foreign understanding of social conditions in Vietnam and thus to supportive policies on the part of the industrial democracies. An increased reverse flow of information into Vietnam about the historical experience of other peoples and the scholarly reflections of intellectuals outside Marxist-Leninist systems is equally needed. Having abandoned economic and political autarky, Vietnam needs to avoid falling back into intellectual autarky. There are voices calling for just this stance toward the rest of the world. One must hope that anti-protectionist forces will continue to prevail.

Notes

1. Do Muoi, *Political Report of the Central Committee, Communist Party of Vietnam, Mid-Term National Conference* (Hanoi: The GIOI Publishers, 1994), p. 10.

2. Ibid., p. 10.

3. World Bank, *Social Indicators of Development: 1994* (New York: Oxford University Press, 1994), p. 373.

4. *The Socialist Republic of Vietnam* (Hanoi: Foreign Languages Publishing House, 1990), p. 57.

5. Judith Bannister, *Vietnam: Population Dynamics and Prospects* (Washington, D.C.: Bureau of the Census, U.S. Department of Commerce, February 1992).

6. Ibid.

7. Bannister, *Vietnam;* see also Jayne Werner, "Women, Socialism, and the Economy of Wartime North Vietnam, 1969–75," *Studies in Comparative Communism* 2–3 (Summer-Autumn 1981).

8. World Bank, *Social Indicators of Development: 1994,* relevant country tables.

9. Pham Xuan Nam, "An Overview of Socio-Economic Impacts of the Renovation in Vietnam," presented at University of British Columbia and National Center for the Social Sciences and Humanities, Round Table on Socio-Economic Impacts of the Renovation in Vietnam (Hereafter UBC/NCSSH Roundtable), Haiphong, December 14, 1993.

10. State Planning Committee and General Statistical Office, *Vietnam Living Standards Survey, 1992–1993* (Hanoi, April 1994); World Bank, Country Operations Division, Country Department I, East Asia and Pacific Region, *Vietnam: Poverty Assessment and Strategy* (Washington, D.C.: World Bank, January 1995), p. 2.

11. World Bank, *World Development Report: 1992* (New York: Oxford University Press, 1992), Table 1, p. 218.

12. General Statistical Office, *Statistical Data of the Socialist Republic of Vietnam, 1986–1991* (Hanoi, Statistical Publishing House, 1992), Table 89, p. 109.

13. World Bank, *Vietnam: Poverty Assessment and Strategy.*

14. Vu Tuan Anh, "Impacts of Economic Policy Reform on Economic Growth and Social Structure Changes in Vietnam," presented at UBC-NCSSH Roundtable, December 15, 1993.

15. World Bank, *Vietnam: Poverty Assessment and Strategy,* p. 7.

16. E.H.G. Dobby, *Southeast Asia* (London: University of London Press, 1956), pp. 288 ff; General Statistical Office, *Economy and Finance of Vietnam: 1986–1992* (Hanoi: Statistical Publishing House, 1994), Table 1, pp. 7–8.

17. James C. Scott, *The Moral Economy of the Peasant: Rebellion and Subsistence in Southeast Asia* (New Haven: Yale University Press, 1976). For a more recent example, Neil L. Jamieson, *Understanding Vietnam* (Berkeley: University of California Press, 1993), pp. 3–6.

18. Scott, *Moral Economy,* p. 78.

19. Ibid., p. 68.

20. Ibid., p. 78.

21. Ibid., p. 81.

22. Ibid., p. 82.

23. Ibid., pp. 201–202.

24. Edwin E. Moise, *Land Reform in China and North Vietnam* (Chapel Hill: University of North Carolina Press, 1983), pp. 205–268.

25. Gareth Porter, *Vietnam: The Politics of Bureaucratic Socialism* (Ithaca: Cornell University Press, 1993), pp. 57–60.

26. Ngo Vinh Long, "Reform and Rural Development: Impact on Class, Sectoral, and Regional Inequalities," in William S. Turley and Mark Selden, *Reinventing Vietnamese Socialism: Doi Moi in Comparative Perspective* (Boulder: Westview Press, 1993), pp. 166–173.

27. Gareth Porter, *Vietnam*, pp. 57–59.

28. Ngo Vinh Long, "Reform and Rural Development," p. 176.

29. Ibid., p. 177.

30. Melanie Beresford, *National Unification and Economic Development in Vietnam* (London: Macmillan, 1989), p. 114.

31. General Statistical Office, *Statistical Data . . . 1986–1991,* Tables 37, 38 and 39, pp. 49–50; see also Ngo Vin Long, "Reform and Rural Development," p. 176.

32. Nguyen Sinh Cuc, "The Actual Economic and Social Situation in Rural Areas of Vietnam Following the 10th Resolution," *Economic Problems* (Hanoi: Institute of World Economy, January-March 1992), pp. 9–16.

33. See, for example, the sections on agriculture and poverty alleviation in World Bank, *Vietnam: Transition to Market—An Economic Report* (Washington, D.C.: Country Operations Division, Country Department I, East Asia and Pacific Region, September 15, 1993).

34. UBC-NCSSH Roundtable, December 14–16, 1993.

35. Trinh Duy Luan, "Social Impact of Renovation in Vietnamese Cities," UBC-NCSSH Roundtable, p. 6.

36. World Bank, *Vietnam:Poverty Assessment and Strategy,* pp. 3–4.

37. Trinh Duy Luan, "Social Impact," p. 8.

38. "Something Smelly in Vietnam's Doi Moi," *The Economist,* June 4, 1994, p. 33.

39. "New Effort to Curb Corruption," *Asian Wall Street Journal Weekly,* December 27, 1993.

40. World Bank, *Vietnam: Transition to Market,* pp. 65–66.

41. Ibid., p. 67.

42. State Planning Committee and General Statistical Office, *Vietnam Living Standards Survey, 1992–1993,* Table 4.2.4.

43. "State Enterprises Face Closure," *Indochina Digest,* June 4, 1993.

44. Nguyen Tri Dung, "Doi Moi and the Woman: Is Vietnam's Female Workforce Reaping the Benefits of Reform?" *Vietnam Investment Review,* July 11–17, 1994, p. 16.

45. Tran Thi Van Anh, "Some Aspects of Household Economy in Hanoi," UBC-NCSSH Roundtable, December 15, 1993.

46. *Indochina Chronology,* 12, 3 (July–September 1993).

47. Adam Fforde and Stefan de Vylder, *Vietnam—An Economy in Transition* (Stockholm, 1988), pp. 119–121.

48. World Bank, *Vietnam: Transition to Market,* p. 161.

49. Ibid., p. 182.

50. *World Bank, Social Indicators of Development, 1994,* p. 373.

51. Ibid.

52. Pham Minh Hac, ed., *Education in Vietnam (1945–1991)* (Hanoi: Ministry of Education and Training, 1991), p. 59.

53. Ibid.

54. Vietnam, Ministry of Education, UNESCO, and UNDP, *Viet Nam: Education*

and Human Resources Sector Analysis. Synthesis Report (Hanoi, October 1992), p. 23.

55. Ashley S. Pettus, "Vietnam's Learning Curve," *Far Eastern Economic Review,* August 18, 1994, pp. 36–37.

56. Nguyen Thien Tong, "Higher Education Reform in Vietnam," prepared for the Eleventh Annual Southeast Asia Conference, University of California at Berkeley, February 26–27, 1994, p. 1.

57. Vietnam, Ministry of Education et al., *Viet Nam: Education,* pp. 33 ff.

58. Nguyen Thien Tong, "Higher Education Reform," pp. 3–4.

59. Vietnam, Ministry of Education et al., *Viet Nam: Education,* p. 24.

60. Personal interviews, August 1992 and August 1993.

61. Bui Cong Tho, "Glimpse of International Cooperation in Education and Training," in Pham Ming Hac, *Education in Vietnam,* p. 171.

62. Ramses Amer, *The Ethnic Chinese in Vietnam and Sino-Vietnamese Relations* (Kuala Lumpur: Forum, 1991); E.S. Ungar, "The Struggle over the Chinese Community in Vietnam, 1946–86," *Pacific Affairs,* Winter 1987–88; Lewis Stern, "The Eternal Return: Changes in Vietnam's Policies Toward the Overseas Chinese, 1982–1988," *Issues and Studies,* July 1988.

63. Murray Hiebert, "Market Test: Cautious Re-emergence by Ethnic Chinese," *Far Eastern Economic Review,* August 1, 1991.

64. Gerald Cannon Hickey, *Shattered World: Adaptation and Survival Among Vietnam's Highland Peoples During the Vietnam War* (Philadelphia: University of Pennsylvania Press, 1993).

65. Murray Hiebert, "Dynamics of Despair: Poverty Condemns Minorities to Margins of Society," *Far Eastern Economic Review,* April 23, 1992.

66. *Indochina Chronology,* 11, 2 (April-June 1992).

67. *Indochina Chronology,* 12, 1 (January-March 1993).

68. Philips Shenon, "Vietnam to Try Dissident Buddhist and Monk Despite U.S. Protest," *The New York Times,* August 18, 1995, p. A7.

69. *Indochina Chronology,* 12, 2 (April–June 1993) and 4 (October–December 1993).

70. *Indochina Chronology,* 11, 4 (October–December 1992).

71. *Indochina Chronology,* 11, 1 (January–March 1992).

72. *Indochina Chronology,* 12, 3 (July–September 1993).

73. Pham Minh Lang, "Scientific Attitude Towards Philosophical and Sociological Trends Outside Marxism," in *Vietnam Social Sciences,* 2, no. 40 (1944), pp. 30–34.

4

The Strategic Predicament

Richard K. Betts

Economically and politically, everything seems to be looking up for Vietnam. In the strategic sphere, however, the country is scarcely more secure than it was during four decades of war. Insecurity exists now not in spite of victory in past wars, but because of it. The only great power now engaged strategically with Vietnam—China—is engaged in a threatening way. Having fought off a succession of other great powers since the 1940s, Hanoi is now free of their military interference, and also free of their military support.

To say that Vietnam is insecure is not alarmist. The country is not likely to be attacked or conquered in the near future. Many states live long and fruitful lives despite insecurity. Indeed, at present there is no crisis or imminent danger. To say that Vietnam is insecure is only to say that it faces an unfavorable imbalance of power, with few options for redressing it, and is vulnerable if others take advantage of its military isolation. Although true that war is an improbable threat to Vietnam today, this provides no reassurance for national security policy. Most wars are quite improbable until they happen.

It is not popular to think about Vietnam in these terms. Inside Vietnam, government and populace are preoccupied with economic renovation.[1] Outside the country, most people who still take balance-of-power politics seriously are not interested in Southeast Asia, and many of those interested in Southeast Asia consider balance-of-power concerns outmoded. When most observers speak of Vietnam and war in the same breath, they are still speaking about the agonizingly prolonged process of getting beyond the last war, not the possibility of a new one. There is not a lot of concern about Vietnam's strategic predicament because most observers focus on *current* problems or *probable* changes, neither of which is the preoccupation of a normal security policy. And there is, of course, much more to foreign policy than security policy and military power.

Nevertheless, virtually all countries have security policies and military strategies. In these terms, Vietnam has a big problem. It has lost the massive economic and military support it once had from the Soviet Union and has no good prospects for finding any other great-power patron. Admission to ASEAN will prove beneficial, but the economic and diplomatic benefits will not translate into meaningful strategic help. While Vietnam has many good reasons to celebrate progress and to look forward to more economic and diplomatic integration in the outside world, it stands alone militarily.

The notion that peace has not yielded security is less difficult to grasp when we recall that peace has been an abnormal condition for the Vietnamese Communist Party and the regime that it established in the North in 1954 and extended to the South in 1975. Throughout the half-century before 1989 they were at peace for only a few years in the 1950s and 1970s. The rest of the time they were consumed by sustained combat not only against their own anticommunist countrymen or weak neighbors in Laos and Cambodia, but against a succession of four great powers: Japan, France, the United States, and China.

This odyssey gave Vietnam's Communists good reason to believe that persistence in the face of powerful enemies pays and that history would confirm their mission. It also gave them good reason for self-confidence. Why then did ultimate success after a half-century of war not bring much more security to the Hanoi government?

Losing by Winning

After 1975 Vietnam's rulers lost the peace *because* they won the war. As Douglas Pike put it:

> The overwhelming victory . . . was ruinous for strategic thinking in Hanoi in a way a less-decisive ending never would have been. The . . . stunning success created among members of the High Command and Politburo such a sense of the superiority of their doctrine that they were unable to treat new strategic needs objectively. . . . The result in each case was grief and injury for Vietnam.[2]

The victory ensured both the sovereignty of the Communist Party and the stagnation of the country's development. The new regime saddled the country with a Marxist economy and lost the chance for normal interaction with the largest economies of the West. When the Carter administration was willing to normalize diplomatic relations, Vietnam insisted that Washington implement the financial aid provisions of the 1973 Paris peace agreement, despite the United States position that Hanoi's conquest of Saigon in 1975 had voided the agreement and the naiveté of the idea that U.S. public opinion would ever permit aid to those who had rubbed American noses in defeat.

By the time Vietnam gave up the demand for reparations, it was too late. The reinvigoration of the Cold War and the invasion of Cambodia had made normalization impossible. The Communists had overestimated the importance of Vietnam to the United States once the United States had lost the struggle over who would govern it.[3] The normal connections between power, victory, and influence were reversed after this war. Washington had lost but did not need anything from Vietnam; Hanoi had won but needed investment from the West. Vietnamese leadership did not fully grasp how much more the victors needed the vanquished than the other way around, and they did not revise their "triumphalist revolutionary view of the world" until the late 1980s. By then, events were making it unmistakably clear that a self-contained market among socialist states could not substitute for integration in the world capitalist market.[4]

Why such miscalculation and change of fortune? First, until 1975 the main strategic problem for Vietnam's Communists was not national security against other countries, but establishing sovereignty over their own country. Second, until 1989 they had powerful sources of external support in the Soviet Union and, for part of the time, China. No matter how bad things got in South Vietnam or Cambodia, Hanoi had enough backing to ensure that it would not be wiped out by a great power. Third, until 1989 Vietnam's leaders could cling to the notion that they were riding the tide of history proclaimed by Marx and Lenin. Ideology was a secular religion. It may have been the only thing capable of sustaining such asceticism and sacrifice for so long.

All three of these conditions are gone, but the change in Vietnam's strategic fortunes is obscured by its past success. The image of Vietnam as a scrappy bantam resisting and ultimately defeating a succession of great powers, a David against the world's Goliaths, or as the Prussians or Israelis of Southeast Asia, has been a powerful one. That past success, however, was associated with the unconventional character of most of the past wars. The Vietnamese Communist Party outlasted the French and Americans in large part because the center of gravity in those wars was the political loyalty and control of the population.[5] Today, the strength associated with a revolutionary independence movement does not apply. First, the animating inspiration of Marxism and the motive it provided for sacrifice are dead.

Vietnam's strategic problems now are normal ones—international rather than internal. Vietnam did perform adequately in the past in conventional military conflict against China and the Khmer Rouge, but the conditions underlying those performances have been steadily eroding. The balance of conventional military power has shifted overwhelmingly against Hanoi.

In the 1990s, for the first time, Vietnam has to make it in the world as a normal state and must do so without benefactors or protectors. It is still economically backward in a region of booming economies. It has powerful adversaries whose power is still growing faster than its own. Its main adversary, China, is not just much stronger, but astronomically stronger. Hanoi's choices for ameliorating these vulnerabilities are quite limited.

The United States, in turn, has been slow to adapt its Vietnam policy to the end of the Cold War. Hardheaded strategic logic should have led Washington to reverse its policy and repair relations with Vietnam as soon as the Warsaw Pact collapsed and Hanoi withdrew its forces from Cambodia, and certainly no later than when the Soviet Union imploded. Earlier, Vietnam could reasonably be seen as a regional "proxy" for Soviet power and thus an obstacle to establishing a balance of power that would be in U.S. interest. When the highest priority was the titanic struggle with Moscow for influence throughout the world, it was advantageous to the West for Vietnam to be weak. Global balance-of-power concerns could also override humanitarian concerns to make Washington oppose Hanoi's invasion of Cambodia. None of these realpolitik reasons to squeeze Vietnam, however, applied once the global contest ended. Indeed, traditional balance-of-power logic should have made the Soviet collapse reverse the U.S. attitude toward China's relationship to Vietnam.

No reversal occurred because the end of the Cold War also freed Washington from the need to put balance-of-power considerations at the fore of its Indochina policy. By that time the only constituencies very interested in Vietnam were those driven by emotion and suspicion still grounded in the wounds of the 1960s; by the 1990s no one else in the United States except the business community (which remained remarkably reticent) cared a whit about Vietnam. After the tragic mistake of grossly inflating Vietnam's importance in the 1960s, the United States compounded the error by dismissing any stake at all in Vietnam in the early 1990s.

Twin strategic mistakes by Hanoi and Washington demonstrate that current policy choices can still only be grasped in the context of the past—the long regional hot war that took place within the long global Cold War. Only now may Vietnam's role in the world be coming into alignment with its intrinsic importance and capabilities, after being exaggerated in the Cold War and denigrated after it ended. Indeed, the international significance of Indochina has been out of kilter for more than half of the twentieth century, ever since it figured prominently in the run-up to war between Japan and the United States.

Vietnam's position in the Cold War was an extension of the pre-Cold War colonial scramble among the great powers. When Japan and France passed from the scene, South Vietnam became a pawn in the global struggle between East and West, a line item on the long balance sheet of the competition over which ideology would come to dominate the world. (North Vietnam was not the same sort of pawn, because after 1954 there was no serious attempt to overthrow its government and bring it into the opposite camp.)

For the United States, the fight over Vietnam was not about Vietnam. Rather it was about what the South's conquest would allegedly mean for the worldwide credibility of the containment doctrine and, thereby, for the tide of history. American blood and treasure were not poured into the country for twenty years because of the country's intrinsic importance—its population, natural resources, productivity, market, or capacity to project military power beyond its borders—but because of its derivative importance as a test case of resolve to prevent an Asian "Munich."[6]

What could lead to a war involving Vietnam in the post-Cold War era? That, after all, is the ultimate question behind any normal national security policy, even if it is often forgotten in periods of amity and stability.[7] When war breaks out, it is usually because two sorts of conflict coexist and cannot be resolved peacefully. These are conflicts over might and right, that is, over the balance of power between the rivals and over whatever substantive interest or value gives life to the rivalry—disputed territory, natural resources, religious or ideological identity of a community, or some other claim. Without a conflict in both dimensions, rivalry is unlikely to produce war.[8]

If there is nothing approaching a balance of power between the opponents—and if they both *understand* which one is dominant and capable of imposing its will—other conflicts of interest will probably be resolved peacefully because it is clear that the weaker of the two has no alternative but to surrender what is in dispute. (This is why attempting to maintain a balance is often seen as both necessary and dangerous—necessary if many countries are to have any effective freedom of action, dangerous because it allows them to think that they might have less to lose from fighting than from conceding in a crisis.) If there is no conflict of interest, the balance of power is irrelevant. Consider Vietnam's prospects in both dimensions.

Strategic Contexts

Can Vietnam get the power it needs to protect its interests? This depends not just on its own efforts, but on what others—especially bigger countries—do. The only power that matters in strategic terms is power relative to adversaries.

The long time in which Vietnam was a major issue in the worldwide balance of power is now long past. The side that won the Vietnam War lost the Cold War. Today, Vietnam is neither pawn nor proxy, because there is no global game, no clash of great powers, even at the regional level. To highlight the change in the country's strategic significance, it would be more apt to say that now Vietnam is not *even* a pawn. Given its population of 73 million, successful economic development that turned Vietnam into another Asian "tiger" would change the strategic calculus. Until then, Vietnam is one of the two major powers in Indochina (along with China), a medium power in Southeast Asia, a minor one in East Asia in general, and of negligible importance on the world scene as a whole. Developments at the lower levels, however, can ramify upward and complicate great-power relations. Similarly, if great-power relations deteriorate for other reasons, the consequences can ramify downward and channel conflict at the lower levels (which is just what happened in the Cold War).

The Vietnamese interest in hegemony over Indochina is natural and typical for countries with weak neighbors and strong enemies. Going back to the war against the French, the need for secure lines of communication, and later for sanctuaries in the war with the Saigon government and the United States, led the Communist leadership to view the three countries of Indochina as, in General Vo Nguyen Giap's words, a "single strategic unit" in wartime. Because the two centers of population in northern and southern Vietnam are "linked by a long, slender central Vietnamese region (only twenty-five miles wide at its narrowest point) that can be easily cut by external enemies, Vietnamese leaders have viewed the mountainous interiors bordering Laos and Cambodia as secure rear areas vis-à-vis more powerful intruders."[9]

After the second Indochina war, as Thailand and China drew closer, the Vietnamese cultivated a big brother relationship with Laos. Hanoi stationed 30–40,000 troops in the country and built an all-weather road to Haiphong in order to give Laotian trade an alternative to transit through Thai territory. A dozen years later, as it was withdrawing from Cambodia, Vietnam also took many of its troops out of Laos. This may have been a conciliatory gesture to China, but it became a necessary retreat. Hanoi has been unable to keep up with the burden of being a patron to its smaller neighbors since it lost the backup of Soviet support and Thai investors invaded Laos.[10]

In the rest of Southeast Asia beyond Indochina, Vietnam is less important than during the Cold War. It has withdrawn from Cambodia. It has cut its military drastically. The armed forces are now at less than half of their peak strength of over a million men (which included an army bigger than that of the United States), and their stocks of weaponry and equipment are decaying. Without Soviet economic backing, the Vietnamese military now lacks reliable access to spare parts and lacks the funds to pay for training of its personnel abroad.[11] Hanoi no longer represents as great a military threat to Thailand as it did through the 1980s—indeed, a proto-détente between the two broke out after 1990—and water buffers still keep Vietnam from posing a military threat to the other states of ASEAN.[12]

The lessened threat simply reflects how Hanoi is falling farther behind in the balance of power. The military establishment has continued to buy weapons and in a few targeted areas to modernize. Compared with its past status and sources of supply, nevertheless, the decline in quantity and quality of forces is quite sharp. At the same time, the other states of Southeast Asia have been modernizing their armed services and deploying progressively larger amounts of state-of-the-art equipment.[13]

In the world beyond Southeast Asia, Hanoi's strategic role and options depend above all on its relationship with China. Vietnam's only remaining global significance is that it is one of a surviving handful of nominally communist states. The other communist survivors, however, are no help. Cuba is far away and tottering itself. North Korea was on bad terms with Hanoi during the Vietnamese occupation of Cambodia and has its hands full in its own neighborhood. And China is Vietnam's main strategic problem, not solution.

For a while it seemed that the threat of "peaceful evolution" gave the communist survivors a logical incentive to "huddle together" as the United States emerged unchallenged as the only worldwide military power. The decline of the Soviet threat reduced barriers to cooperation, and some local states worried about the possibility of a renewed Sino-Vietnamese alliance. And Hanoi even dumped pro-American Foreign Minister Thach in 1991. But China did not prove receptive to huddling. The Vietnamese military in particular pushed for rapprochement with Beijing. The September 1990 Chengdu summit raised the possibility of cooperation, but on terms that would require Hanoi to coordinate its foreign policy with China. After the November 1991 Beijing summit, China turned away Vietnamese feelers for a closer security relationship and suggested that the two countries could be "comrades but not allies." And soon China went on to press its claims in territorial disputes between the two countries.[14]

Like China, Vietnam has retained but loosened political Leninism while more or less shedding economic Marxism. If this shift generates more economic growth it will generate more power, but not necessarily more security. Compared to China, Vietnam is much farther behind in the economic

Table 4.1.

The Decline in Vietnam's Power Potential in Relation to China since the Last War between Them

		Vietnam	China	Ratio
Population	1978	51.5	958.8	.05
(millions)	1994	72.7	1,201.2	.06
GNP*	1978	7.6	131.5	.06
GDP**	1993	17.6	507.5	.03
(U.S.$ billions)				
GNP per capita*	1978	248	230	1.08
GDP per capita**	1993	800	2,200	.36
(U.S.$)				

Sources: 1978: *World Military Expenditures and Arms Transfers 1989* (Washington, D.C.: U.S. Arms Control and Disarmament Agency, October 1990), pp. 42, 70.

1993–94: *The Military Balance 1994–1995* (London: International Institute for Strategic Studies, October 1994), pp. 170, 192.

* Estimated, 1988$

** Purchasing power parity estimate, 1993$.

NB: Economic data for these countries are notoriously soft, and properly comparable statistics across time are not readily available. Incommensurate data (GNP, GDP, and purchasing power parity estimates) are used because Arms Control and Disarmament Agency (ACDA) data are not available beyond 1991, and International Institute for Strategic Studies (IISS) data for 1978 are less recent estimates than those provided by ACDA. The point of the table is to compare changes in ratios rather than the absolute changes from 1978 to 1993.

shift. This means that in the decade and a half after the Sino-Vietnamese war of 1978–79, the tremendous absolute gap in power between the two countries was compounded by a relative gap in growth rates and per capita income. The relative gap is not yet closing and could even widen further (see Table 4.1).

Although allowance must be made for significant inadequacies in the data, the changes indicated in Table 4.1 are all bad. The ratio of total economic product is roughly twice as unfavorable to Vietnam as it was at the time of the last war, and the ratio of per capita product is three times worse than it was. The only index in which disparity was reduced was population growth. That would reduce the disparity in power potential only if it was matched with improvement in relative economic efficiency. Since the comparison in the latter dimension shows a huge decline in Vietnam's relative position, the faster rate of population growth represents a fall in relative power, not a rise. Even if bad data overstate the trends by a wide

Table 4.2.

Vietnam and China in 1994: Actual Military Power

	Vietnam	China	Ratio
Active military manpower (millions)	.572	2.93	.2
Main battle tanks	1,300	7,500–8,000	.16–.17
Light tanks	600	2,000	.3
Towed artillery	2,300	14,500	.16
Combat aircraft	190	4,970	.04
Frigates, destroyers, and submarines	7	105	.07
Defense budget (U.S.$ billions)*	.435	6.7	.06
1992 Defense expenditures (U.S.$ billions)*	.72	24.3	.03

Source: The Military Balance: 1994–1995 (London: International Institute for Strategic Studies, October 1994), pp. 170, 171, 173, 192, 193.
   *Purchasing power parity, estimate.

margin, Vietnam's relative power is significantly lower now than it was the last time China invaded.

Changes override any comfort that might be taken from the outcome of that Sino-Vietnamese War. The Chinese People's Liberation Army (PLA) did perform poorly when it invaded, although it penetrated an appreciable distance into the country. Even then, however, Vietnam benefited from a cushion it no longer has. Part of the reason that Hanoi weathered the attack well was that Beijing adopted a strategy of limited aims at the outset to give Moscow an excuse for restraint.[15] In the time since, the Chinese military has been streamlined, improved, and better equipped, while Vietnam's armed forces have declined and lost vital outside assistance.[16] Meanwhile, the People's Republic of China (PRC) has moved to develop force-projection capability as its military doctrine has shifted from preoccupation with all-out war against great powers to limited wars on its land and sea periphery.

The ratios in Table 4.2 are of limited use as indicators, since effective military power cannot be judged from a few static indices.[17] They are so lopsided, however, that they make it clear that Vietnam can pose no offensive threat to China and that Vietnam's defensive options are questionable too, even assuming a tremendous tactical advantage for forces operating from defensive positions. Present naval and air capabilities would not allow much of a contest in the South China Sea (Eastern Sea, to the Vietnamese), although Vietnam has an advantage in distance from main bases to the Spratly Islands. For assessing Vietnam's potential to defend itself in its mainland border area the ratios must be discounted somewhat, because China could not bring as large a portion of its military to bear in an attack on Vietnam as Vietnam could deploy in defense against such an attack. Many of the PRC's forces are deployed far from its southeastern borders, and Beijing still lacks the logistical capability necessary for any of its forces—land, sea, or air—to support operations at long distances.

As an indication of potential power, the comparisons are more ambiguous. The question is not whether Vietnam could rival China's power, but whether it has an alternative to being utterly submerged by it. On this question, the two highest of the ratios tabulated—military manpower and GDP per capita—are significant. If Vietnam could narrow the gap in economic performance while maintaining the size of the current force (which, like China's, is much reduced from the earlier norm) and modernizing it, a respectable counterweight to the PLA in the border area would be quite feasible given the tactical advantages of a defensive posture. In the face of progressive modernization of Chinese forces, however, as well as the prospect of improved Chinese logistics, Vietnam would still not have a promising option for autonomous self-defense. All these trends together put a much higher premium in Vietnam's security policy on stabilizing relations with China, either through accommodation or by finding some other source of countervailing power to replace the deterrent effect of the old Soviet alliance.

Is countervailing power available? Probably not enough. The hypothetical possibilities are the United States, Japan, a resurgent Russia, India, a well-integrated alliance of ASEAN countries, or some combination of these five. None looks very plausible. Consider the standard strategic solution of a great-power alliance (multilateral possibilities will be explored later). Russia is out of the picture for now; Japan self-consciously avoids normal strategic behavior that goes with being a great power; and the United States shows no interest.

Most obviously, there is no self-interested reason *yet* for any of the great powers to aggravate the security dilemma by lining up against Beijing, making the potential China Problem an actual one any sooner than necessary. None has an interest in worsening relations with a huge power—and a nuclear one at that—for the sake of a small one that has little to offer. An anti-Chinese alliance becomes plausible only if tensions grow between Beijing and other capitals for other reasons. In that case, an economically developed and militarily reinvigorated Vietnam would not be a trivial partner in an attempt to balance China.

Among the great powers, India might be the least unlikely bet for Hanoi.[18] Apart from Pakistan, which has been markedly inferior in conventional military potential since it was dismembered by India in 1971, China has been the principal threat that preoccupies strategists in New Delhi. Apart from Russia, India is the only great power that shares a substantial border—and a history of armed clashes over disputed territory—with China. Hanoi and New Delhi have had friendly military relations, including exchanges of personnel, ministerial-level visits, and ship visits, but any sort of real alliance relationship remains hypothetical.[19] Moreover, India could do little to help Vietnam strategically unless it were to plan to mount an offensive against China in the event that the latter attacked Vietnam. Otherwise, the value of an Indian alliance to Hanoi would be comparable to the value of the French and British alliance to Poland in 1939. India is not close enough, and lacks compensating logistical capacity, to assist Vietnamese defensive operations. A credible guarantee that India would attack China is hard to imagine.

If the United States is to be militarily engaged in Southeast Asia—a very big *if*—Vietnam could be as good a partner as any. Since leaving the bases in the Philippines in 1992, Washington lacks significant military installations in the region for the first time in the twentieth century. When countries that were traditionally more friendly—Thailand, Malaysia, and Indonesia—turned away the modest option of allowing floating U.S. supply depots in their waters, U.S. interest in the possibility of access to port facilities in Cam Ranh Bay grew (although Russia has not given up the base agreement that allows it to stay in Cam Ranh until the year 2004).[20] It is still fanciful to think of an American return, but stranger things happen in international politics.

Venues of Conflict

What substantive conflicts of interest could evoke the danger of war for Vietnam? Against the French, Japanese, Americans, and anti-Communist Vietnamese, the main such issue for the leaders who came to rule in Hanoi was their sovereignty over the country itself. For the Americans, Soviets, and Chinese, the issue was the epochal struggle between two transnational ideologies over the future of the world. Those questions are passé. The last two wars Vietnam fought were not over these issues, but over local influence and territorial control—the war against the Khmer Rouge in Cambodia and against China in northern Vietnam. These two conflicts remain sources of tension, but the more dangerous potential dispute is over the ownership of the islands in the South China Sea known in the West as the Spratlys.

The Sino-Vietnamese war of 1978–79 resulted more from tensions over Hanoi's alignment with Moscow, invasion of Cambodia, and treatment of ethnic Chinese citizens than from border disputes per se.[21] Intermittent combat and frequent shelling continued in the border area for a decade after that war, however, until lessening tension gave way to an effective ceasefire at the end of 1988.[22] Both sides also now have a substantial interest in stability of the border because of the dramatic growth in trade that has developed across it, although this interest is quite asymmetrical—greater to Vietnam than to the PRC. (It is also a double-edged interest: the border trade increases available consumer goods but depresses local production.)[23]

Nevertheless, there are historic and contemporary grounds for questioning the northern border. The French administration in the colonial period ceded land the Vietnamese considered theirs to the Qing dynasty and border markers were subsequently moved farther, to Chinese advantage. In the 1990s, China reportedly set up a customs post well inside what the Vietnamese considered their side of the border. In 1992 officials in Hanoi claimed that China occupied 8,000 hectares of Vietnamese territory.[24] Latent border disputes, tractable in themselves, could assume larger proportions if some other catalytic event raised tensions.

In 1978, that event was the Vietnamese invasion of Cambodia. Now, having withdrawn after a decade of trying to pacify the country and accepting the subsequent United Nations project to engineer a transition to new government in Cambodia, it seems clear that Hanoi will avoid entangling itself there again.[25] That resolve could be tested if there are new pogroms against the Vietnamese population in Cambodia. Deputy Foreign Minister Le Mai insisted in 1994 that Vietnam was committed to multilateral solutions for preserving the country's stability, even regarding the Vietnamese minority.[26] But the odds that there would be any serious multilateral response are quite low in the wake of experiences in Somalia, Rwanda, and Bosnia in the time since the United Nations Transitional Authority in Cambodia (UNTAC) mission was undertaken. In that event Hanoi would be in a bind. If the Khmer Rouge can be kept marginalized, however, it is hard to envision how any other instability in Cambodia (and some significant and long-lasting measure of instability there is virtually inevitable) would provoke renewed Vietnamese intervention. If Cambodia can be kept neutral and its instability can be kept short of the genocidal explosion of the 1970s, it can provide a valuable buffer between Vietnam and Thailand. Keeping the buffer from becoming a source of tension, however, may not be easy as long as the old strategic asymmetry persists—the Thais dominate the area economically, while Vietnam dominates it militarily.

In the 1990s the world has gradually become aware that the conflict over the Spratly Islands (known as the Truong Sa Archipelago to Vietnam, and the Nansha Islands to China) could become more than a sideshow spat, and at the least a significant occasion for miscalculation.[27] Yet few observers in the United States, at least, are aware of how much conflict these islands have *already* generated over the past two decades.

From 1958 through the war against the United States, Hanoi accepted the PRC's claim to territory in the South China Sea and only reversed itself in 1976. By that time, however, Beijing had already seized the Paracels, driving South Vietnamese forces out in January 1974. Almost immediately, the Republic of China on Taiwan and the Philippines jumped in and an armed clash seemed imminent.[28] Since then, China has persisted in its claims, calling for negotiations, but ignoring the claims of others and penetrating farther into the area.

At first glance it is hard to see why Vietnam or China would choose international confrontation over concession or compromise on a matter of such limited significance as a bunch of uninhabitable rocks and reefs. Should either one risk war over a territorial issue that seems primarily one of principle? Should China risk alienating other maritime nations, including the United States, whose navies worry about transit rights and sea lines of communication? The Spratlys, however, have potential economic significance, including oil deposits and other minerals as well as fishing grounds. Explicit concern for dealing with China's expanding population by exploiting the sea for economic purposes has played a major role in the country's increased interest in the area in recent decades. After surveying PRC studies and official statements, John Garver warns, "westerners should be wary of attributing their skepticism about *Lebensraum* to China's leaders."[29]

In this conflict Vietnam might benefit diplomatically from the lack of international consensus on China's claims. For political reasons it may not be in Beijing's interest to resolve the issue decisively, since it is of low priority in comparison to other objectives that might be damaged by a showdown with the Philippines, Malaysia, Taiwan, and Brunei in addition to Vietnam. The lack of consensus that may restrain China temporarily, however, could also be a problem for Vietnam, as the four-way imbroglio of February 1974 indicates.

Neither Hanoi nor the other claimants who oppose Beijing are likely to be able to prevent the Chinese from consolidating control of the Spratlys if the decision is taken in Beijing to do so. Only the U.S. Navy could do that, and Washington has no commitment to go to war with a nuclear-armed power over those reefs and rocks. Although some in American naval circles invoke the importance of protecting transit rights as a reason to contest Chinese claims to the Spratlys, there is no plausible reason to expect a strategic consensus for doing anything. Washington even failed to back Malaysia or its ally the Philippines in the mid-1970s when China took the

Paracels, and more recently it tacitly agreed to the joint venture in the South China Sea between an American company, Crestone, and China.[30]

In regard to a prospective Chinese move against the Spratlys, Major General Vu Xuan Vinh, director of the Vietnamese Foreign Ministry's external relations department, said, "I'm sure the U.S. will not let China expand so much."[31] Was that a prediction or a prayer? The closest thing to such a commitment to fight China over the Spratlys was the controversy over defending Quemoy and Matsu in the 1950s. Quemoy and Matsu were more substantial islands (inhabited even!), Washington and China were at the peak of their Cold War antagonism, and China had no nuclear weapons, yet the prospect of military embroilment with the mainland over Quemoy and Matsu evoked tremendous controversy in the United States even then, and Eisenhower never did make a definite decision to defend the islands.

There is nevertheless some uncertainty about what U.S. policy would be toward a full Chinese attempt to grab the Spratlys, because the issue has not been faced at high levels in Washington, and in some future context of escalating tension the situation could prove quite volatile. This makes it dangerous but also may contribute at least marginally to deterring China from decisive action. All in all, however, Vietnam has weak options for pressing its claims in the islands against a determined Chinese move. This reaffirms the reasons Hanoi has to reach an accommodation—what before 1938 might have been called appeasement with less embarrassment than it could be today—unless it can enlist a strong alliance commitment.

Multilateral Options

Vietnam has four general options, in principle, for handling the threats to its security that emanate primarily from China. In order of probability, from least to highest, these are: collective security, a coalition of medium powers in the region, alliance with a great power, or accommodation with Beijing. The best strategic bet in principle would be the third, but as discussed above, this does not look very promising in practice. Consider the other possibilities.

In the immediate aftermath of the Cold War there was a resurgence of optimism about prospects for the old ideal of collective security, whereby states would commit themselves to outlaw aggression and come to the aid of any victim of aggression. The Persian Gulf War represented something close to the fulfillment of that ideal, although not all that close.[32] Since then the halfhearted and impotent efforts of the United Nations and North Atlantic Treaty Organization (NATO) to end the war in Bosnia have deflated optimistic expectations about how well multilateral organizations might guarantee any nation's security.

In the Gorbachev era the Soviet Union promoted collective security schemes for Asia, but with little result. Since then commentators have referred to the possibility of building a "security community" along the lines suggested years ago by Karl Deutsch: "attainment, within a territory, of a 'sense of community' and of institutions and practices strong enough and widespread enough to assure . . . dependable expectations of 'peaceful change' among its population."[33] There is a crucial difference, however, between that vague ideal and an explicit commitment by all member states in a security community to defend each other.[34] While there has been ample interest throughout the region in developing multilateral discussion mechanisms and economic agreements, there has been negligible movement toward widespread undertaking of mutual military obligations.[35]

Although hardly anyone would take seriously the notion of an Asia-wide collective security system, a multilateral coalition limited to the Southeast Asia region based on ASEAN might seem less unrealistic to analysts from afar. With Vietnam admitted to ASEAN, could it not be a party to such an expansion of the organization's mission? There are no indications, however, that anything like that development is in the cards. There has been multilateral security activity in ASEAN, but on matters such as antipiracy operations that do not involve joint planning for combat against other states. Even before taking Vietnam into the organization, the differences in interest of the members have been enough to block explicit commitment to mutual defense.[36] ASEAN is seen by many as a confidence-building factor in the region, but many of the conditions that made the Conference (now "Organization") on Security and Cooperation in Europe (OSCE) seem relevant to security in Europe are missing in Southeast Asia.[37] Indeed, the reference for strategic purposes would be NATO, not OSCE.

Southeast Asia has experience with an analogue to NATO, and it did not fare well. That was the Southeast Asia Treaty Organization (SEATO), which was not activated in the main war that occurred during its existence, the war in Vietnam, and which went out of business twenty years ago. The reasons that SEATO was misconceived are not entirely irrelevant to the post-Cold War situation:

> The Manila Treaty was an effort, more than anything else, at deterrence without the basic conditions for a convincing strategy of deterrence being satisfied. It was created to demonstrate allied unity in a region where allied interests diverged and, in some instances, were obviously incompatible. . . . It was the misapplication of an alliance strategy that had worked in Europe under different conditions, but in Southeast Asia signified the kind of misperception that advertised fragility. . . . Rather than demonstrating strength,

SEATO displayed weakness and for the period of its existence contributed to the emergence of the illusion of security. . . .[38]

Vietnam might count on help from Indonesia, the most anti-Chinese member of the association, but Indonesia could do next to nothing to counter a Chinese attack on the mainland. The member of ASEAN best positioned to collaborate militarily with Vietnam against China—Thailand—is aligned in the reverse direction, far more interested in having China's help against Vietnam.

The most forthright agreement for military support in the area is the Five Power Defense Arrangement among Britain, Australia, New Zealand, Malaysia, and Singapore, which was revived in the early 1990s. Bilateral conflicts among ASEAN states block even this sort of less than full-blown alliance.[39] Considering the slow pace at which consideration of Vietnam's admission to ASEAN even in its nonmilitary form occurred, the notion that the organization might bolster Hanoi's military position is hard to take seriously (although it can certainly provide useful political support).[40]

Multilateralism has so far proved empty in regard to restraining conflict over the Spratlys. When the PRC promulgated its legal claim in February 1992 and landed troops on Da Ba Island and then in June on Da Lac Reef, ASEAN foreign ministers expressed concern and called for "restraint by all parties." ASEAN did nothing further when China simply responded with rhetoric to the effect that it was not an expansionist power.[41] These events and responses make the point. For the principle of collective security to work, it must be based on commitment to international law. But consensus on the policy application of such law—especially in regard to identifying who is an "aggressor" state—is rare, even among states with far more cultural and political affinities than are shared by the states of Asia.[42]

Vietnam's prospects for getting others to shore up its security, whether through multilateral or bilateral support, look bleak. If it cannot beat the Chinese, should it join them? This could be done in two ways: offering cooperation in mutual interest, or simply truckling. The former would clearly be preferable, but the latter could still be better than a showdown that Hanoi would probably lose; "Finlandization" would wound Vietnamese *amour propre,* but it might guarantee survival. Hanoi tried the first possibility but, as discussed above, without success. The May 1992 deal with Crestone and other initiatives to press maritime territorial claims against Vietnam brought the cooperative strategy to a dead end for Hanoi.

What about simply conceding China's claims, abandoning interest in minor territories for the sake of preserving basic territorial integrity, and avoiding any grounds for provocation of China? For a cool, rational, and cautious strategist this might well seem the least bad alternative. It would be uncharacteristic, however, for a regime with the history of constant combat and resistance to great powers that the Hanoi regime has had. Movement in this direction, if it occurs, is less likely to be a deliberate, consensual, consistent policy than a hesitant, fitful, constantly debated one.

Conclusion

The Vietnamese state today is the direct extension of the revolutionary movement that strove for decades to take control of the country. The problems faced by a state in international relations are always different in important ways from the problems faced by an independence movement or a domestic political party. These differences are extreme for Vietnam. For most of its history the party-regime struggled constantly against high odds, against far larger and more powerful enemies, and succeeded. If standard international balance-of-power logic had dominated the calculations of Hanoi's leaders, they would probably have given up long before 1975. The strategic problems of the post-1975 world, however, are far more similar to standard balance-of-power logic than to the ideological and political context of the earlier struggles.

If Vietnam wishes to pursue its interests in the manner that a medium power often does, rather than accept the dependency and severe limitations on freedom of action of a weak state in the shadow of a local leviathan, there are no low-risk strategies available. The least unlikely hope for great power support might be India, but the most useful support would be from the United States. At present this option is unrealistic because neither country—the United States especially—is interested in it. Developing a tacit alliance against China is premature at best and risks worsening the problem it aims to cope with. As long as it is possible to avoid a new cold war in Asia, everyone involved has an incentive to do so.

At the same time, the only reasons for not melting the ice in U.S.-Vietnamese relations faster have been matters of history, emotion, and domestic politics, not strategy. During the Cold War, when Hanoi extended Soviet influence, it made sense for Washington to want Vietnam to be weak and vulnerable and China to be strong and vigorous. Shorn of the connection to a hostile superpower, however, Vietnam is no threat to U.S. interests, and the old interest in its weakness is gone. At the same time, the potential of trouble coming out of Beijing must loom larger to Washington than it did when both capitals shared a common negative interest in contesting Moscow's reach. If there is any power likely to need balancing in Asia in the early twenty-first century it is not Moscow's or Hanoi's, but Beijing's.

Managing strategic diplomacy for rapprochement between old enemies while simultaneously avoiding unnecessary provocation of China is not something that Hanoi and Washington can bring off easily. If neither sees good reason to raise risks of conflict in order to contain the growing 800–pound gorilla of East Asia, it will not happen. Nor is it by any means obvious that it should happen. If Vietnam wishes to assert its rights, however, and the United States wishes to assert its influence in the way to which it became accustomed after 1941, some form of cooperation in this direction will before long become a logical choice.

Notes

1. Of the eight "Main Tasks in the Years to Come" discussed in the Communist Party Central Committee's report in 1994, six points (and 33 pages) concerned domestic economic and political matters, while only two points (and 2 pages) concerned foreign relations and national defense. Communist Party of Vietnam, *Political Report of the Central Committee: (7th Tenure) Mid-Term National Conference* (Hanoi: GIOI Publishers, 1994), pp. 25–60.

2. Douglas Pike, *PAVN: People's Army of Vietnam* (Novato, CA: Presidio Press, 1986), p. 255.

3. In 1979 Zbigniew Brzezinski was calling Vietnam an "Asian Cuba," a proxy for Soviet power, and by that time normalization with Vietnam would have antagonized China, with whom Washington was developing an anti-Soviet entente. Raymond Garthoff, *Detente and Confrontation* (Washington, D.C.: Brookings Institution, 1985), p. 701. The Vietnamese had believed that the United States would concede on reparations because they thought it was "in a weak and defensive posture in Southeast Asia. They thought the United States needed friendly relations with Vietnam to 'stabilize the region' and to permit U.S. oil companies to recover their former concessions." Gareth Porter, *Vietnam: The Politics of Bureaucratic Socialism* (Ithaca: Cornell University Press, 1993), p. 200.

4. Porter, *Vietnam: Politics of Bureaucratic Socialism*, p. 190. Market exchange and profit were not the main priorities for most of Vietnamese Communist history. Before the mid-1980s, the foreign policy of Vietnam "was carried out in *dau tranh* (struggle) terms, so that foreign relations are treated strategically—like protracted military conflicts—over an extended period of time." Clark D. Neher, *Southeast Asia in the New International Era* (Boulder: Westview Press, 1994), p. 199. See also Pike, *PAVN*, chaps. 9–11.

5. The final North Vietnamese victory over Saigon in 1975 was a completely conventional one. By that time, however, Saigon's American protector had gone home after failing to eliminate the Communist Party's ability to prevent consolidation of the South Vietnamese government's control of the countryside. If political organization and discipline had not been the hinge of the earlier war, overwhelming U.S. power and economic resources poured into support of the client government in Saigon would have carried the day, or the Saigon government would have been able to subvert the Hanoi regime within North Vietnam as effectively as the Communists subverted the government in the South. For contrasting arguments on which aspects of the war were cen-

tral—conventional or counterinsurgency strategies—see Harry Summers, *On Strategy: A Critical Analysis of the Vietnam War* (Novato, CA: Presidio Press, 1982) and Andrew Krepinevich, *The Army and Vietnam* (Baltimore: Johns Hopkins University Press, 1986) and the analysis in Douglas Blaufarb, *The Counterinsurgency Era* (New York: Free Press, 1977). Although internal opposition to the Hanoi regime was effectively eliminated after 1975, sporadic or limited armed resistance continued in a few areas even into the 1990s. See Carlyle A. Thayer, *The Vietnam People's Army under Do Moi,* Pacific Strategic Paper No. 7 (Singapore: Institute of Southeast Asian Studies, 1994), pp. 12–13.

6. See Leslie H. Gelb with Richard K. Betts, *The Irony of Vietnam: The System Worked* (Washington, D.C.: Brookings Institution, 1979), and Richard K. Betts, "The United States: Global Deterrence," in James Morley, ed., *Security Interdependence in the Asia Pacific Region* (Lexington: D.C. Heath/Lexington Books, for the Columbia University East Asian Institute, 1986). Other analogies were also salient. See Yuen Foong Khong, *Analogies at War: Korea, Munich, Dien Bien Phu, and the Vietnam Decisions of 1965* (Princeton: Princeton University Press, 1992).

7. There are important elements of security besides those directly related to the use of force, but if the concept of national security is to be coherent enough to be analytically useful, matters associated with threats to the state's political autonomy must remain the essential concern. The prevalent desire to "broaden" the concept of security risks making it synonymous with other categories such as foreign policy or international relations in general (in which case security becomes conceptually redundant) or human safety (in which case medicine might as well be included).

8. Geoffrey Blainey argues in *The Causes of War,* 3rd ed. (New York: Free Press, 1988) that all causes can be reduced to disagreements about the balance of power, because all conflicts of interest are "varieties of power" (chap. 10).

9. Michael Leifer, "Vietnam's Foreign Policy in the Post-Soviet Era," in Robert Ross, ed., *East Asia in Transition: Toward a New Regional Order* (Armonk, N.Y.: M.E. Sharpe, 1995). Quotations from Porter, *Vietnam: Politics of Bureaucratic Socialism,* pp. 185–86.

10. William S. Turley, " 'More Friends, Fewer Enemies': Vietnam's Policy Toward Indochina-ASEAN Reconciliation," in Sheldon W. Simon, ed., *East Asian Security in the Post-Cold War Era* (Armonk, NY: M.E. Sharpe, 1993), pp. 189–190; Leifer manuscript, p. 7; Porter, *Vietnam: Politics of Bureaucratic Socialism,* pp. 201, 208; Michael R. Chambers, *Realignments in Indochina: The Development of the Sino-Thai Alignment, 1975–79* (Pew Case Study in Diplomatic Training 1994).

11. In 1987 the manpower total was 1,260,000, and the army 1,100,000; by 1994 the figures were 572,000 and 500,000. *The Military Balance: 1987–1988* (London: International Institute for Strategic Studies, Autumn 1987), p. 175; *The Military Balance: 1994–1995* (London: International Institute for Strategic Studies, October 1994), p. 192. As in China, much of Vietnam's military is now preoccupied with business activities rather than combat readiness.

12. See Thayer, *Vietnam People's Army,* pp. 22, 69.

13. See David Saw, "Politics and Defence Modernisation in Southeast Asia," *Military Technology* (April 1992).

14. Carlyle A. Thayer, "Comrade Plus Brother: The New Sino-Vietnamese Relations," *Pacific Review* 5, no. 4 (1992), p. 403; Ramses Amer, "Sino-Vietnamese Relations and Southeast Asian Security," *Contemporary Southeast Asia* 14, no. 4 (March 1993), p. 325; Thayer, *Vietnam People's Army,* p. 68; Carlyle A. Thayer, *Vietnam's Developing Military Ties with the Region: The Case for Defence Cooperation,* Working Paper No. 24 (Canberra: Australian Defence Studies Centre, June 1994), p. 10; Carlyle A. Thayer, "Sino-Vietnamese Relations: The Interplay of Ideology and National Interests," *Asian Survey* 34, no. 6 (June 1994), pp. 518–523.

15. Soviet statements to diplomats suggested that the USSR would not intervene as long as the Chinese attack remained limited. King C. Chen, "China's War Against Vietnam, 1979: A Military Analysis," *Journal of East Asian Affairs* 3, no. 1 (Spring/Summer 1983), pp. 249–252.

16. "The estimated current dollar value of total military assistance to Vietnam, overwhelmingly from the Soviet Union, shot up from $100 million in 1977 to $3.4 billion in 1979 and averaged nearly $1.7 billion a year from then until 1987. Soviet economic and military aid together accounted for about 20 percent of the country's GNP." Turley, " 'More Friends, Fewer Enemies,' " p. 175.

17. Moreover, estimates of defense spending are hard to make and in some respects are deceptive when compared with data for more modern militaries and economies. See Andre Sauvageot, "Vietnam, Defence Expenditure and Threat Perception," in Chin Kin Wah, ed., *Defence Spending in Southeast Asia* (Singapore: Insitute of Southeast Asian Studies, 1987), p. 285, and Thayer, *Vietnam People's Army Under Doi Moi,* pp. 32–36.

18. Many Western strategists still do not count India as a great power. This is hard to explain on grounds other than ethnocentrism. It is the second most populous country in the world, with a growing economy, has demonstrated and perhaps clandestinely deployed nuclear weapons capability, and fields conventional military forces larger than those of most of the other great powers and in many respects equal or superior to China's in quality.

19. Thayer, *Vietnam's Developing Military Ties,* pp. 9, 11.

20. Charles Morrison, "US Security Relations with Southeast Asia: Possibilities and Prospects for the Clinton Administration," *Australian Journal of International Affairs* 47, no. 2 (October 1993), p. 239; Thayer, *Vietnam's Developing Military Ties,* p. 4; Elaine Sciolino, "With Thai Rebuff, U.S. Defers Plan for Navy Depot in Asia," *New York Times,* November 12, 1994, p. 6; Patrick E. Tyler, "Vietnamese Hint the U.S. Could Use Port Again," *New York Times,* November 24, 1994, p. A12. Chinese spokesmen declared their opposition to U.S. presence in Cam Ranh, ibid.

21. See Robert S. Ross, *The Indochina Tangle: China's Vietnam Policy, 1975–1979* (New York: Columbia University Press, 1988) and Anne Gilks, *The Breakdown of the Sino-Vietnamese Alliance, 1970–1979* (Berkeley: Institute of East Asian Studies/Center for Chinese Studies, 1992).

22. Thayer, *Vietnam People's Army,* pp. 11, 20.

23. "The impact of improving economic relations between the two countries is far more pronounced.in Vietnam than in China. . . . Vietnam would be less anxious about capitalist investment in its economy than it would be about Chinese investment. . . . China's investment would easily be portrayed as a security risk . . . the dilemmas posed by the China trade are felt more intensely in northern Vietnam than in the South. . . . The problems of transformative investment are the South's primary concern, and as a result it is more worried about domination by Japan of its new foreign-financed modern economy than it is about market competition from China." Brantly Womack, "Sino-Vietnamese Border Trade," *Asian Survey* 34, no. 6 (June 1994), pp. 498–505, 509, 510.

24. Porter, *Vietnam: Politics of Bureaucratic Socialism,* p. 187; Frank Frost, *Vietnam's Foreign Relations: Dynamics of Change,* Pacific Strategic Paper No. 6 (Singapore: Institute of Southeast Asian Studies, 1993), p. 38; Murray Hiebert, remarks to the Columbia University Southeast Asia Seminar, November 3, 1994. See Chang Paomin, "The Sino-Vietnamese Territorial Dispute," *Asia Pacific Community* (Spring 1980), pp. 130–159.

25. A decade of occupation was a huge drain. In the words of Paul Quinn-Judge, "Cambodia has turned Vietnam, one of the world's poorest countries, into an aid donor." Quoted in Sauvageot, "Vietnam, Defence Expenditure and Threat Perception," p. 286.

26. Henry Kamm, "Christopher to Meet Hanoi Counterpart," *New York Times,* July 10, 1994, p. 10. Legitimization by multilateralism may have also helped Washington edge back toward involvement in the security of the new Cambodian regime. By 1994 the United States was giving "non-lethal" military assistance (road building, de-mining) to the Cambodian army and was considering sending arms. Philip Shenon, "Pentagon Sends Trainers and Equipment to Cambodian Army," *New York Times,* July 28, 1994, p. A6.

27. See my arguments in "Wealth, Power, and Instability: East Asia and the United States After the Cold War," *International Security* 18, no. 3 (Winter 1993/94), pp. 65, 76.

28. For a brief history of the claims, clashes, and negotiations in the South China Sea, see chapters 5 and 7.

29. John W. Garver, "China's Push Through the South China Sea: The Interaction of Bureaucratic and National Interests," *China Quarterly,* no. 132 (December 1992), pp. 1000, 1018–1020. See also Samuel S. Kim, "Mainland China in a Changing Asia-Pacific Regional Order," *Issues and Studies* 30, no. 10 (October 1994), pp. 33–34.

30. Charles McGregor, "Southeast Asia's New Security Challenges," *Pacific Review* 6, no. 3 (1993), p. 271.

31. Quoted in William Branigin, "Vietnam's Enterprising Army," *Washington Post National Weekly Edition,* October 25–31, 1993, p. 13. Another Vietnamese analyst noted hopefully that the western great powers "would not stand with their arms folded to see China turn Asia into its 'sphere of influence.' " Chu Cong Phung, "Some Aspects of China's Foreign Policy towards Asia Pacific," in *Asia-Pacific and Vietnam-Japan Relations,* Papers from the Second Workshop (Hanoi: Institute for International Relations, September 1994), p. 57.

32. Richard K. Betts, "Systems of Peace or Causes of War? Collective Security, Arms Control, and the New Europe," *International Security* 17, no. 1 (Summer 1992), p. 26.

33. Karl W. Deutsch *et al., Political Community and the North Atlantic Area* (Princeton: Princeton University Press, 1957), p. 5.

34. See Amitav Acharya, "The Association of Southeast Asian Nations: 'Security Community' or 'Defense Community'?," *Pacific Affairs* 64 (Summer 1991).

35. Jusuf Wanandi, "Asia-Pacific Security Forums: Rationale and Options from an ASEAN Perspective," in Desmond Ball, Richard L. Grant, and Jusuf Wanandi, *Security Cooperation in the Asia-Pacific Region,* Significant Issues Series, vol. 15, no. 5 (1993).

36. Sheldon W. Simon, "U.S. Policy and the Future of Asian-Pacific Security," *Hitotsubashi Journal of Law and Politics,* Special Issue (June 1994), pp. 56–57.

37. Jason D. Lewis, "Southeast Asia—Preparing for a New World Order," *Washington Quarterly* 16, no. 1 (Winter 1993), p. 190.

38. Leszek Buszynski, *SEATO: The Failure of an Alliance Strategy* (Kent Ridge, Singapore: Singapore University Press, 1983), p. xi.

39. Richard Stubbs, "Subregional Security Cooperation in ASEAN," *Asian Survey* 32, no. 5 (May 1992), pp. 405–408.

40. Martin Gainsborough, "Vietnam and ASEAN: The Road to Membership?" *Pacific Review* 6, no. 4 (1993). For Vietnam, membership "would serve a political purpose. Hanoi sees closer association with ASEAN as a means of giving it more clout in its dealings with Beijing." Ibid., p. 385. Vietnam resisted ASEAN for a long time because it saw the organization as a creation and agent of U.S. imperialism. This attitude reversed in 1978 when the Chinese threat became primary.

41. Thayer, "Sino-Vietnamese Relations," p. 526.

42. Betts, "Systems for Peace or Causes of War?," pp. 16–18, 25–26.

The Opening to the World

5

Coping with China

Tatsumi Okabe

The Legacy of Resentment

As an "Indochinese" country, Vietnam has been strongly influenced by the two great civilizations of Asia: India and China. The impact of China has been especially heavy in Vietnam's northern part, which, in fact, was occupied by China for a thousand years up to the tenth century. Since then, there have been frequent Chinese invasions, so that historical relations have left a legacy of mutual resentment. Only after the French arrived in the late nineteenth century was the border with China defined and demarcated, and only then did China cease to be "threatening" to Vietnam—for a time.

From Comradeship to Confrontation: 1945–78

These traditional relations began to change as the Communist movement caught the attention of East Asian intellectuals. Ho Chi Minh, who visited China many times in the course of directing his communist-oriented independence movement, made Southern China a "homeland" of the Vietnamese revolution.[1]

To be sure, in the early years following the establishment of the Democratic Republic of Vietnam in 1945, Ho was cautious about acknowledging his affiliation with the Communist Chinese. After all, the Chinese were caught up in their own struggle and their own future did not then seem so assured. But by 1950 the situation had changed. The Chinese Communists had won their war and established their rule in Beijing. They, like the Soviet Russians, were now in a position to help Ho, and in his struggle with the French he desperately needed all the help he could get. Accordingly in that year full diplomatic relations were established. Over the years, China claims that it gave Vietnam more than U.S.$20 billion and sent more than 20,000 advisers and 300,000 soldiers.[2]

As "close as lips and teeth" was the phrase often used to describe the new relationship between the two nations as party delegations met in "comradely" conclave and official visits were frequently exchanged. Underneath these professions of solidarity, however, differences of interests persisted, as clearly revealed at the Geneva Conference in 1954.

During the conference, Zhou Enlai, the Chinese prime minister, made a remarkable effort to end the Indochinese war by agreeing with the West to partition Vietnam into two parts. The Communists secured the area north of 17 degrees north latitude as their base, expecting future reunification.[3] This was regarded as a great achievement for the Communist camp at the time, but later, at the height of the Sino-Vietnamese conflict in the late 1970s, the Vietnamese made public their anger. They charged that China had compromised at Geneva, thereby obstructing the Vietnamese from unifying the country by persevering in the war against France.[4]

The Geneva agreement was signed just three months after the historic defeat of the French at Dien Bien Phu. As seen from the Chinese side, the victory at Dien Bien Phu was accomplished with massive aid, both material and human, from China. For example, according to the Chinese, General Chen Geng led a military advisory group to Vietnam to assist in the struggle, and later General Wei Guoqing prepared and commanded the whole operation at Dien Bien Phu.[5] This made the Chinese particularly angry over the Vietnamese resentment of Zhou's success in Geneva.

Another disagreement surfaced at the conference when Vietnam argued that the three Indochinese countries were "an integrated entity." Both China and the Soviet Union opposed this view and suppressed it, China seeing this as a bid for an expansionist "Indochinese Federation."

In the decade that followed, when Sino-Vietnamese relations were at their best, new problems arose. There were differences over relations with the Soviet Union (the attitude to be taken toward Soviet "revisionism," for example) and over the attitude to be taken toward the United States.[6] Many of these differences fed into the problem most fundamental for Hanoi: what strategy the North should pursue in its effort to "liberate" the South and what assistance it could expect from China.

Hanoi preferred a strong offensive and called on China to supply more sophisticated weapons. China was not prepared to supply such weapons. On the other hand, it did not want Hanoi going to Moscow for them either, lest Hanoi should incline to Moscow in the Sino-Soviet dispute.[7] In addition, since Mao Zedong reportedly feared an invasion by the United States of China itself, he was anxious to keep the United States engaged in the South.[8] The Chinese recommendation for Hanoi, therefore, was a strategy of protracted war.

Hanoi's problems became more acute after the entry of the United States into the war in 1965. Hanoi was hoping for a joint Soviet-Chinese response, only to be met, not only with the refusal of China to undertake such an action, but also with China's turning to Vietnam's enemy with a policy of detente. In 1971 China invited Henry Kissinger and in 1972 President Richard Nixon to Beijing and shortly thereafter negotiated the Shanghai Communique.[9] Behind the "lips and teeth," anger mounted.

Hanoi's victory in 1975 did little to ease the tension. China continued to assist Vietnam for several more years, but at reduced levels.[10] The demands of its own economic development were becoming more pressing. In any event, the strategic conflicts with Vietnam were becoming more serious.[11] The difference in their policies toward the Soviet Union were increasing, with China growing more hostile toward it and Vietnam more friendly. In addition, conflicting definitions of the land border and conflicting claims to the Spratly Islands began to be pressed; conflicts among their respective proteges in Laos and Cambodia were becoming increasingly violent.[12]

The immediate issue that provoked confrontation was Vietnam's policy toward the ethnic Chinese in Vietnam.[13] According to the Chinese, there was an understanding between China and Vietnam in 1955 that the nationality of the Chinese residents in Vietnam should be solved by their own will. In fact, when the Ngoh Dinh Diem regime of South Vietnam forced ethnic Chinese to adopt Vietnamese nationality in 1956, North Vietnam criticized the South and supported China. After the war ended in 1975, Hanoi started to force the Chinese to take Vietnamese nationality, thereby endorsing Diem's policy of 1956.[14] China accused Vietnam of oppressing the ethnic Chinese and expelling them from their jobs. Many Chinese, even those who had Vietnamese nationality, fled to China by land. The total number of refugees was over 200,000.[15]

The Vietnamese explained that the campaign that led to the mass exodus of ethnic Chinese was a part of a "class struggle" and suggested that the flight had been encouraged by China. Some Vietnamese argued that China planned to use Southeast Asian ethnic Chinese for China's expansion into Southeast Asia.[16] During 1954 and 1956 China had already established a policy of separately dealing with Chinese nationals residing in foreign countries (*Huaqiao*) and foreign nationals of Chinese origin (*Huaren*). The distinction was blurred during the Cultural Revolution and again became ambiguous with the adoption of an open-door policy. China called on both groups to express their "nationalism" (meaning to invest in China). The ambiguity of this policy, however, cannot fully explain the Chinese exodus in 1978.

In that year, Vietnam joined the Soviet-led Council for Mutual Economic

Assistance (COMECON), further clarifying its stand on the Sino-Soviet conflict. China retaliated by severing all assistance to Vietnam. In July at the Fourth Plenum of the Fourth Congress of the Vietnamese Communist Party, Vietnam declared that its "consistent primary task is to rapidly win a political and military victory in its southwest border area [the border with Cambodia]" and that China was "the most immediate and most dangerous enemy" and was a "new target of Vietnamese operations."[17]In November of that year, Vietnam signed a Treaty of Friendship and Cooperation with the Soviet Union in preparation for the invasion of Cambodia. The Vietnamese army crossed the disputed border with Cambodia in December 1978, initiating what would be a thirteen-year struggle in Cambodia. China, as an enemy of Vietnam, sided with the losing Pol Pot regime, as did the ASEAN countries, which were very much concerned about the possibility of further aggression by Vietnam in Thailand and beyond.

The Years of Hostility: 1979–90

Vietnam successfully expelled the unpopular Pol Pot regime in a very short time, established the pro-Vietnam Heng Samrin regime in Phnom Penh, and called for a "battle alliance" of the three Indochinese countries. It had already concluded a Treaty of Friendship and Cooperation with Laos. China was outraged. It denounced Vietnam as the "Cuba of the East," charging it with carrying out proxy activities for the Soviet Union. China also accused Vietnam of being a "small hegemonist" with an ambition to form a "Federation of Indochina" and thereby gain hegemony in Southeast Asia.[18] Vietnam, of course, denied the charge.

In early 1979, Deng Xiaoping visited the United States. On January 30 he revealed his plan to punish Vietnam to the Senate Foreign Relations Committee and to President Jimmy Carter and appears to have received de facto approval. This contrasted with the tense reaction of Japanese leaders who heard the same plan from Deng some days later on his way back to China.[19] China also must have had some confidence that the Soviet Union would not intervene, at least militarily, in a war between China and Vietnam,[20] although China prepared for such a contingency along its northern border.[21]

On February 17 that year Chinese armed forces initiated a "self-defensive counterattack" across the Vietnam border, and after occupying Lanson on March 5, withdrew behind the border. Although the war was called defensive, it is clear that Chinese intentions were, first, to constrain Vietnamese action in Cambodia by threatening the northern part of the country and, second, to "punish" Vietnam for not only violating the international code of nonaggression, but also for expelling the pro-China Khmer Rouge regime from Phnom Penh. The ideological affinity that had existed between the major doctrines of the Khmer Rouge and China's Cultural Revolution no longer existed in 1979. Still, the geographical position of Cambodia was an asset for China in opposing Vietnam. The common interests of China and the Pol Pot faction, therefore, continued until the ceasefire in 1991.

According to China, the Sino-Vietnamese war achieved the expected results. Vietnam, however, continued to stay in Cambodia for ten years afterwards. The Heng Samrin (chairman of the National Council) or Hun Sen (prime minister) regime effectively existed all these years. In addition, the losses China suffered were unexpectedly heavy,[22] leading some quarters of the People's Liberation Army of China to call for rapid military modernization.[23]

After China's withdrawal, verbal exchanges escalated. Vietnam published its "China White Paper," accusing China of being a historical aggressor as well as a persistent obstructor of the unification of Vietnam. China responded by charging that even during the height of Chinese assistance and friendship the Vietnamese persisted in praising historical heroes of the anti-China resistance.[24]

Throughout the prolonged war in Cambodia, China was an active player. It provided most of the military assistance that kept the Khmer Rouge in the field and encouraged them to join with the popular Prince Norodom Sihanouk, whom China also supported, and Son Sann, the former premier, to form a united anti-Vietnamese front. It was this front that established the Coalition Government of Democratic Kampuchea (CGDK) that won extensive international support and that occupied the Cambodian seat in the United Nations until the UNTAC-managed election.

For nine years the war dragged on. Vietnam controlled most of Cambodia and its government. That government ruled most of the country and did not want to see any change. The Pol Pot faction, being among the most infamous genocidal regimes in history, depended on Sihanouk's prestige among the Cambodian population. Sihanouk, on his part, did not have enough resources to oppose Vietnam. He had no other way than allying with his former staunch enemy, Pol Pot. In order to harass the Vietnamese, China, with the help of Thailand, continued to assist anti-Vietnam forces, especially the Khmer Rouge. ASEAN countries made support for the coalition government a "rallying point" for strengthening the unity of their organization. The war itself was also useful in that it diverted the attention of Vietnam and China away from themselves. Although there was a common understanding that Vietnam was a "short- and medium-term enemy" while

China was a "long-term enemy," the attitudes of the ASEAN countries were not identical. Singapore and Thailand tended to emphasize the immediate danger; Indonesia and Malaysia were easier on Vietnam, hoping it would remain a future buffer against China.

Normalization

The situation in Cambodia was stalemated until the late 1980s, when the ravages of the war, the failures of the socialist system, and the loss of essential financial support from its Soviet and East European allies forced Vietnam to make a fundamental change of direction. The war in Cambodia was terminated, the economic reform known as *doi moi* was undertaken, and the doors were opened to peaceful engagement with the world community. It was in this context that the decision was taken to try to put relations with China on a new footing.

This decision seems not to have been arrived at easily. Observers agree that Vietnam's leaders were for some time divided, those calling for accommodation with China being opposed by others, notably Foreign Minister Nguyen Co Thach, who advocated closer ties with the West.[25] In the end, Thach was removed and an omnidirectional policy was adopted, one that involved pursuing detente with both China and the United States at the same time.

In 1988 the reference to China as a hegemonist was removed from the Vietnamese Constitution. In 1989 the engagement of the Vietnamese forces in Cambodia that so angered the Chinese was ended.

For its part, China, suffering from the international isolation imposed after the Tiananmen incident in June 1989, also saw the desirability of detente. Unofficial contacts picked up. Cross-border trade was resumed. In September 1990, in the context of the Cambodian peace negotiations, a secret meeting between leaders of the two countries was held in Chengdu, China. Jiang Zemin, Li Peng, Nguyen Van Linh, Do Muoi, and Pham Van Dong attended.[26] After the meeting, exchanges between the two countries became frequent. The most publicized was the visit of General Vo Ngyuen Giap to China to attend the Asian Games in Beijing, where he met Li Peng and reconfirmed his old personal friendship with the Chinese leaders.[27] On the occasion of an informal meeting of the Supreme National Council of Cambodia held in Beijing in mid-1991, Prime Minister Hun Sen of the State of Cambodia visited China. Hun Sen had been regarded as a "puppet" of Vietnam and one who had sharply confronted the "pro-China" Khmer Rouge.

The situation was rapidly changing. After the conclusion of the Paris

Peace Accord on Cambodia in October 1991, China declared an end to its aid to the Khmer Rouge and in July 1992 invited the Phnom Penh hardliner Chea Sim to visit, making it clear that China had split with the Pol Pot faction.

Finally in November 1991, two weeks after the conclusion of the Paris Accord on Cambodia, official relations between Vietnam and China were restored. By normalization, however, the Vietnamese do not mean to signal a return to the heady days when they saw the Chinese as comrades in a struggle of global proportions. The two countries are, of course, intensely interested in each other's reform policies. As Nguyen Van Linh and Vo Van Kiet remarked on the occasion of Jiang Zemin's visit in November 1994, one of the things that draws the two countries together is the similarity of their situations and the possibility therefore of "learning" from each other. Each is trying to transform a planned economy into a market economy. Each wants to be integrated into the world market. Each is trying to preserve its political system of dictatorship by a single party. Each shares the view that for reform and economic development a peaceful international environment is indispensable. Each is trying to develop mountainous border areas and is eager to participate in the Mekong River Development Plan. But party relations have not been restored. Representation is by formal diplomatic establishments. Conflicts persist. The most serious are these involving conflicting territorial claims all along the Sino-Vietnamese land border and out into the Gulf of Tonkin and the South China Sea. Toward the end of 1992 when Li Peng visited Vietnam, both sides agreed to seek solutions to these issues peacefully, and a negotiating process was put in place.[28] In 1993, an Agreement of Fundamental Principles on Territorial Conflicts was concluded with Vietnam at the deputy ministerial level, mainly to solve border disputes in the Gulf of Tonkin. A fourth round of negotiations was held in April 1995. But progress has not been notable.

Typical of the land border disputes is that concerning Friendship Pass, which is one of the main connections between the two countries. Here, according to the Vietnamese, China moved the border 300 meters inside what Vietnam considered to be its territory. As a result, though the rail link at the Friendship Pass was repaired in 1993, it was still suspended for "technical" reasons as of 1994. Another land connection was opened in April 1994. This is Moncai-Dongxing bridge, which the writer passed over in August 1994. Cross-border trade was active, but the Vietnamese seemed less enthusiastic about it than the Chinese, perhaps due in part to lingering resentment from the war in 1979. The Vietnamese also fear Chinese economic domination and the possible danger of "peaceful evolution" from China (southern China is much more liberal than Vietnam).

Conflict in the South China Sea

Unquestionably the most serious conflict involves the Spratly Islands* in the South China Sea. There are four archipelagoes in the South China Sea, but relevant here are the Paracels and the Spratlys, notably the latter. Both Vietnam and China have submitted massive amounts of ancient materials in order to prove their respective claims to these islands, but what is more relevant is the legal situation in the years immediately before the dispute occurred.

In 1939, when the Japanese Imperial Army seized the Paracels from China and also occupied most of the Spratlys, China's identification of these islands was uncertain.[29] Japan claimed that the Spratly group it occupied was *terra nullius*. It named the group the Shin'nan Islands and placed them under the administration of Kaohsiung City, Taiwan, which was then under Japanese rule. The sphere of Shin'nan was a little smaller than the present Spratlys, excluding from the latter Royal Charlotte Reef, James Shoals, Prince of Wales Bank, and Vanguard Bank, among other islets—in other words, excluding most of the areas claimed by Malaysia, part of the Vietnamese continental shelf, and some of the islets claimed by the Philippines and Brunei.[30]

After Japan surrendered in 1945, the Republic of China, then the legitimate government of China, took over the Paracels and Shin'nan from Japan and stationed troops on Itu Abu island, which is the only island to produce fresh water in the Spratlys. At the San Francisco Peace Conference in 1951, neither Chinese government was invited, so Japan renounced its possession of Taiwan, Penghu, the Paracels and the Spratlys (in the Japanese text, the latter are referred to as Shin'nan) without naming a new possessor. The same clause was included in the peace treaty between Japan and the Republic of China in Taiwan, though the People's Republic of China declared that the title to those islands renounced by Japan should belong to China. Hence legally speaking, the problem remains whether these areas have any legitimate possessor or not.

Some have applied the no possession theory to Taiwan and Penghu to justify the independence of Taiwan, but Taiwan and Penghu have been effectively governed by the Republic of China—or the "Taiwan authority," as Beijing prefers to call it. In the case of the Spratlys, the Kuomintang

---

*The Spratly Islands are called Nansha by the Chinese and Troung Sa by the Vietnamese. While claimant countries often use different names to refer to the individual island reefs and shoals of the area, the names used here and in subsequent chapters are those customarily used internationally.

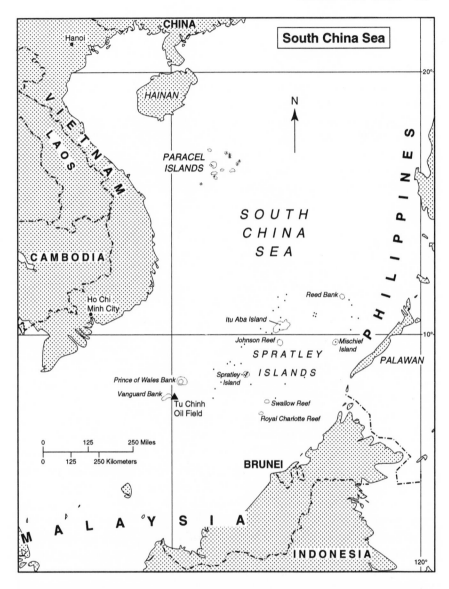

army withdrew from Itu Aba island in 1950 after its defeat in the civil war on the mainland.

During this early postwar period, the parties concerned today took a rather passive attitude toward the title to the islands. This was merely common sense when the territorial waters were limited to three nautical miles. The occupation of the islets was no more than a costly vanity. The principal incident occurred in 1956, when Taipei hastily reoccupied Itu Aba after

Tomas Cloma, a Filipino, claimed title to the Reed Bank (thence called the Kalayaan or Freedom Island Range by the Philippines) in the northern part of the Spratlys. China and South Vietnam also protested Cloma's action. He withdrew but left a precedent, on which in 1971 President Ferdinand Marcos claimed part of the Spratlys for the Philippines.

Attention picked up in the early 1970s, when the possibility of exploiting seabed oil in the vicinity of shoals and on other atolls came to the fore and when progress in the negotiations on the United Nations Law of the Sea suggested that littoral states would be able to expand their exclusive economic zones to 200 nautical miles from shore.

China focused its attention first on the Paracels, then occupied by South Vietnamese armed forces. On January 11, 1974, China protested what it called South Vietnam's invasion of the South China Sea islands.[31] On January 15, fighting occurred between the South Vietnamese and Chinese navies. A few days later, China overcame the South Vietnamese and since then has occupied all of the Paracels. According to the Chinese, the government in Hanoi at the time did not oppose the Chinese action.[32] In fact during this period, when Hanoi was relying heavily on the Chinese for support, the Hanoi authorities seem to have recognized the Spratlys and the Paracels as Chinese territories. Three bits of evidence for this are often cited by China.[33] The first is a statement by Vietnamese Deputy Foreign Minister Ung Van Khien to Chinese Deputy Foreign Minister Li Zhimin in which the former indicated that Vietnam had recognized the Paracels and the Spratlys as Chinese territory since the days of the Song dynasty. The second is Pham Van Dong's letter dated September 14, 1958. It supported China's statement, extending its territorial waters twelve nautical miles. The statement clearly mentioned the Paracels and Spratlys by name as belonging to China. Third, in May 1965, the (North) Vietnamese Foreign Ministry criticized the United States for defining "part of China's Paracels" as a "fighting operation area."[34]

When victory was finally attained over the South, however, Hanoi was anxious to pick up all the pieces and claims left by the fallen regime. It acknowledged later that it had indeed previously acquiesced in China's claims to the islands but argued that times since then had changed.

> At that time, Vietnam had to struggle against American intervention and aggression. . . . During this period, China regarded American imperialism as its main enemy and firmly supported the anti-American war of the Vietnamese people and was the "Vietnamese people's great rear base." China was one of the biggest aid donors to Vietnam. In the anti-American struggle, China and Vietnam became real friends. Relations between the two were "as close as lips and teeth." . . . During this period of opposing a much stronger enemy,

the more Vietnam could let China fight hand in hand with Vietnam, the more advantageous for Vietnam to prevent America from using these two archipelagoes, and avoid attacks from the South China Sea [the East Sea in Vietnamese]. We have to understand the above statements in this spirit.[35]

With this rationale, in 1975 Vietnam asserted its claims to both the Paracels and the Spratlys and physically took possession of the six Spratly islands that the former South Vietnamese regime had occupied. In later years other islands were added.

Meanwhile, the Philippines had occupied three islets in 1971 and expanded its claims further to include Mischief Reef, which became a source of conflict with China in early 1995. In 1983 Malaysia announced its occupation of Swallow Reef. China did not respond immediately, but in 1987 it held two naval exercises in the Spratlys for the first time. In March of the following year, during what were explained as research activities, Chinese warships clashed with Vietnamese warships in the area of Johnson Reef and sank two of them. At this time, China occupied six shoals and acquired a base to extend its presence farther.

In February 1992, China promulgated a Territorial Waters Law in which it stated that the South China Sea Islands, together with the Diaoyutai Islands (claimed also by Japan and called by it the Senkaka Islands), belonged to China and declared its right to expel by any means those who violated Chinese sovereignty. It moved promptly in May in the same year to grant an oil exploration concession to Crestone, an American company, in an oil field that is called Tu Chinh by the Vietnamese and is adjacent to an existing Vietnamese oil field. Vietnam regards this area as part of its own continental shelf. The action was, therefore, very provocative. It is reported that President Randall Thompson of Crestone told reporters that "China has promised the full support of its navy to protect Crestone."[36] At the time the threat perceived by Vietnam was multiplied because the United States still maintained an embargo against Vietnam, so that Vietnam saw the move as part of a united front by China and the United States against it. China also moved quickly to consolidate its presence in the area by planting a territorial marker on Da Lac Reef (if Da Lac is Nanxun, as China claimed, the marker had already been planted in 1989), and by taking possession also of Da Ba Island.

These Chinese actions have caused great apprehension, not only in Vietnam, but among the ASEAN claimants as well. After all, while China, Taiwan, and Vietnam occupy only 7, 1, and 24 respectively of the more than 100 named islands,[37] each of them claims sovereignty over the entire archipelago, including the 8 occupied by the Philippines, the 3 by Malaysia, and the 1 by Brunei. And as the controversy has gone on, the appreciation of their economic value (according to one estimate, recoverable oil deposits in the Spratlys are between three and five billion tons) and their strategic significance in the midst of the major sea lanes connecting the Indian and the Pacific oceans has increased.

The ASEAN Foreign Ministers' Conference in July 1992 announced ASEAN's South China Sea Declaration, calling for peaceful settlement of the issue. China has tried to dampen concern over the "China threat" and the fear of a Sino-Vietnamese clash that has been spreading throughout the region. Jiang Zemin, Li Peng, and Qian Qichen have repeatedly emphasized their desire for a peaceful settlement of the conflict and proposed to develop the area jointly by shelving the sovereignty issue. In 1993 many other Chinese leaders, including the military, visited Southeast Asian countries to assure them of China's peaceful intentions. Most of the heads of states of ASEAN countries also visited China that year, concluding economic agreements and projects.

But Vietnam's fear that its infant industries would be overwhelmed by the booming Chinese economy only grew stronger, and the "threat of China" continued to be a favorite topic to discuss with foreign visitors. Vietnamese leaders talked much about China's "betrayal" of its pledges of peaceful settlement of disputes, of joint development, and of respecting the status quo before a final solution is achieved.[38]

In October 1994, the conflict between Vietnam and China over the Spratlys was further inflamed by Vietsovpetro drilling in the same Tu Chinh oil field where the Crestone company also is drilling.[39] To this, Vietnam responded that the area was on the continental shelf of Vietnam and Crestone's contract with China was null and void.[40] Mobil also is drilling in Tu Chinh. At the same time, conflict occurred in the Tonkin Gulf.[41]

In early 1995 China protested a Russo-Vietnam joint geological survey in the Spratlys that caused renewed controversy on the sovereignty issue.[42] In February 1995, Filipinos found Chinese installations on Mischief Reef that they alleged were for military purposes. (China said they were shelters for fishermen.) This incident could not but involve Vietnam. The Vietnam Foreign Ministry, insisting that disputes should be peacefully resolved and that no parties should take actions to complicate the issue, declared that China's action was serious. It also criticized China's expansionism.[43] It is reported that both Vietnam and China sent more troops to the Spratlys.

China's establishment of an Ocean Agency in Hainan Province in March 1995 intensified the concerns of ASEAN countries and Vietnam. In early April a deputy ministerial level consultation was held between China and the ASEAN countries in Hangzhou, China; but little appears to have been accomplished, China continuing to maintain that the disputes should be negotiated on a bilateral basis.[44] Chinese Foreign Minister Qian Qichen reiterated in a press conference at the annual National People's Congress that there was no question about China's sovereignty over the Spratlys, but that China had restrained itself and advocated "shelving the disputes and developing the area jointly."[45] Meanwhile, fear of the rising influence of the Chinese military has grown.[46]

Vietnam's Search for Support

Convinced that the "China threat" is real, but anxious to avoid hostilities, Vietnam is exploring the possibilities of international strategic support. It is, first of all, trying to draw closer to ASEAN, which shares Vietnam's concerns about China's ambitions in the Spratly Islands. China, it is argued, would hesitate to attack the island interests of an ASEAN-related Vietnam, since such an attack would antagonize the countries of ASEAN, which China looks on as development models and as potential allies in its struggle with the big countries in the Asia-Pacific region.[47] Such was at least some of the thinking that led Vietnam to sign the ASEAN Treaty of Amity and Cooperation in July 1992.

That full membership in ASEAN would quickly follow, however, was not obvious. Some of the ASEAN countries welcomed the Vietnamese initiative, perhaps for economic and security reasons. Others did not. Some in Singapore, for example, were worried that Vietnam's admission would make ASEAN consensus more difficult to achieve.[48] Some in Thailand shared this view.[49] Some in Indonesia, although supporting Vietnam's membership, made it clear that they had no intention of getting involved in the long-standing Vietnam-China rivalry.[50]

In Vietnam also there were doubts about the wisdom of seeking membership. First of all, there were lingering ill feelings toward certain ASEAN states, especially Thailand. Second, as the least developed country in ASEAN, Vietnam feared that it might be at a disadvantage in the ASEAN Free Trade Area (AFTA), which is an inseparable part of ASEAN. Third, there was apprehension about the financial burden of attending the hundreds of meetings held by ASEAN each year and even more of hosting some of these meetings. Fourth, there was uneasiness about the shortage of personnel who could speak English, the official language of ASEAN.[51]

But both sides pressed ahead. In July 1994 the ASEAN ministers declared their readiness to process Vietnam's application; in October the formal application was submitted; and at the July 1995 ASEAN Ministers Meeting, full membership was accomplished.

Vietnam's policy of normalization with the United States can also be understood as partly motivated by the search for friends to help in the deterrence of China. Clearly U.S. presence and involvement in the region is seen as crucially valuable to the small countries in the Spratly Island dispute.[52] Although Vietnamese officials are circumspect in expressing these views, the chief of the American Bureau of the Vietnamese Foreign Ministry is reported to have said in April 1994, "Normalization with the United States contributes a great deal to the stability and security of the [Southeast Asian] region";[53] and Nayan Chanda, deputy editor of the *Far Eastern Economic Review,* reports that in April 1995 a well-informed Vietnamese opined "that the government is counting on . . . eventual strategic ties with the U.S. to counter the threat from a resurgent China."[54]

The U.S. response has been guarded but not unsympathetic. Although strategic ties between the United States and Vietnam are not now foreseeable—Deputy Secretary of State Trobe Talbot said in July 1994 at the ASEAN Foreign Ministers' Meeting that "the United States takes no position on territorial claims"; nevertheless, he also said that the United States "strongly opposes the use of force to resolve them."[55] In October 1994 Admiral Richard Macke, then commander in chief of the U.S. Pacific Command, went a little further in remarks in Hanoi, saying that he expected U.S. military cooperation with Vietnam once relations were normalized.[56]

The U.S. Defense Department followed this up with the following more general explanation:

> Our interest is in the peaceful solution of territorial and other disputes. Our ability to protect the vital sea lanes in the Pacific and Indian Oceans enhances regional prosperity. . . . At the same time, there is a danger from potentially destabilizing political transitions throughout the region. Leadership and generation transitions could intersect in unpredictable ways with the dynamic security and economic trends in the region. In addition, the danger of proliferation of weapons of mass destruction, emerging nationalism amidst long-standing ethnic and national rivalries, and unresolved territorial disputes could combine to create a political landscape of potential instability and conflict. America's engagement in regional security must take these changes into account.[57]

This is not to suggest that Vietnam is identifying China as a main enemy and attempting to forge a united front against it. International strategic support is only one of Vietnam's new foreign policy objectives. Equally important is its search for international economic support, which, Vietnam believes, requires an omnidirectional diplomacy, one that eases the political tensions with China—as with all countries—as much as possible and engages it economically. In 1994 the Vietnamese stopped using the term "China threat"; and in November of that year, in spite of Taiwan's heavy involvement in the Vietnamese economy, Vietnam reaffirmed its adherence to the "one China" policy, acknowledging Taiwan to be a part of China" and the PRC as "the sole legitimate government of China." China, for its part, also is pursuing detente, as was made clear by Jiang Zemin's visit to Vietnam in November 1994 and in China's warm congratulations on the sixty-fifth anniversary of the Vietnamese Communist Party in February 1995.[58] Both sides look forward to increased trade, the Chinese provinces of Guangxi and Yunnan being particularly interested in including Vietnam in their economic development strategies.

Vietnam's approaches to ASEAN and to the United States need to be seen not only in the context of Vietnam's strategic policy vis-à-vis China, but also as part of its development policy to integrate its economy with the most vibrant economies in the world.

How successful will this new policy toward China be? When, if ever, are Vietnam and China likely to find a compatible path together? One cannot be sure. The legacy of ancient resentments continues to bubble, and current disputes seem intractable. But both sides are seeking detente, and economic ties are growing. In any event, Vietnam is not as alone as it was. In these circumstances the probability that the South China Sea will become a major flash point in Asia seems remote. Equally remote, however, seems to be the probability of the conflict's being peacefully resolved in the foreseeable future. The combination of intimacy and conflict that have characterized Vietnam-China relations for centuries shows no signs of waning.

Notes

1. Guo Ming, ed., *Zhong-Yue Guanxi Yanbian Sishinian (Forty Years' Evolution of Sino-Vietnamese Relations)* (Guangxi: Guangxi Renmin Chubanshe, 1992), pp. 9–15.

2. Guoji Wenti Yanjiu, Bianjibu (editorial staff of *International Studies*), "Zhong-Yue Guanxi de Zhenxiang" (The Truth about China-Vietnam Relations), *Peking Shuho*, October 13, 1981 (originally published in *International Studies*, no. 2, 1981) (hereafter cited as "Truth").

3. For bargaining over the latitude, see ibid., p. 50.

4. Socialist Republic of Vietnam, Foreign Ministry, *Chugoku hakusho; Chugoku o kokuhatsusuru* (Tokyo: Nicchu Shuppan, 1979), pp. 27–40. A Japanese version of *The Truth about Vietnam-China Relations over the Last Thirty Years* (Hanoi, October 1979) (hereafter cited as "White Paper").

5. Guo Ming, *Zhong-Yue*, pp. 33–39, and Renmin Ribao and Xinhua News Agency, "Betonamu no Etchukankei Hakusho wo Hyosu (2)" (A criticism on the White Paper of the Vietnamese Foreign Ministry on Vietnam-China relations, Part 2), *Renmin Ribao*, November 21, 1979, as published in Japanese in *Pekin Shuho* (Beijing review), December 4, 1979 (hereafter cited as "Criticism," Part 2).

6. Guo Ming, *Zhong-Yue,* pp. 67, 99–101.

7. Eugene K. Lawson, *The Sino-Vietnamese Conflict* (New York: Praeger, 1984), p. 86.

8. Ibid., pp. 35, 39. Also see Shu Ken'ei (Zhu Jianrong) "1965 nen no Ra Zuikyou-Lin Pyou shomei ronbun ni kansuru atarasii kenkyu—'ronso' denaku 'shutaiteki tenkan' no kanosei" (A new study on articles signed by Luo Ruiqing-Lin Biao—a possibility not of a 'controversy,' but a 'self-transformation'), *Ajiya Kenkyu* (Asian studies), December 1993, pp. 77–83.

9. Lawson, *Sino-Vietnamese Conflict,* pp. 134ff, 240ff.

10. "Truth."

11. Guo Ming, *Zhong Yue,* p. 118.

12. Ibid., pp. 160–161; and "Criticism" Part 3, as published in Japanese in *Peking Shuho* (Beijing review), December 11, 1979.

13. Guo Ming, *Zhong-Yue,* pp. 118–133.

14. Ibid., p. 132.

15. Ibid., p. 123.

16. Ibid., p. 133.

17. Ibid., p. 163; and "Truth," in *Peking Shuho* (Beijing review), October 20, 1981.

18. Guo Ming, *Zhong-Yue;* "White Paper," in *Peking Shuho* (Beijing review), October 27, 1981; and "Criticism," Part 3, in *Peking Shuho* (Beijing review), December 11, 1979.

19. Min Li, *Zhong Yue Zhanzheng Shinian Neimu* (Inside Stories of the Ten Years' Sino-Vietnamese War) (Chengdu: Sichuan University Press, 1993), pp. 4–7; Zhang Weiming et al., *Zhong Yue Zhanzheng Milu* (Secret Memorandum of the Sino-Vietnamese War) (Hong Kong: Cosmos Books, Ltd., 1993), p. 29.

20. Min Li, *Zhong Yue,* pp. 16–18.

21. Zhang Weiming et al., *Zong Yue,* p. 29.

22. Ibid., p. 35. Reportedly the number of dead or injured was 63,000 on the Chinese side and 62,000 on the Vietnamese side.

23. You Ji, "A Test Case for China's Defense and Foreign Policies," *Contemporary Southeast Asia,* March 1995, pp. 376ff.

24. "Truth," in *Peking Shuho* (Beijing review), October 13, 1981.

25. Carlyle A. Thayer, "Vietnam Coping with China," *Southeast Asian Affairs 1994* (Singapore: Institute of Southeast Asian Studies, 1994), pp. 354ff; and Guo Ming, *Zhong-Yue,* p. 212.

26. For more details, see Carlyle A. Thayer, "Sino-Vietnamese Relations, the Interplay of Ideology and National Interests," *Asian Survey,* June 1994, pp. 513–528.

27. Min Li, *Zhong Yue,* pp. 80–81.

28. A knowledgeable Vietnamese scholar said that this was a major change.

29. Takeshita Hidekuni, "Minami Shina Kai Funso no Keii to Ryoyuken Mondai" (A History of South China Sea Disputes and the Territorial Problem), *Ajia Torendo* (Asian Trend), no. 3, 1992, p. 72.

30. Ibid., pp. 65–68.

31. Han Zhenhua et al., eds., *Woguo Nanhai Zhudao Shiliao Huibian* (Collection of historical materials on the South China Sea of Our Country) (Dongfang Chubanshe, 1988), p. 451.

32. Lawson, *Sino-Vietnamese Conflict,* pp. 277–279.

33. Guo Ming, *Zhong-Yue,* pp. 146–147.

34. Han Zhenhua, *Woguo Nanhai,* pp. 543–544.

35. Guo Ming, *Zhong-Yue,* pp. 207–208.

36. *New York Times,* June 18, 1992, cited in Takeshita, *Minami Shina Kai Funso,* no. 4, p. 88.

37. According to Yosakushu (Yang Zouzhou), *Funso Nansa Shoto* (Conflict: Spratly Islands) (Tokyo: Sinhyoron, 1994), the number of islands, shoals, etc., named by the Republic of China is 106. According to a list comparing Chinese and international names in Han Zhenhua, *Wogue Nanhai,* pp. 704–719, the number is 191.

38. Interviews with Vietnamese officials and scholars in Hanoi in 1993.

39. *Tonan Ajia Geppo* (South East Asia monthly bulletin), October 1994, p. 18.

40. *Far Eastern Economic Review,* March 16, 1995, p. 58.

41. *Tonan Ajia Geppo,* October 1994, p. 18.

42. *Tonan Ajia Geppo,* January 1995, p. 20.

43. *Yomiuri Shinbun,* February 11, 1995.

44. *Asahi Shinbun* and *Nihon Keizai Shinbun,* April 4, 1995.

45. *Renmin Ribao,* March 11, 1995.

46. *Yomiuri Shinbun,* March 25, 1995.

47. For the Vietnamese change of perception of the region, see Masaya Shiraishi, "Betonamu no Ajia Taiheiyo Ninshiki" (Vietnam's Perception of the Asia-Pacific Region) in Tatsumi Okabe, ed., *Posuto reisen no Ajia Taiheiyo* (Asia Pacific Region in the Post-Cold War Era) (Tokyo: Nihon Kokusai Mondai Kenkyujo, 1995), pp. 193, 198–199.

48. Lianhe Zaobao (Singapore), October 18, 1994, cited in *Sankei Shinbun,* October 19, 1994.

49. Sukhumbhand Paribatra, "From ASEAN Six to ASEAN Ten: Issues and Prospects," *Contemporary Southeast Asia,* December 1994, p. 255.

50. Remark of Jusuf Wanandi of the Jakarta-based Centre for Strategic and International Studies, quoted in *Far Eastern Economic Review,* March 16, 1995, p. 20.

51. Interview with a Vietnamese scholar in August 1994.

52. Hoang Anh Tuan, "Vietnam's Membership in ASEAN," *Contemporary Southeast Asia,* December 1994, p. 269.

53. *Nihon Keizai Shinbun,* April 28, 1995.

54. *Far Eastern Economic Review,* May 4, 1995, p. 24.

55. *Business Times,* July 27, 1994, quoted in Tuan, "Vietnam's Membership in ASEAN," p. 268.

56. *The Straits Times,* October 27, 1994.

57. U.S. Department of Defense, Office of International Security Affairs, *United States Security Strategy for the East Asia-Pacific Region* (Tokyo: American Embassy, 1995), p. 20.

58. *Renmin Ribao,* February 1995.

6

Detaching from Cambodia

Seki Tomoda

Although the Vietnamese had struggled for centuries with the Laotians and the Khmer for living space in the Indochina peninsula, the imposition of French rule over the entire area in the nineteenth and twentieth centuries brought a new sense of common purpose. The young communist leaders of the 1930s became convinced that independence could only be achieved by a unified struggle. Out of this conviction was born the Communist Party of Indochina; and while in 1951 separate parties were formed in Vietnam, Laos, and Cambodia, each was originally dedicated to a peninsulawide revolutionary strategy and to the maintenance of a "special relationship"—under Vietnamese leadership.

But time has dealt harshly with this ambition. Khmer nationalists refused to accept it, and the international community, particularly the Chinese, made clear they would not tolerate what appeared to be an effort to create a greater Vietnam. Vietnam was forced therefore, as a fundamental element in its turnabout in the 1980s, to withdraw from Cambodia, end party-to-party relations, and proclaim henceforth its renunciation of the "special relationship." In the years that have followed, the detachment seems clean. But the question remains: Once Vietnam gets on its feet, how long can it remain detached from neighbors who line its strategic western border, whose lands continue to attract Vietnam's expanding population, and whose capacities to govern seem so unsure?

The Old "Special Relationship"

When Ho Chi Minh set out to elaborate a strategy to combat French domination, he viewed Indochina as a single battle theater. In Cambodia and

Laos he established branches of his Indochinese communist movement and later made them headquarters for commanding guerrilla war against local French troops. According to this strategy, priority would be given to the revolution in Vietnam, the success of which would provide momentum for revolutions in the other two countries. If the idea of an Indochina federation was officially abandoned at the Second Congress of the Communist Party of Indochina in 1951, when it was decided to create an independent communist party in each of the three countries, that decision had little effect on the perception of Indochina as a strategic entity. Throughout the two wars in Indochina, Hanoi continued to follow the original strategy, pursuing the idea of an Indochina federation and requesting its Cambodian and Laotian comrades to dedicate themselves to the Vietnamese cause. The Vietnamese concept, however, created resentment among some of these comrades. The most visible example was the revolt of a dissident group of the Cambodian Communists, consisting mainly of young nationalistic intellectuals who had studied in Paris, and who later became the Khmer Rouge.

Did the end of the Vietnam War really put an end to the idea of an Indochina federation? The answer is yes and no. Nguyen Co Thach, the former minister of foreign affairs, reasserted recently that with the end of the Vietnam War the idea of Indochina federation was replaced by the concept of an association among the three countries. He said: "We fought against the French with the solidarity of the three Indochinese countries. After the departure of the French, the Americans tried to dominate Indochina with the same strategy as the French one and we fought accordingly. However, after 1975 when the war in Vietnam ended, we no longer needed a federation in Indochina." He then added, "Later, as our strategic enemy— China—tried to divide Indochina, the close association of the three countries became indispensable."[1]

What, then, was the difference between association and federation? Although the two formulations differed in a legal sense, the substance apparently remained the same: a sort of political and military union presumably with the predominant role to be played by Vietnam. The resolution adopted by the Fourth Congress of the Communist Party of Vietnam (CPV) in 1976 reiterated Hanoi's Indochinese policy: "to preserve the special relationship between the Vietnamese people and the peoples of Laos and Cambodia, and to strengthen military solidarity, mutual trust, long-term cooperation and mutual assistance in all fields . . . so that the three countries, which have been associated with one another in the struggle for national liberation, will be associated forever with one another in the building and defense of their respective countries."[2]

If the China factor was, as Nguyen Co Thach put it, the main reason for

Vietnam to seek a strategic association or alliance of the Indochinese countries and for its tilt toward Moscow after the end of the Vietnam War, there can be little doubt that these actions alarmed Beijing and stimulated an increasingly aggressive response. According to this author's private conversations with informed Chinese sources in 1980, Mao Zedong, in his final days in 1976, described to other Chinese leaders the lessons from the Vietnam War. Among these was the realization that since the peninsula was attached to the Chinese land mass, if it were united and allied with an unfriendly power, it would inevitably constitute one of the most serious threats to Chinese security. Mao's "last words" were a revealing reflection of how Chinese leaders viewed the situation in Indochina. This assessment apparently was shared by Deng Xiaoping, his successor, though he denied many of Mao's policies in other fields.

For Vietnam, successive events occurring since the early 1970s made Beijing's intentions in the region suspicious. President Nixon's visit to China in 1972 was a real shock for Hanoi. The degree of Vietnam's concern was noted by two Japanese officials who visited Hanoi a few days before Nixon's departure to Beijing. Throughout the discussions with the Japanese diplomats, Vietnamese officials showered them with questions on Sino-American relations as well as the impact of the rapprochement on Chinese relations with the USSR.[3] Later, in 1974, when Chinese troops attacked the Paracel Islands, which had been under South Vietnamese control, Hanoi was deeply upset. Suspicions about Chinese ambitions in the South China Sea rose to such an extent that one Vietnamese source described the Chinese attack as the starting point of the third Indochina war.[4]

Tensions remained high in September 1975 when Le Duan, then the first secretary of the CPV, visited Beijing. The Chinese asked him, as a condition for continuing military aid to Vietnam, to agree to an antihegemony—meaning, in fact, an anti-USSR—clause to be inserted in the joint declaration. Le Duan promptly rejected the clause and left the Chinese capital without issuing any communique. One month later in Moscow, Le Duan confirmed to Soviet leaders that Vietnam shared "completely" the USSR assessment of the international situation and expressed Vietnamese support for the Soviet's external policy.[5] In December 1976, the Fourth Congress of the CPV purged the Political Bureau and the Central Committee of individuals with "Chinese connections," revealing a critical shift within the leadership to those favoring the Soviets.[6]

In July 1977, Hanoi concluded a treaty of friendship and cooperation with Vientiane, thus making the first step toward formal establishment of a "special relationship" in Indochina. The effort was completed in 1979 with the conclusion of a similar treaty with the newly established pro-Hanoi regime in Phnom Penh soon after the collapse of the Khmer Rouge's rule in Cambodia.

The Vietnamese invasion of Cambodia, begun at midnight, December 24, 1978, was the decisive turning point both for bilateral relations between Vietnam and Cambodia and for the triangular relations among the PRC, the USSR, and Vietnam. A new structure of regional confrontation became evident. A dual rivalry divided Cambodia: the antagonism between China and the USSR, on the one hand, and the "brother enemy" confrontation between pro-Soviet communists and pro-Chinese ones, on the other, with the Beijing-Khmer Rouge alliance politically backed by ASEAN as well as the Western capitals.

There was a consensus in Hanoi to conduct a massive military operation in order to topple the Khmer Rouge regime in Phnom Penh. In Hanoi's view, the regime constituted a serious threat due to its aggressions along the Vietnamese border that seemed tinged with the radical nationalist claim to the former Khmer territories in the southern part of Vietnam. The Vietnamese leaders, however, differed on tactics. General Vo Nguyen Giap, the defense minister, advocated sealing the Thai-Cambodian border in advance of the capture of Phnom Penh in order to cut off the retreat of the Khmer Rouge. General Van Tien Dung, then chief of the general staff of the People's Liberation Army (and a rising star for his role in the "Ho Chi Minh Campaign" to capture Saigon in 1975), wanted to attack the capital first, and his view won out. Today many Vietnamese experts believe that the absence of strong resistance by the Khmer Rouge was a trap, set up with Chinese advice, to draw Vietnamese troops into a protracted war.[7]

After the fall of Phnom Penh in January 1979, Vietnam concluded in February a treaty of friendship and cooperation with the newly established government in Phnom Penh. Thus, Hanoi moved swiftly to set up a strategic alliance in Indochina based on a network of "special relations." This was, in fact, a politico-military triangle with Vietnam as protector of Laos and Heng Samrin's Cambodia. Significantly, the network was closely linked to Moscow through the Vietnamese-USSR treaty signed in November 1978, one month before the Vietnamese campaign against Cambodia. The treaty provided protection for Vietnam. The Soviet Union thereby firmly established its presence in Indochina, and the nightmare that Beijing had long feared became real. Was Hanoi, then, really prepared to accept Soviet influence in order to prevail in Indochina? It seems Hanoi was caught in a dilemma. After the end of the Vietnam War in 1975 Hanoi shifted its priority from war to economic reconstruction. This was why Pham Van Dong, then the prime minister, visited France and later the ASEAN capitals. It is also why Nguyen Co Thach, then the deputy foreign minister, engaged in long and difficult talks for normalization with the Carter administration. Nguyen Duy Trinh, then the foreign minister, visited Tokyo on the eve of the invasion of Cambodia in December 1978 for negotiations on economic aid. At the same time the Vietnamese were preoccupied with the increasingly provocative acts of the Khmer Rouges in Cambodia as well as the deterioration of relations with Beijing. After long debate, their answer to the dilemma was to secure Soviet support.

Although Hanoi concluded the treaty of friendship and cooperation with Moscow in November 1978, Vietnam did not count on Soviet military intervention in case the Chinese attacked Vietnam. Nguyen Co Thach has confirmed that,

> We concluded the treaty with the Soviet Union as we needed to have a friend in order to face the threat of the Chinese strategy, which was to oppose the USSR as an enemy at the global level and Vietnam as an enemy at the regional level. What we sought in a treaty was not Soviet intervention but only its political assistance, as we know big powers do not like to intervene in the conflicts of smaller nations. The Soviets themselves found the treaty useful because it reinforced the Soviet position vis-à-vis China, which claimed that the USSR was its main adversary. As for a Chinese attack, we certainly anticipated one, but we did not believe Chinese troops were strong enough to conquer all of Vietnam, as China had committed itself to the four modernization efforts domestically, on the one hand, and its military capabilities were extremely reduced because of the disaster of the Cultural Revolution, on the other.[8]

If the need to have friends pushed Hanoi to accept the strategic alliance with Moscow, it seems that the Vietnamese today look back on this choice with bitter skepticism. The lesson Vietnam learned, a Vietnamese source admitted privately, was that it had embedded itself too deeply in big-power relations. For example, he continued, the Americans rejected normalization with Vietnam in 1978 because they found Hanoi closely allied with the USSR, while they normalized relations with Beijing as the PRC was opposed to the Soviets. That is why, he said, Vietnam should free itself from dated views on relations with big powers.[9]

"New Thinking" and the Withdrawal from Cambodia

During the 1980s the international power structure underwent a sweeping transformation that directly affected relations in Indochina. For Vietnam this transformation began in March 1982, when Leonid Brezhnev, then the secretary general of the Soviet Communist Party, announced publicly in a speech at Tashkent that for the first time Moscow was ready for the amelioration of relations with the PRC. The debate engendered within the Vietnamese party continued until 1986, when the CPV's Sixth Congress adopted the *doi moi,* or renovation, policy for economic reform. Even prior to Brezhnev's Tashkent speech, the Soviet leader had expressed privately to his three Indochinese counterparts assembled in the Crimea in September 1981 for an informal summit meeting that the Soviets intended to ameliorate relations with the PRC and had urged them to alter their policy toward ASEAN from one of confrontation to one of good-neighborliness for the sake of resolving the Cambodian problem. The abrupt change in Soviet policy toward China and Cambodia was a real shock to the Vietnamese leaders.[10]

The debate that followed in the Central Committee plenum in Hanoi lasted 25 days—the longest in the history of the party—and included the delicate questions of whether to withdraw quickly from Cambodia or stay longer, awaiting the consolidation of Phnom Penh's capacity to face the Khmer Rouge threat. Vietnam started a partial withdrawal from Cambodia in 1982, described at the time as a "proof of good will" but later explained as a response to the Heng Samrin regime's increasing capability of assuming larger responsibility for the war effort.[11] In fact, it might well have been an indication of a compromise reached between the two schools in Hanoi, one for quick withdrawal in order to end international isolation and the other, mainly supported by the military, for a continued Vietnamese armed commitment in Cambodia.

In any event, in 1982 Hanoi paid careful attention to the trend of Sino-USSR relations, which moved steadily toward detente. As early as October 1982 Beijing and Moscow resumed meetings at the deputy foreign minister level, which had been broken off after the Soviet invasion of Afghanistan three years before. Seven meetings were held before 1985, when Mikhail Gorbachev came to power in Moscow. Beijing asked Moscow to meet three conditions for the normalization of relations: a significant reduction of Soviet troops stationed along the Sino-USSR and Sino-Mongolian borders, the withdrawal of Soviet troops from Afghanistan, and an end to support for the Vietnamese occupation of Cambodia.

Following Gorbachev's announcement in July 1986 in Vladivostok that the Soviet Union would start withdrawing troops from Afghanistan before the end of the year and that it was ready to discuss withdrawal from Mongolia, Beijing concentrated its diplomatic efforts on the third condition, the withdrawal of Vietnamese troops from Cambodia. Regarding Vietnamese reactions to the Soviet policy shift, it was significant that Le Duan had signalled official agreement with Gorbachev in the joint communique issued when they met in Moscow in June 1985, one year before the latter's speech in Vladivostok. The communique recognized "the need for the normalization of relations with the PRC for the sake of peace in Asia and the world."[12]

The shift in Vietnam's policy toward Cambodia unveiled at the Sixth Congress of the CPV, held in December 1986, marked one of the biggest turns in the course of Hanoi's post-Vietnam War policy evolution. The shift had become clear in August 1985 at the eleventh conference of the foreign ministers of Indochina held in Phnom Penh. The joint statement expressed the desire for normalization with the PRC as well as the intention, publicly mentioned for the first time, to complete the withdrawal of the Vietnamese troops from Cambodia before 1990 in order to "facilitate the political solution" of the Cambodian conflict.[13] In view of the Vietnamese perception that the conflict in Cambodia was basically the result of Beijing's strategy, Hanoi's shift in its Cambodian policy was naturally related to a change in its China policy. Hanoi's new approaches in these two respects were confirmed in the political report of the Sixth Congress of the CPV:

> We hold that the time has come for the two sides to enter into negotiations to solve both immediate and long-term problems in the relations between the two countries. Once again we officially declare that Vietnam is ready to negotiate with China at any time, at any level and in any place to normalize the relations between the two countries . . . We fully support the People's Republic of Kampuchea's readiness to negotiate with opposition individuals and groups to realize national concord on the basis of excluding the criminal genocidal Pol Pot gang. We stand for the continued withdrawal of Vietnamese army volunteers from Kampuchea and at the same time are ready to cooperate with all parties concerned so as to proceed toward a correct political solution on Kampuchea.[14]

With respect to the new Cambodian policy, the decision was then made to the effect that, as long as Cambodia remained neutral, independent, peaceful, and nonaligned, the burden should be left to the Cambodians. It meant in practice the "Khmerization" of the conflict. The military seemed reluctant to accept the policy changes, especially the withdrawal. Nevertheless, the broader shift in the perception of the international situation, on the one hand, and the deeper deterioration of the economic situation, on the other, pushed the leadership in Hanoi to proceed with the policy changes.[15]

"The general current in the world then was aiming at peace in Cambodia," Nguyen Co Thach recalled recently, "and we thought it was in Vietnam's interest to facilitate the peace process by withdrawing troops from Cambodia." And he added, "The economic difficulties we experienced in those days were very serious and inflation was approaching a three-digit peak in 1987."[16] Therefore, the need to end international isolation, which had accelerated economic difficulties, was all the more pressing.

As background to the Cambodian policy shift, other sources in Hanoi pointed to the profound change of international perception that took place at the Sixth Congress. According to one source, the key phrase in the political report was: "In the coming years, the tasks of our party and state in the field of external affairs are to strive to combine the strength of the nation with that of the epoch."[17]

What was meant by the "strength of the epoch"? In a 1990 article Gareth Porter interpreted it as "the new potential for rapid industrialization through participation in the global division of labor—whether among socialist nations or in the broader capitalist system." He argued that "Vietnam was moving away from the traditional view of the world as a struggle between two camps for dominance to one in which states with different systems faced similar challenges in a single overarching economic system."[18]

Although Porter's interpretation dealt with the emerging basic change of Hanoi's world view in general, the more limited political as well as economic implications of the "strength of the epoch" might have been the structural changes in the international environment, namely, the improvement in relations between Moscow and Washington as well as the end of the antagonism between Moscow and Beijing, on the one hand, and the startling economic dynamism becoming visible in the Southeast Asian nations, on the other.

In order to escape international isolation and take advantage of structural changes in external conditions, Hanoi launched a new diplomatic offensive consisting of four parts: to get out of the Cambodian quagmire, to improve relations with ASEAN countries, to normalize relations with the United States, and to normalize relations with the PRC. In regard to Cambodia, the above-mentioned efforts at Khmerization were pursued.

As for relations with ASEAN countries, initial efforts toward rapprochement had begun following the Fourth Congress of the CPV in 1976, with poor results. Later Hanoi's efforts centered on establishing closer relations with Indonesia, which was more vigilant to Chinese threats than other ASEAN countries were. At the eleventh conference of foreign ministers of Indochina in 1985, however, Hanoi for the first time attempted to improve relations with Bangkok and ceased to accuse the Thais of involvement in a Chinese expansionist scheme. At the same time the new Vietnamese posture was interpreted as a shift from a strategy of trying to divide ASEAN countries into anti-Chinese and pro-Chinese groups to one of seeking rapprochement with them as a whole.

Thus, Nguyen Co Thach, then the Vietnamese foreign minister, and

Mochtar Kusumaatmadja, then the Indonesian foreign minister, proposed a dialogue between all Cambodian parties concerned in the form of a cocktail party in the July 1987 joint communique. This led to the Jakarta Informal Meeting One (JIM I) in July 1988 and the JIM II in February 1989. Nguyen Van Linh, then the secretary general of the CPV, expressed for the first time the Vietnamese desire to adhere to ASEAN when he met with Raul Manglapus, then the foreign minister of the Philippines, in November 1988. Coincidentally, a surprising shift in Thailand's Indochinese policy occurred with the advent of the Chatichai Choonhavan government in August 1988. By ending its hardline posture toward Vietnam and the Phnom Penh regime and advocating rapprochement, Thailand seriously jeopardized the coordinated ASEAN position in the Cambodian peace process. At the same time, Chatichai's new approach helped to ease to some extent the international isolation from which Vietnam had tried to break free. Hanoi had already made overtures to Thailand, with Nguyen Co Thach visiting Bangkok three times beginning in June 1988, even before Chatichai came to power. The Vietnamese officials were quoted as saying that Thach's willingness to talk to the Thais was a signal from Hanoi that it intended to give Thailand a role in determining the future of Cambodia.[19] Hanoi's efforts bore fruit.

Chatichai's initiative was essentially motivated by the economic aim to convert Indochina "from a battle field to a market." The rapid growth of the Thai economy since the mid-1980s (averaging 9.8 percent annually from 1986 to 1990)[20] enabled the policymakers in Chatichai's government to see Indochina as a promising trade and investment center in which Thailand could play a leading role. The new orientation of Thailand's Indochina policy first became visible with changes in its Cambodian policy. Chatichai Choonhavan invited Hun Sen, the prime minister of the Vietnamese-backed Phnom Penh government, to Bangkok in January 1989 as his "private guest." In view of the long-standing Thai position of isolating the Phnom Penh government, Chatichai's gesture was clear evidence of the bold change.

Thailand's policy shift also encouraged Japan to revise its policy of alignment with the tripartite opposition government headed by Prince Norodom Sihanouk. Tokyo sent a high-ranking official in charge of Indochina policy to Phnom Penh in February 1990, the first time since the beginning of the Cambodian conflict, and it opted to cooperate closely with Bangkok in its Cambodian policy. The Tokyo Conference on Cambodia was held in June of that year; and from July to October 1993, Japanese officials met three times with Khmer Rouge representatives in Bangkok and Phnom Penh, pressing them to observe the second phase of the cease-fire agreement.[21]

Compared with relations between ASEAN countries and Vietnam, progress in Sino-Vietnamese relations remained minimal. When the foreign ministerial dialogue, suspended in 1979 after the Chinese invasion of northern Vietnam, was resumed in January 1989, the Chinese limited the discussions to the Vietnamese withdrawal from Cambodia, refusing to deal with normalization. In the absence of normalization with the PRC, the Vietnamese effort to end international isolation was not complete.

The withdrawal of the last group of Vietnamese forces from Cambodia in September 1989 constituted confirmation of the definitive change in Vietnam's Cambodian policy that had evolved since 1985. It was Heng Samrin of the People's Republic of Kampuchea (PRK) who first announced in January 1989, on the occasion of the Indochinese foreign ministers' conference, that Vietnam would complete its withdrawal before September 1989 on the condition that a political solution would be reached in advance. However, three months later, in April, Hanoi announced the withdrawal within the same time limit, this time without any condition attached. According to Nguyen Co Thach, it was Hanoi's belief that the Cambodian situation was stabilized to the extent that the Khmer Rouge would never be able to return to Phnom Penh. That enabled Hanoi to reach the conclusion that Vietnam could completely withdraw its troops whether a peace agreement were reached or not.[22]

What Nguyen Co Thach did not mention was that the biggest reason behind the unconditional withdrawal was to prove to the international community Vietnam's desire for peace in Cambodia. The Vietnamese withdrawal constituted one of the basic conditions that had to be met before the United States and Japan, as well as the PRC, would modify their stance toward Vietnam. By withdrawing, Hanoi presumably expected progress on such issues as the lifting of the American embargo against Vietnam, the start of talks on U.S.-Vietnamese normalization, and the resumption of Japanese economic assistance, as well as normalization talks with Beijing. This expectation was betrayed, however. Once the Vietnamese withdrawal was completed in September 1989, the Americans, the Chinese, and the Japanese insisted on a further condition—the achievement of a comprehensive solution in Cambodia—in order to put final pressure on Hanoi to accept the framework proposal drafted by the UN Security Council.

In any event, it seems that the evolution in Hanoi's perception of security in general also played a not-negligible role in the decision for an unconditional withdrawal from Cambodia. The CPV's Political Bureau adopted in May 1988 the so-called Resolution 13 on External Policy. The existence of the resolution, which remained unpublished, as is the case with Political Bureau resolutions, became known from an interview with Nguyen Co Thach, then a Politburo member and foreign minister, published in January

1990 in the first issue of *International Relations,* a new magazine issued by the Foreign Ministry. Under the title "The Change of the World and Our New Thinking," Thach asserted that: "Global productive capacity is highly developed and the world is becoming an integrated market. We have the opportunity to make use of the world's production capacity, and we ought to do so. As Resolution 13 on external problems described it, we have to make maximum use of the world market in order to raise our underdeveloped economy to the level of the average rate of the development in the world within a relatively short period of time such as twenty or twenty-five years."[23]

Analysts of Resolution 13 concluded that it supported the concept of comprehensive security in which the conditions of security in contemporary international relations are perceived to consist of three factors: strong economic might, an appropriate military defense capability, and enlarged relations of international cooperation. The analysts pointed out the remarkable contrast of this new security perception, as formulated in Resolution 13, with the traditional Vietnamese concept based upon the inevitability of war between socialist and capitalist forces.[24] The resolution appears to have been bitterly fought over, and as for its implementation, Thach revealed in the above-mentioned interview, "We had to assist in the fight between the old and the new thinkers for more than a year."

In spite of resistance by conservatives, the fact that unconditional withdrawal was implemented as planned showed that the new security thinking finally prevailed among decision makers in Hanoi. In other words, Vietnamese leaders were determined to demonstrate before the international community their strong willingness to resolve the Cambodian conflict in order to end international isolation and participate in the "integrated world market." It is significant that the process of the complete withdrawal from Cambodia went side by side with efforts aiming at normalization with the United States and the PRC. Since the basic reason for the establishment of a "special relationship" in Indochina had been designed to counter a strategic threat from China, the new thinking confirmed its demise.

Vietnam's Policy of Detachment

Since the signing of the Paris peace agreements in October 1991 Hanoi has followed a determined policy of noninterference in Cambodia. The Khmer Rouge continued to protest that Vietnamese troops remained on Cambodian territory, but these claims were rebuffed by the United Nations Transitional Authority in Cambodia (UNTAC) as unverified. The Khmer Rouge also accused the Hun Sen government and the coalition royal government established after the promulgation of the new constitution of being "Vietnamese puppets." It is true that there was no firm evidence that ties did not continue to exist between Vietnamese agencies and the Cambodian security and intelligence apparatus. Nevertheless, as far as Hanoi's official policy was concerned, the Vietnamese were determined to concentrate their efforts on national economic development and avoid any possibility of involvement in the Cambodian internal quagmire.

The detachment Hanoi imposed upon itself with respect to Cambodia was reflected in a statement that the Vietnamese Foreign Ministry issued on the eve of the Cambodian elections in May 1993:

> . . . The Government of the Socialist Republic of Vietnam reaffirms its consistent policy, that is, to scrupulously implement the Paris peace agreement and strictly respect Cambodia's independence and sovereignty, and the right of the Cambodian people to determine their own destiny . . . the Government expresses its willingness to recognize a new government in Cambodia to be elected by a constituent national assembly.[25]

According to Vietnamese sources, the statement implied Hanoi's readiness to accept any kind of electoral results, since the Vietnamese had ceased to favor specific political forces in Cambodia. In fact, in June 1993 when General Sin Son, former security chief of the State of Cambodia (SOC), and Prince Norodom Chakrapong, one of Sihanouk's sons and the SOC's former deputy prime minister, escaped to Vietnam after the abortive secessionist movement of the seven eastern provinces, Hanoi bluntly pushed them back to the Cambodian side of the border. In late March 1994 when Tie Banh and Tie Chamrath, the co-defense ministers of the royal government in Phnom Penh, came to Hanoi to ask for military assistance, the Vietnamese government reportedly refused the request. A Vietnamese high official later confirmed the report, saying:

> They did not ask for our military aid in the formal discussion but they referred to it during conversations in the corridor. We told them we had to abide by the Paris agreement. The Vietnamese government is ready to give economic assistance. As for military aid, we welcome the international community to provide it; but for Vietnam, as a neighbor of Cambodia, the position is delicate.[26]

Hanoi's attitude, as expressed in these statements, indicated its determination not to get reinvolved in Cambodian internal affairs. As another Vietnamese source put it, "Even if the Khmer Rouge were to return to power in Phnom Penh (though that is improbable), Vietnam would never interfere in Cambodia."[27] How do the Vietnamese view the future course of the Cambodian situation? One Vietnamese official described three scenarios: (1) the Khmer Rouge problem is resolved by peaceful means, such as national reconciliation, the two parties in the present governing coalition, the Cambodian People's Party (CPP) and the royalist National Front for an Independent, Neutral, Peaceful and Cooperative Cambodia (Funcinpec) and economic and social conditions stabilize; (2) the situation persists in which the Khmer Rouge problem remains unresolved, while the CPP and Funcinpec are forced to cooperate, and economic and social conditions remain unstable; or (3) King Norodom Sihanouk dies and an intensified power struggle ensues in Phnom Penh, eventually leading to the eruption of civil war.[28]

For this official, the first of the scenarios was "desirable," though the second one was more probable than the first. Taking into account the fact that both the international community and the Cambodian people were firmly opposed to a resumption of conflict in Cambodia, the third scenario was difficult to envision. The assessment developed here implies that Hanoi views the future evolution of the situation in Cambodia with a degree of pessimism, though it does not anticipate a return to civil war.

The relatively negative assessment of the Cambodian situation did not hinder the Vietnamese from pursuing a low-profile policy toward its neighbor, a policy that Nguyen Co Thach summarized in the following four principles: (1) to strictly abide by the Paris agreement, (2) to respect the independence and sovereignty of Cambodia, (3) to oppose intervention by any foreign power, and (4) to maintain amicable relations with Cambodia.[29] Conversations with a number of knowledgeable sources, including officials in Hanoi, confirmed these points. The basic line seems to be that now that the Vietnamese have withdrawn from Cambodia, it is up to the Cambodians and the international community to try to solve the problems that remain.

In confirmation of this change, the announcement of the end of party-to-party relations was made in 1991. This coincided with decisions taken at the Extraordinary Congress of the People's Revolutionary Party of Kampuchea (PRPK) on October 18, 1991, during which it changed its name to the Cambodian People's Party, accepted a multiparty system, and abandoned Marxism-Leninism. Chea Sim, number two in the leadership hierarchy until the congress, rose to number one, becoming chairman of the Central Committee. He replaced Heng Samrin, who was given the title of honorary chairman of the Central Committee. At the same time Hun Sen, who had been number three, became number two as the vice chairman of the Central Committee. In the same year at the Seventh Congress of the Vietnam party, the new foreign policy of diversified relations launched at the Sixth Congress of the CPV in 1986 was codified more fully.

The demise of party-to-party relations with the CPP ended Hanoi's ideological obligation to help the former brother party in Cambodia; and that was why, as one Vietnamese source suggested, Hanoi intended thereafter to have good relations with all Cambodian factions except the Khmer Rouge. The "new foreign policy," as another official called it, was directed to realizing an association with the Southeast Asian nations and to securing integration into the international community within the minimum time. To get involved in regional conflicts was too much for an underdeveloped nation such as Vietnam, he added.[30] In short, the special relationship with Cambodia and the dream of an Indochinese federation were dead.

Cambodia's Nationalistic Response

It is true that the State of Cambodia was under Hanoi's overwhelming influence for more than a decade since the Vietnamese invasion of Cambodia and its installation in 1979. Just before the start of the invasion, Hanoi set up a front organization, the National United Front for the Salvation of Kampuchea (NUFSK), headed by Heng Samrin and on the basis of which the People's Revolutionary Council, the new government, was organized. Hanoi also reactivated the PRPK, the pro-Vietnamese Cambodian communist party, with Pen Sovan, who had stayed in Vietnam since the Geneva Agreement in 1954, as the first secretary. The Cambodian leaders of the new ruling institutions in Phnom Penh, however, were drawn from different groups: as Gareth Porter puts it, the "outsider group," consisting of those who stayed in Hanoi after the Geneva Agreement and who were, during the initial years until late 1981, more influential, and the "insider group," including Heng Samrin, Chea Sim, and Hun Sen, who had not left the country and were former Khmer Rouge dissidents.[31] The non-communist intellectuals who had survived the Pol Pot years in Cambodia formed a third group, which became the biggest one after the Fifth Party Congress in 1985. Many of the third group presumably associated themselves later with Hun Sen's moderate reformers. The declining influence of the "outsider group" in the leadership—only pro-Hanoi members remained in the Central Committee after the Fifth Party Congress in 1985—later resulted in the rise of a more or less nationalistic orientation in Phnom Penh's relations with Vietnam.

Manifestation of Phnom Penh's nationalism toward Vietnam went side by side with the shift in Hanoi's Cambodian policy. According to Vietnamese sources, leaders in Phnom Penh became fearful of eventual abandonment for the first time in 1982, when Vietnam started the partial withdrawal of troops from Cambodia.

In 1987, when the Jakarta Informal Meeting One (JIM I) for the first time assembled all Cambodian parties around a table for discussion, Hanoi had a difficult time persuading the SOC to participate. The SOC leaders were afraid of the eventuality that they might have to share power with other factions; and, according to the Vietnamese assessment, it was at the two meetings between Norodom Sihanouk and Hun Sen, then the prime minister, in 1987 and 1988 in France, that the SOC, desperate to strengthen its domestic support, began to think about an independent approach to the resolution of the conflict based upon cooperation with Sihanouk. The shift of the SOC's position indicated the widening distance between Hanoi and Phnom Penh.[32]

Discussions with former SOC officials in Phnom Penh, too, confirmed the widening gap with Hanoi. As a Cambodian high official put it, "The SOC matured politically around 1985 and 1986. That was why it began to develop an independent external policy without Vietnamese help. We Cambodians were fed up with being viewed as Vietnamese vassals and hoped to be recognized by the international community as an independent political entity." At the same time the official criticized Vietnam's decision of unconditional withdrawal from Cambodia in 1989, opining that it had induced a less compromising attitude on the part of the tripartite coalition government than before, resulting in the failure of the first Paris international conference on Cambodia.[33]

The Paris peace agreement reached in October 1991 definitively put an end to Phnom Penh's dependence on Vietnam. Instead, the government of Cambodia began to look toward the international community not only for assistance in its efforts at national reconstruction but for financial survival itself. And to deal with the threat of the Khmer Rouge, it placed its confidence in the possibility of military assistance from certain Western and Southeast Asian countries. The power structure in Phnom Penh, too, has changed. The government itself is not under the unique control of the pro-Vietnamese CPP any more. The CPP continues to occupy substantial positions both at central and provincial levels. But the posts of key ministers and deputy ministers are shared by Funcinpec and to a lesser degree by the Buddhist Liberal Democratic Party (BLDP), the two former members of the CGDK, the anti-Vietnamese tripartite coalition government which had fought against the Vietnamese and Phnom Penh government for more than a decade. In the National Assembly Funcinpec occupies the majority.

A remarkable example of the changed attitude of Phnom Penh toward Vietnam is the immigration law approved overwhelmingly by the National Assembly in late August 1994, by which Phnom Penh dared to undermine the status of several hundred thousands of ethnic Vietnamese living in Cambodia as well as to block the safe return of thousands of ethnic

Vietnamese fishermen who had escaped to Vietnam in 1993 for fear of armed attacks by the Khmer Rouge guerrilla troops. Hanoi protested the law and wrote to Boutros Boutros-Ghali, UN secretary general, and to King Norodom Sihanouk in Beijing asking for their intervention. Boutros-Ghali and Sihanouk requested Phnom Penh to amend the bill, but Phnom Penh has not budged.

A forecast of the future evolution of Phnom Penh's attitude toward Vietnam needs to take into account the complex political situation that has emerged after the return to peace. Funcinpec and the BLDP, the two parties sharing power with the CPP in the royal government and the National Assembly, are basically much more nationalistic than the CPP. Furthermore, given the historical resentment against Vietnam deeply anchored in the population and the need to compete with the anti-Vietnamese propaganda campaign energetically undertaken by the Khmer Rouge, the royal government is likely to continue to feel obliged to take a nationalistic stand toward Vietnam.

This, however, does not necessarily imply that Phnom Penh is bound to be against Vietnam. The Cambodian concern about a Thai connection at the local level with the Khmer Rouge and about Thailand's economic expansion into Cambodia, does not allow Phnom Penh to let relations with Vietnam deteriorate.

The Outlook

In the coming years, bilateral relations between Vietnam and Cambodia will not constitute a factor of vital importance for the external relations of either country. As Norodom Sihanouk has put it, Vietnam, the lion, will not be interested in Cambodia, the small kitten. Vietnam's major concerns, now and in the future, will be how to resist expansionist pressure from the northern dragon, China, and how to participate as fully and quickly as possible in the "integrated world market."[34] The goal is to catch up to its ASEAN neighbors.

Cambodia, for its part, will be preoccupied for some years with domestic concerns, specifically its political and military battle against the Khmer Rouge and the reconstruction of its devastated country.

The possibility for more positive relations would seem to depend therefore on whether a framework of multilateral economic relations can be devised for the subregion. The Indochinese peninsula, including Myanmar, has enormous economic potential, given its population of more than 184 million.[35] Effective cooperation among nations in the peninsula could transform this potential into actual economic strength.

The formation of a "golden quadrangle" in the upper-Mekong River region, including Yunnan Province in the PRC, parts of Myanmar, Laos, and Thailand, the construction of trans-Indochina highways and electric power supply lines, or the establishment of a forum for the comprehensive development of Indochina, proposed by Kiichi Miyazawa, former Japanese prime minister, may lay the basis for greater economic cooperation. Membership in ASEAN, too, may help Indochinese countries integrate their economies faster and lessen the threat they have traditionally perceived from each other.

But one should not be too optimistic. Even in the broader region of East Asia, although economic prospects for the short and medium range are undoubtedly bright, the longer term future of the region remains uncertain. It is simplistic to believe that economic development is bound to lead to lasting political stability. In fact, the emergence of a middle class, the natural consequence of economic development, is likely to make new political claims that for at least a transitional period will upset the political and social order. Moreover, nobody can be certain whether it is possible to construct a system of economic interdependence that is solid enough to deter these nations from engaging in a struggle for influence.

In Indochina there are also other questions that remain unresolved. Will Vietnam be ready to accept the economic influence of Thailand, its historical rival, prevailing in Indochina? Is it unrealistic to imagine that the linking of the economies of Yunnan province with those on the western part of the peninsula, that is, parts of Myanmar, Laos, and Thailand, may come into competition with Vietnamese economic influence in the eastern part of Indochina in the future? Would Laos and Cambodia, caught between the two dynamic subregional economies, be able to play effective—dissuasive—roles as buffer countries? The history of Cambodia demonstrates how difficult it is to be a stable buffer. And although relations between Vietnam and Cambodia have improved as a result of the former's shift in favor of economic development, no one can know how long the relative calm will last.

Potential disputes abound. First of all, the annual growth rate of the Vietnamese population is increasing, from 1.6 percent in 1989 to 2.2 percent in 1990 and 3.0 percent in 1991.[36] The World Bank estimates that the population of Vietnam will increase to 82 million in 2000 and 116 million in 2025.[37] And it is a historical fact that demographic pressures have prompted Vietnamese to move westward toward the vast, flat, and fertile terrain of Cambodia. If the two countries cannot find accommodation on the problem of the Cambodian immigration law, which threatens to undermine the status of hundreds of thousands of ethnic Vietnamese in the country, the continued spillover of Vietnamese across the border will inevitably invite harsher reaction from Cambodia in the future. The long-standing controversies over demarcation of the land and the Gulf of Siam, too, remain potentially explosive.

Thus, the key question remains: How long will Vietnam's policy of detachment from Cambodia be viable? It will take more than two decades at least for Vietnam to catch up with its ASEAN neighbors. And when Vietnam eventually finds its economy strong enough, geopolitical logic suggests that it will once again turn its attention to Cambodia.

Will Vietnam then revive its old idea of Indochina federation? On this particular point, the answer seems to be no. First of all, this author's conversations with Vietnamese officials and experts cited above indicated that Hanoi may well have learned a lesson from the disastrous failure of its previous efforts to form a "strategic alliance" among the three Indochinese countries. Vietnam today is well aware that the risks of such an effort definitively outweigh the merits. Second, the generation influenced by the grandeur of the revolution is being replaced by a more pragmatic one. Third, it appears less likely that two of the three major players in the subregion — China and Thailand — would allow Vietnam, the third one, to occupy a privileged political position in Indochina.

More likely is a struggle between Thailand and Vietnam for economic influence in Cambodia and Laos, once Vietnam has attained Thailand's economic level. Then the Vietnamese attention to Cambodia, in addition to border disputes and Vietnamese migration, would be based on economic concerns. Politically, Hanoi would try to deter the Phnom Penh regime from a pro-Bangkok stance, which might enhance Thai economic superiority in Cambodia.

The Vietnamese withdrawal from Cambodia in 1989 marked the conclusion of an historical epoch in Indochina. For the time being, Vietnam and Cambodia seem destined to go their own ways. But eventually, unless a network of economic cooperation can bind the peninsula together, a resumption of Thai-Chinese-Vietnamese rivalry for influence seems inescapable.

Notes

1. Author's interview with Nguyen Co Thach in Hanoi in August 1994.

2. *Fourth National Congress of the Communist Party of Vietnam: Documents* (Hanoi, Foreign Language Publishing House, 1977), pp. 248–249.

3. Author's interview with Mr. Wasuke Miyake, former Japanese diplomat, in Tokyo in July 1994. Miyake and Kichisaburo Inoue, another Japanese diplomat, made a secret visit to Hanoi in early February 1972 when Miyake was director of the First Southeast Asia Division of the Ministry of Foreign Affairs in charge of Vietnam.

4. Author's conversation with a Vietnamese source, who asked not to be identified, in Hanoi in August 1994.

5. *Tonan Ajia Geppo* (Southeast Asia monthly bulletin), Tonan Ajia Chosakai

(Council of Southeast Asian Studies), Tokyo, September 1995, pp. 9–12, and October 1975, pp. 10–14. In addition, William J. Duiker, *China and Vietnam: The Roots of Conflict* (Berkeley: Institute of East Asian Studies, University of California, 1986), pp. 63–65.

6. Thai Quang Trung, *Collective Leadership and Factionalism—An Essay on Ho Chi Minh's Legacy* (Singapore, Institute of Southeast Asian Studies, 1985), p. 73.

7. Author's conversation with a Vietnamese source, who asked not to be identified, in Hanoi in August 1994.

8. Nguyen Co Thach, interview cited above.

9. Author's conversation with a high official of the Vietnamese Foreign Ministry in Hanoi in August 1994.

10. *Far Eastern Economic Review,* September 18, 1981, pp. 11–13; and Tadashi Mio, "Vetonamu sensogono Soetsu kankei" (Evolution of Soviet-Vietnamese Relations after the Vietnam War), *Kokusai Mondai (International Problems),* Japan Institute of International Affairs, No. 316, July 1986, pp. 36–39.

11. Communique carried by the Vietnam News Agency (*VNA*) on the conclusion of the sixth Indochinese foreign ministers' conference in Ho Chi Minh City, July 7, 1982, and the author's interview of a Vietnamese official in charge of Cambodia in Hanoi in August 1994.

12. *VNA,* June 29, 1985.

13. *Nhan Dan,* August 17, 1985, cited in the semi-monthly magazine of the Communist Party of Japan, *Sekai Seji: Ronpyo to Shiryo* (World Politics: Commentaries and Materials), September 1–15, 1985, p. 16.

14. *Sixth National Congress of the CPV: Documents* (Hanoi, Foreign Language Publishing House, 1987).

15. Author's conversation with a Vietnamese source, who asked not to be identified, in Hanoi in August 1994. The interlocutor pointed out that the progress in Sino-Soviet relations was not the definitive factor that induced the transformation of Vietnam's policy.

16. Nguyen Co Thach, interview cited above.

17. Author's conversation with a Vietnamese source, who asked not to be identified, in Hanoi in August 1994.

18. Gareth Porter, "The Transformation of Vietnam's World View: From Two Camps to Interdependence," *Contemporary Southeast Asia,* Vol. 12, No. 1, June 1990, pp. 7–8.

19. *Far Eastern Economic Review,* December 17, 1988, p. 42.

20. Asian Development Bank, *Asian Development Outlook,* 1991, Manila.

21. Author's conversation in Tokyo with Mr. Tadashi Ikeda, former director general of the Asian Affairs Bureau, Japanese Ministry of Foreign Affairs, May 23, 1995.

22. Nguyen Co Thach, interview cited above.

23. Takayuki Ogasawara,"Dai 6–kai Vetonamu Kyosanto Taikaigo no Vetonamu gaiko—atarashii kikai to furui chosen" (Vietnam's Foreign Policy after the Congress of the CPV—New Opportunities and Old Challenges), *Posuto reisen no Indoshina (Indochina in the Post-Cold War Era),* Japan Institute of International Affairs, 1994, p. 91. Ogasawara translated the interview from *Quan He Quoc Te (International Relations),* Hanoi, January 1990, p. 6. See also Ogasawara,"Vetonamu gaiko ni okeru 'shin shiko' no taito" (Emerging "New Thinking" in Vietnam's Foreign Policy), *Gaiko Jiho* (Journal of Foreign Affairs), No. 1268, May 1990, Tokyo.

24. Ibid. See also Gareth Porter, "Transformation of Vietnam's World View," pp. 10–15.

25. Voice of Vietnam, June 3, 1993; FBIS-EAS-93–105, June 3, 1993.

26. Author's conversation with a high official of the Defense Ministry in Hanoi in August 1994.

27. Author's conversation with a Vietnamese source, who asked not to be identified, in August 1994.

28. Author's conversation with an official in charge of Cambodia in the Foreign Ministry in Hanoi in August 1994.

29. Nguyen Co Thach, interview cited above.

30. Author's conversation with a high official of the Foreign Ministry in Hanoi in August 1994.

31. See Gareth Porter, "People's Republic of Kampuchea—Politics in a Dependent State," *Indoshina wo meguru kokusai kankei (Indochina in Transition—Confrontation or Co-prosperity?)*, Japan Institute of International Affairs, 1988, pp. 127–129.

32. A Vietnamese source confirmed this assessment in a conversation with the author in Hanoi in August 1994.

33. Author's conversation with a high official of the Foreign Ministry, who asked not to be identified, in Phnom Penh in August 1994.

34. Norodom Sihanouk and Jean Lacouture, *Pekin kara mita Indoshina* (Tokyo: Saimaru Shuppankai), p. 192. This is a Japanese translation of *L'Indochina Vue de Pekin—Entretiens avec Jean Lacouture,* Paris: Editions du Seuil, 1972.

35. World Bank, *World Development Report 1992.*

36. United Nations, *Statistical Year Book for Asia and the Pacific, 1992.*

37. World Bank, *World Development Report 1992.*

7

Joining ASEAN

Donald S. Zagoria

During the past five years, Vietnam has made a spectacular transformation in its foreign policy from confrontation with its neighboring states in the Association of Southeast Asian Nations (ASEAN) to cooperation and association with them. In 1994, the ASEAN group invited Vietnam to join their organization and on July 28, 1995, Vietnam acceded to membership. This urge for membership in the Southeast Asian community seems to be driven by two felt needs: one, to secure support in its enduring struggle with China; the other, to participate in the economic growth that its neighbors have been enjoying.

The Security Factor

Throughout the troubled 2,000–year history between the two neighboring states, Vietnam has either had to endure Chinese colonization or to fight for its independence. Viewed in this historical context, China's recent efforts to "teach Vietnam a lesson" in 1979 after Vietnam invaded Cambodia with Soviet support are part of a well-established historical tradition. Such actions can be explained by what Western analysts would call balance-of-power theory, that is, that China will not accept the Vietnamese domination of Indochina, particularly when that domination is aided by a hostile big power such as the Soviet Union was at the time. Or these actions can be explained in historical terms, that is, that the Chinese have over the centuries come to expect a pattern of Vietnamese accommodation and deference to Chinese interests. The two explanations are not incompatible.

For its part, Vietnam, while struggling for independence in China's huge shadow, has developed a certain style of dealing with China that is a mixture of firmness and flexibility—firmness in defending its separate identity, and flexibility in seeking a way to avoid confrontation with China. Out of this complex history, too, many Vietnamese have drawn a lesson, which was explained to author Nayan Chanda in these terms:

> In all of history, we have been secure from China in only two conditions. One is when China is weak and internally divided. The other is when she has been threatened by barbarians from the north. In the present era, the Russians are our barbarians.[1]

The Russian or Soviet factor was critical for Vietnam in balancing Chinese power during the Cold War. During the early part of the Cold War, Vietnam successfully played off China against Russia in the Sino-Soviet alliance.[2] In the latter part of the Cold War era, after China and the Soviet Union split, Vietnam allied itself with Moscow against Beijing in an effort to dominate Indochina, a region that Vietnam saw as indispensable to its own security.

But the collapse of the Soviet Union in 1991 and the end of the Cold War, as well as the withdrawal of Soviet (and later Russian) military and economic assistance to Vietnam made it impossible for Vietnam to balance Chinese power in this manner. Moreover, the combined opposition to its hegemonial ambitions in Indochina from the United States, Europe, Japan, and ASEAN, as well as China, forced Vietnam to abandon this strategy by the late 1980s, when it agreed to withdraw from Cambodia and to sign the Paris peace agreements.

By the early 1990s, therefore, Vietnam had to come up with a new strategy for coping with China. Initially, there seems to have been a debate within the top Hanoi leadership over two conflicting options. The "pro-China" lobby in Hanoi, led by older party officials and some military leaders, stressed the common ideological ties of the two communist one-party states, and the fact that they allegedly shared a common external threat from the West, particularly the United States, which supported a strategy of "peaceful evolution."[3] The "realist" faction in the Vietnamese party leadership countered that although Vietnam and China shared a common ideology and political system, this did not prevent China from seeking expansionist goals at Vietnam's expense. For a time during the early 1990s, the pro-China lobby in Hanoi seemed to gain the upper hand. Finally, in November 1991, Sino-Vietnamese relations were fully normalized at both party and state levels. An eleven-point joint communique laid out the basis of state and party relations.

The honeymoon in Sino-Vietnamese relations did not last long, however.

By 1992, relations between the two countries were seriously troubled, largely by China's continued assertiveness in the South China Sea, where China's claims overlap those of the Republic of China on Taiwan, the Philippines, Malaysia, and Brunei, as well as of Vietnam.[4] Since then the conflict has continued to escalate, a recent incident occurring in early 1995 when China took a step that marked a major turning point in its relations not only with Vietnam but with the entire region. Beijing established a presence in the Spratlys on Mischief Reef, which lies within the 200–nautical-mile exclusive zone off the Philippine coast. China also left marker claims on other reefs within this Philippine zone. Manila immediately protested the moves, destroyed a number of the markers, seized four Chinese fishing boats, and arrested 62 Chinese fishermen. This was the first time in any of its disputes over the Spratlys that China sought to enforce a claim and establish a semipermanent presence within the generally accepted 200–mile zone of another claimant. It was therefore an alarming act not just for the Philippines but for the other Southeast Asian nations as well.[5]

The impact of these events has been to strengthen the hands of the realists. By May 1993, a Vietnamese Foreign Ministry official told a Western scholar:

> There are three possible ways of organizing our relations with China: (1) confrontation, (2) satellite status similar to North Korea, or (3) a median position between the two. Satellite status provides no guarantees. North Korea was sacrificed by China when it turned to South Korea. Also, even if Vietnam were to be a good satellite, China would not leave us alone. They will always pressure us and try to dominate Southeast Asia. We tried for a full year to forge new relations with China but we failed.... China follows its own national interests. That game is the nature of international politics.[6]

Having lost its Soviet ally to balance China, having been unable to resolve its territorial issue with China, and being unwilling to accept "satellite" status, Hanoi felt it had only one practical option for dealing with China: to cultivate good relations with ASEAN and other regional states, as well as the United States, in an effort to deter China from acting unilaterally in the South China Sea. As another Vietnamese Foreign Ministry official put it:

> [by improving relations with ASEAN and other regional states] Sino-Vietnamese relations will be meshed within the much larger regional network of interlocking economic and political interests. It is an arrangement whereby anybody wanting to violate Vietnam's sovereignty would be violating the interests of other countries as well. This is the ideal strategic option for Vietnam. It is also the most practical.[7]

Skeptics will say that ASEAN is a very weak reed for Vietnam to rely on in balancing China. The ASEAN countries have neither the military power nor the will to contest China's claims in the South China Sea. Still, Vietnam must be mindful of the fact that the ASEAN states were successful in exerting diplomatic and political pressure against Vietnam during the 1980s both at the United Nations and in other fora and that this pressure ultimately played a role in forcing Vietnam to withdraw from Cambodia. If the ASEAN states were able to use their political and diplomatic weight in conjunction with other great powers to restrain Vietnam, why can they not use comparable diplomatic pressure to restrain China in the Spratlys?

The ASEAN Response

The six ASEAN states (Indonesia, Malaysia, Singapore, Brunei, the Philippines, and Thailand) have in the past been far from unified in their approach to and view of China. As one keen student of the region has put it: "the states of Southeast Asia are not homogeneous in terms of their proximity to China or the degree to which their societies have been able to assimilate their resident Chinese."[8] Moreover, the Southeast Asian states are aware that their own power resources are limited and that they will not be able to deal to their satisfaction with an aggressive China at any time soon. The best strategy is to engage China as a participant in regional affairs and to increase the incentives for China to play a peaceful and constructive role. This was, in fact, one of the principal motivations in ASEAN's decision in 1993 to begin the ASEAN Regional Forum security dialogue involving China and the other major powers in the region.

Nevertheless, the Southeast Asians are "united in their fear of China as a growing regional power."[9] And although it will be difficult to form a unified diplomatic front against Beijing, if they could develop such a front, it could be extremely effective diplomatically. China would not then be able to play off the Southeast Asian states against each other, as it has tried to do in the past.

To be sure, the Southeast Asian states have somewhat differing interests in and perceptions of China. Thailand views Vietnam, not China, as its traditional rival for influence on the Indochinese peninsula. Particularly after Vietnam invaded Cambodia in 1978, the Thais developed close ties with China, considered by Bangkok to be a natural ally against Vietnamese expansionism. Particularly now that the United States, Thailand's other great power ally during the Cold War, has withdrawn from the Philippines and distanced itself from Southeast Asia diplomatically, the Thais are unlikely to want to jeopardize their close relationship with China. Moreover,

Thailand itself does not have territorial claims in the South China Sea conflicting with those of China. Also, to this day, despite Vietnam's withdrawal from Cambodia, Thai leaders continue to look warily upon Vietnam. The two countries still have fishing and border disputes, and the lack of mutual trust has hindered the development of economic relations. Thailand, despite its proximity to Vietnam, still lags far behind other Southeast Asian nations in developing trade and investment relations with Vietnam.

Singapore, a Chinese city state, has also demonstrated in the past a reluctance to antagonize China. And Singapore's senior minister, Lee Kuan Yew, has quite recently gone out of his way to play down China's aggressiveness on the Spratlys issue. In a lengthy interview with the Singapore *Straits Times* on May 13, 1995, Lee said that he did not think China's building of structures on Mischief Reef "necessarily means that China is becoming aggressive," adding that China's actions were more "like a big dog going up against a tree, lifting his leg to mark the tree, so that smaller dogs will know that a big dog has been there, and to take note of that." China's actions, said Lee, were just a "little one-upmanship." When asked whether ASEAN was now starting to put up a common front against China, Lee said: "If I am sure that I belong to a pack [of dogs] that's got a big dog, I would consider a nip. If we are all small dogs, it may be wiser just to bark."[10]

Nevertheless, there are a number of indications that China's relentless assertiveness in the South China Sea is gradually leading to the development of a united front in ASEAN. Prior to the Mischief Reef incident, ASEAN had been careful not to make the Spratlys dispute multilateral and to go along, however reluctantly, with Beijing's desire to leave the issue to bilateral negotiations between China and other disputants. The Mischief Reef incident has, however, marked a turning point and seems to have goaded ASEAN into presenting a united front to China on the South China Sea issue.

In early April 1995 at a meeting with Chinese officials in Hangzhou, China, senior ASEAN officials raised the Spratlys issue with the Chinese. The discussion reportedly lasted more than two hours and extended late into the night. At this meeting, ASEAN, for the first time as a group, expressed its concern in "terms that were unusually forceful," said Philippines Foreign Affairs Undersecretary Rodolfo Severino.[11] At this meeting, ASEAN officials, including those from nonclaimant states, made it clear to China that the occupation of Mischief Reef and similar sorties could destabilize the region.

The Mischief Reef incident has, in fact, even roused the United States to action. Until now, the U.S. position has been that it was not involved in territorial conflicts in the South China Sea. But on May 10, 1995, the Clinton administration State Department issued a statement that did not mention China by name but warned that "a pattern of unilateral actions and reactions in the South China Sea has increased tensions in that region. The United States strongly opposes the use or threat of force to resolve competing claims and urges all claimants to exercise restraint and to avoid destabilizing actions."[12] The administration also dispatched a senior national security official, Stanley Roth, to the Philippines to consult President Fidel Ramos about his problems with the Chinese.

ASEAN's approach toward China in the future will depend to a considerable extent on Indonesia, the largest and potentially most powerful state in ASEAN. In the past few years, Indonesia, which considered itself a non-claimant state, sought to mediate the Spratlys dispute by holding a series of unofficial forums that included government officials from China and the other claimant states. But now Indonesia's position is changing. In July 1994, Indonesia asked China to clarify why it included Indonesia's rich Natuna gas field in its map of claims to a broad swath of the South China Sea.[13]

The Chinese have not replied, and the Indonesians find this behavior galling. "China tells us they still adhere to their historic claims, but does that mean it is claiming the islands or the sea bed or the water? They can never give us a straight answer," says the Indonesian Foreign Ministry's maritime law expert.[14]

The fact that Indonesia has sent China a diplomatic note on the Spratlys issue means that Indonesia is no longer "on the fence," says one ranking official. "Before, we considered ourselves as outsiders. But now we have taken a look at the charts and we have seen the way China seems to be moving south and we are growing more concerned. What Chinese leaders say and what happens in the field are different."[15] What particularly worries and puzzles the Indonesians is that Beijing has not so far made any effort to placate regional concerns—and even seems to go out of its way to fuel them.

There are also signs of change in the attitude of the other ASEAN states toward China. Both Malaysian and Singapore officials have spoken out strongly, and in the Philippines the press has been filled with calls for the government to take more forceful action.

One result of this revived suspicion about China's long-term intent in the region will probably be to speed up ASEAN's plans to develop a common political front by bringing all ten of the countries in the region under ASEAN's umbrella. As mentioned, Vietnam joined the group on July 28, 1995. There now seems to be a growing consensus on the need to bring about a closer association of all ten Southeast Asian states. This would include, in addition to the ASEAN seven, Laos, Cambodia, and Burma. Burma was included in the July 1994 Annual Ministerial Meeting as a guest of the host country, Thailand. That meeting was particularly historic in that it was the first time in ASEAN's 27–year history that foreign ministers from all ten Southeast Asian countries participated. At that meeting, Thai Prime Minister Chuan Likphai led a chorus of calls for a "greater ASEAN." He declared that the time was drawing near for the regional group's former ideological foes, the Indochinese states and Burma, to become full members of ASEAN. "ASEAN must strive to evolve into a truly region-wide body [and] it is important that we complete this process as speedily as practicable," said Chuan in his opening address.[16] And Malaysia's Foreign Minister Badawi said that ASEAN cannot remain a six-member organization. "It must become ten—the sooner the better."[17]

In sum, the small and medium powers of Southeast Asia are moving toward creating a "greater ASEAN," one that includes Vietnam, Cambodia, Laos, and Myanmar, while expanding security dialogue with the great powers and increasing security cooperation among themselves in an effort to get better control of their new strategic environment now that the Cold War is over. They want to ensure that it is they, and not the great powers, who determine the fate of their region. China's recent assertiveness on the Spratlys is bound to increase the sense of urgency in this regard.

The Economic Factor

In addition to its need to cope strategically with China, there is a second important factor that will dictate that Vietnam moves toward peaceful accommodation with its Southeast Asian neighbors in the decades ahead. This is the dynamic of "catching up" economically.

Southeast Asia has been a region of major economic winners and losers in recent decades.[18] The losers have been the Indochinese states of Vietnam, Cambodia, and Laos plus Myanmar, all cases in which the ruling authorities have been committed to doctrines of economic management by command. The winners have been the ASEAN states of Indonesia, Thailand, Malaysia, and Singapore, where the national leaderships have proceeded pragmatically in guiding mixed economies with large and growing private sectors.

Virtually all the communist or former communist states came to the conclusion in recent years that they had no alternative other than to open up to the world economy and to move to a market economy. Otherwise they would lag behind their neighbors and rivals indefinitely and the system itself might not survive. Gorbachev and his closest advisors came to this conclusion in 1985; Deng Xiaoping had already come to this realization in the late 1970s. Deng said at the time that the opening up of China's economy to the outside world was a matter of "life or death" for the Chinese Communist Party.

The Vietnamese Communist leaders came to this very same conclusion by 1986 when they embarked in earnest on the path of market economics they called *doi moi*. This economic transformation was driven by a growing perception of the widening gap in wealth and power between Vietnam and its regional neighbors. The sense of urgency to overcome this gap has deepened as the Vietnamese leaders and population become increasingly aware of its dimensions. Prime Minister Vo Van Kiet, for example, warned the National Assembly in October 1994 that even if "we can reach the target of $450 per capita in the year 2000, the development gap between our country and most of the other regional countries will still be widening. It's a matter of life or death."[19]

The regional per capita income figures confirm the Vietnamese prime minister's point. In 1990, Singapore had a per capita of $11,160; Malaysia was at $2,320, Thailand at $1,420; the Philippines at $730, and Indonesia, the most populous country in Southeast Asia, at $570.[20] Vietnam, despite a doubling of its rice production since 1989 and a substantial increase in exports, had still lifted its per capita income only from $150 in 1987 to $230 a year in 1994.[21] Thus, even after a decade of economic liberalization, Vietnam's per capita income was only about one-sixth that of its neighbor and potential rival, Thailand, and one-tenth that of Malaysia. Moreover, Vietnam's population, which was 66 million in 1990, was growing at a rate of 2.1 percent per year. Several other governments in the region, including Indonesia and Thailand, had recorded population growth rates of under 2 percent a year between 1980 and 1990. This is one of the reasons they both had very high annual growth rates.

Hanoi's only hope to reduce the gap with its regional neighbors is to continue the huge and swift economic transformation it began in the early 1990s. Prior to that time, Vietnam relied on the Soviet Union and its East European satellites for about 80 percent of its two-way trade, as well as for cheap oil, military assistance, and other types of subsidies. During the past few years, Vietnam has been forced to find new trading and investment partners. It has done this with considerable speed and success. Table 7.1 shows that by 1993, East Asia accounted for 62 percent of Vietnam's exports and 82 percent of its imports, while the former Soviet Union, now the Commonwealth of Independent States (CIS), accounted for only 5 percent of Vietnam's exports and 2 percent of its imports.

Table 7.1.

Vietnam: Direction of Trade (1993)

	% of total trade	
	Exports	Imports
Asia (total)	62	82
NIEs (South Korea, Taiwan, Hong Kong, Singapore)	21	54
ASEAN-4*	7	9
Europe	18	11
CIS	5	2
Others	15	5

Source: International Monetary Fund, cited by Turley, "Vietnamese Security in Domestic and Regional Focus" (1995).

*ASEAN-4 refers to the four ASEAN developing economies as of 1993 (Indonesia, Malaysia, Philippines, and Thailand), excluding Singapore as economically more appropriately considered with other Newly Emerging Economies (NIEs).

Singapore has become a particularly important trading partner for Vietnam. In 1993, bilateral trade between the two countries reached $1.3 billion. This represents somewhere between 25 percent and 30 percent of Vietnam's total trade of more than $5 billion a year. Malaysia, too, has become an important trading partner. In 1992, the volume of two-way trade reached $100 million.

Vietnam's East Asian neighbors have also become the most important sources of foreign investment in Vietnam. As Table 7.2 indicates, as of late 1994, the Asian NIEs (Taiwan, Hong Kong, Singapore and South Korea) and Japan were the five leading investors in Vietnam. And Japan was poised to substantially increase its level of investment. Among the ASEAN countries, Singapore and Malaysia were out in front. Singapore has set up an Indochina Assistance Fund to train local managers and help rebuild Vietnam's infrastructure. It also has plans to develop the port of Vung Tau, and Singapore's senior minister, Lee Kuan Yew, has twice visited Vietnam and produced a report on developing Vietnamese infrastructure. Malaysia has offered Vietnam assistance in developing rubber technology, energy, agricultural processing, and telecommunications. It has also raised the possibility of joint oil exploration, its state-owned oil economy, Petronas, has been awarded a 20 percent stake in the development of the offshore Dai Hung oil field.

Vietnam has a particularly strong interest in increasing its trade and investment relationship with Japan, which has the most powerful economy

Table 7.2.

Vietnamese Foreign Capital Investments over U.S.$100 Million by Country of Origin, to December 24, 1994

	No. of Projects	Total Capital (U.S.$ millions)
Taiwan	179	1,964
Hong Kong	171	1,788
Singapore	76	1,070
South Korea	97	884
Japan	73	783
Australia	42	655
Malaysia	31	581
France	58	534
Switzerland	14	463
Britain	15	376
Netherlands	16	348
United States	28	270
Thailand	43	236
Indonesia	11	160
Russia	34	125

Source: The Vietnam Business Journal, XXX, 1, January/February 1995, 9, as cited by Turley, "Vietnamese Security in Domestic and Regional Focus" (1995).

in the region and the potential to be Vietnam's major source of development assistance. Japan is likely to play a prominent and increasing role in the development of Vietnam's economy. Former Prime Minister Miyazawa proposed a plan for the comprehensive development of Indochina in January 1993. In February 1995 Japan hosted the Forum for Comprehensive Development of Indochina to discuss the development of mainland Southeast Asia: Vietnam, Laos, Cambodia, Myanmar, Thailand, and Yunnan province in southern China. Proposals discussed included roads linking southern China to Bangkok and roads linking Thailand, Laos, and Vietnam.[22]

Japan's official development assistance (ODA) to Asia has increased in recent years, and by 1992 Vietnam was among the ten largest recipients of Japanese assistance.[23] At least some Japanese Foreign Ministry specialists believe that as ASEAN graduates from Japanese economic assistance, the Indochinese peninsula, including Vietnam, should become an important new target for Japanese assistance. They are convinced that financing economic development in Indochina is a worthy project for at least two reasons. First, now that ASEAN is already developing, Indochina has become the "last frontier" in East Asia for investment. Labor costs in Indochina are significantly lower than in most of the ASEAN states. Second, if East Asia as a whole is to be more stable, prosperous, and secure, Indochina must become more prosperous.[24]

Apart from being valuable trading partners and sources of investment and technical assistance, Vietnam's Asian neighbors are attractive to Hanoi for yet another important reason. They do not impose human rights conditions on trade or aid and they do not demand democratization.

Developing Ties with Individual ASEAN States[25]

Indonesia

Good relations between Vietnam and Indonesia have their roots in the struggles that the two countries waged to free themselves from colonial rule. Of all ten Southeast Asian countries, only Indonesia and Vietnam had to fight for their independence. This has left a bond of sympathy between the two countries. The Indonesians have long believed that the Vietnamese leaders were motivated more by nationalism than Marxism and that Vietnam therefore could be a potential ally against China, which, in their view, is the chief long-term security threat to the region. The Indonesians believe that Hanoi became an unwilling ally of the Soviet Union only after it had been rebuffed by the West and threatened by China. Sooner or later, they argued, even during the Vietnamese occupation of Cambodia in the 1980s, Vietnam would reassert its historic independence and play a constructive role checking the spread of Chinese power and influence in Southeast Asia.[26]

Throughout the Cambodian conflict, which led to a deep estrangement between Vietnam and ASEAN, the Indonesians consistently tried to play the role of mediator by maintaining an official dialogue with Vietnam. This strained Indonesia's relations with Thailand. Nevertheless, Jakarta kept its channel to Hanoi open in an effort to find a solution that would reduce China's opportunity to interfere in the region. Ultimately, Indonesia's efforts led to the creation of UNTAC, the UN-led multilateral peace process that culminated in the free election of a Cambodian government in the early 1990s.

It is not surprising, therefore, that the visit by Indonesia's President Suharto to Hanoi in November 1990 was the first by any ASEAN leader since 1977, the year before Vietnam's invasion of Cambodia. Following Suharto's visit, there was a succession of high-level visits between the leaders of all the ASEAN states and Vietnam, which have contributed to a steady warming of relations.

The timing of Suharto's visit was suggestive. It came three months after Indonesia normalized relations with China during a visit to Jakarta by China's Premier Li Peng in August 1990. Suharto made a state visit to

China in November 1990 to reciprocate Li Peng's visit, and he then went on to Vietnam. This visit to Vietnam immediately after China was evidently intended to signal Indonesia's interest in balancing China by strengthening ties with Vietnam.[27]

During his visit to Hanoi, Suharto agreed to set up a joint ministerial-level committee to promote mutual ties, and Indonesia and Vietnam signed agreements on economic, trade, scientific, and technological cooperation. Since Suharto's visit, economic relations between Vietnam and Indonesia have sprouted. Indonesia has begun to invest in Vietnam's oil and gas industry. The volume of two-way trade has grown by a factor of seven since 1986 to $220 million in 1992.

Security ties also are developing. In January 1992, the assistant commander in chief of the Indonesian Armed Forces, Teddy Rusdy, paid a visit to the Vietnamese defense minister, General Doan Khue, in Hanoi. Rusdy later described the talks as a "new step" in the relationship between the armies of the two countries, and he called for further military exchanges.

Indonesia and Vietnam share a common concern about China's claims to roughly 80 percent of the South China Sea. The extensive Chinese claims cut through large sections of Vietnam's Blue Dragon oil field and Indonesia's Natuna gas reserves.

Malaysia

Malaysia assumed a cautious, but not overly hostile attitude toward Vietnam during the Cambodian conflict. Like Indonesia, it believed that Vietnam was motivated primarily by nationalism and would ultimately free itself from dependence on the Soviet Union. Even during the Cambodian conflict, Malaysia maintained dialogue with the Hanoi leadership in the hopes that Vietnam would not become isolated.

Since Vietnam's Prime Minister Vo Van Kiet visited Kuala Lumpur in January 1992, high-level contacts and economic cooperation between the two countries have grown steadily. In April 1992, Malaysian Prime Minister Mohamed Mahathir spent five days in Vietnam in order to promote investment and trade. He was accompanied by nearly 200 officials and businessmen. Since then, Malaysia has emerged as the seventh largest investor in Vietnam, and it has entered discussions with Hanoi about expanding petroleum exploration, rehabilitating rubber estates, and promoting tourism.

Mahathir has frequently expressed the view that a stable and prosperous Vietnam would serve the interests of the entire region. And the Malaysian prime minister's outspoken criticism of Western values and interference in the internal affairs of Third World countries has struck a sympathetic chord with the Vietnamese leaders.

Vietnam has announced its support for Malaysia's controversial proposal to develop an East Asian Economic Caucus (EAEC), an all-Asian regional forum, which has been vigorously opposed by the United States because of its racially exclusive overtone.

Malaysia and Vietnam do have overlapping territorial claims in the South China Sea but both countries seem to regard China's claims as more threatening. Hanoi's confidence in Malaysia is indicated by its decision to award Petronas, Malaysia's state-owned oil company, a contract to explore for oil in Vietnam's southern continental shelf, where there are also territorial disputes between the two countries.

Singapore

During the Cambodia conflict, Singapore was ASEAN's most hard-line opponent of Vietnamese expansionism. But with the signing of the Paris peace agreement and the end of the Cold War, Singapore has abandoned its hostility to Vietnam. Singapore's senior leader, Lee Kuan Yew, visited Vietnam in April 1992, and during the course of his visit he counseled the Vietnamese on the operation of a market economy. The Vietnamese leaders said later that the Lee visit marked a turning point in relations between the two countries. Since then, Lee has visited Vietnam several times and on one occasion brought with him a number of Singapore's business and government leaders. By the mid-1990s, Singapore had emerged as Vietnam's second largest trading partner, next to Japan, and by itself accounted for about one-quarter of Vietnam's entire trade turnover. Singapore has also become the third largest investor in Vietnam after Taiwan and Hong Kong.

Philippines

Because the Philippines are far removed geographically from mainland Southeast Asia, their leaders looked with relative indifference on the Vietnamese invasion of Cambodia. They went along with the ASEAN policy toward Vietnam largely in order to maintain ASEAN unity. The lack of interest in Vietnam was also caused by unstable political and economic conditions in the Philippines itself during the Marcos and Aquino eras, which caused the Philippines to look inward.

The improvement of ASEAN-Vietnamese relations during the 1990s has enabled the Philippines to improve relations with Vietnam. What may well accelerate this relationship is a common interest in a peaceful resolution of the Spratly Islands dispute. Although both Vietnam and the Philippines have overlapping claims to more than a dozen reefs and atolls in the archipelago, both countries have always considered China's massive claim on the South China Sea, not their own more limited claims, as the most serious threat to their security. Both states recognize that China is their common problem. As mentioned, this recognition was given added urgency by the confrontation between China and the Philippines over Mischief Reef in early 1995.

Even before the Mischief Reef incident, Philippine President Fidel Ramos had been the first ASEAN leader to appeal for Vietnam's admission. And as early as 1992, when Vietnamese Prime Minister Vo Van Kiet visited Manila, he and President Corazon Aquino expressed their commitment to the peaceful settlement of the Spratlys dispute and pledged to avoid unilateral actions that would exacerbate tensions in the South China Sea.

Thailand

Thailand and Vietnam have been traditional rivals on the Indochinese peninsula for several centuries. During the Cold War, external powers fed their suspicions of each other. And after Vietnam invaded Thailand's neighboring state, Cambodia, in 1978, Thailand felt particularly threatened. The Thais, therefore, began to look for external allies to balance Vietnam. The two most logical candidates were the United States and China. The United States had supported Thailand during the Cold War, and the Thais considered China to be a natural ally against Vietnamese expansionism.

To this day, despite the end of the Cambodian conflict, the Thai and Vietnamese leaders look upon each other warily. The two countries still have fishing disputes that have resulted in several hostile clashes. The disagreement over the site of a Vietnamese consulate in Thailand has still not been resolved. Vietnam requested Udon Thani as the preferred location because there are some 50,000 Vietnamese living in the area, but the Thai military refused because of their lingering suspicion that these residents might be "fifth columnists."[28]

The lack of mutual trust has also hindered the development of economic relations. Despite Thai rhetoric about turning Indochina from a battlefield into a marketplace, Thailand still lags behind Singapore, Malaysia, and Indonesia in developing economic relations with Vietnam. Part of the reason for this gap apparently has to do with the wariness of the Vietnamese, but part also has to do with the reluctance of Thai business circles.

Despite these negative signs, there are also some promising developments. According to one observer, Thai foreign policy is increasingly being driven by economics and by a regional vision.[29] This vision, articulated by a number of Thai civilian and military leaders, emphasizes developing economic relations with neighboring states, including Vietnam, Laos, and Cambodia, and bringing them into the wider community of Southeast Asian states. It is notable that Thai Prime Minister Chuan Likphai led the chorus of calls for a "greater ASEAN" at the July, 1994 meeting in Bangkok of the ASEAN foreign ministers.

There are indications that the civilian leadership in Bangkok is also determined to demonstrate its autonomy in relation to China. The Thai leaders invited the Dalai Lama to Bangkok in February 1993, after having refused him entry in 1984, 1987, and 1990. Thai army chief Vimol Wongwanich criticized the visit on the grounds that it would send the wrong signal to China. But Thai civilian leaders were quick to defend the invitation.

The Thais also seem to be in the process of readjusting their relations with the United States. Trade disputes have come to play a prominent role in the post-Cold War relationship, and prominent Thais have proclaimed that Thailand will no longer behave like a docile younger brother.

As a result of its new regional vision, a more independent stance toward China, and cooling relations with the United States, Thailand is quite likely to attach increased importance to developing stable relations with all its Southeast Asian neighbors, including Vietnam.

In sum, Vietnam has rapidly improved its relations with each of the ASEAN states since the end of the Cambodian conflict. Vietnam has become increasingly dependent on trade and investment ties with its ASEAN neighbors. And there is the gradual emergence of the sense of a common threat from China. Vietnam's perceptions of ASEAN have changed dramatically, and so have the perceptions of Vietnam among the ASEAN leaders. None of the ASEAN leaders, with the possible exception of some of the Thai military, any longer view Vietnam as the main threat to Southeast Asian security.

The Impact of Vietnam's Membership in ASEAN

Despite the favorable developments in relations between Vietnam and ASEAN outlined above, there still remain a number of obstacles to close relations between Vietnam and the ASEAN states, and many of these obstacles will remain in spite of Vietnam's admission to ASEAN. Historic rivalries, conflicting national ambitions, territorial disputes, differing threat perceptions, different levels of economic development, different political systems, and many other factors will feed mutual suspicions.

To begin with, despite the apparent emergence of a united front against China on the Spratly issue, attitudes toward China vary considerably among the ASEAN states and astute Chinese diplomacy should be able to play on these differences. Singapore is a Chinese city state with a large and growing stake in "Greater China's" economic progress. It has little interest in confronting China on the South China Sea issue. This was made clear by Lee Kuan Yew's interview with the Singapore *Straits Times* in which he went out of his way to play down China's aggressiveness.[30]

Similarly, Thailand, for geostrategic reasons, must still want to cultivate good relations with China out of fear that Vietnam may one day resume its hegemonic designs on Cambodia and Laos.

Vietnam will therefore need to be careful as an ASEAN member to assure the other members that it is making efforts to accommodate China's reasonable interests and demands. Otherwise Vietnam's membership could drive a deep wedge in the ASEAN organization and polarize it between "hawks" and "doves" on China.

Another obstacle to Vietnam's integration into ASEAN will be Vietnam's ambitions and its own political and ideological style. While Vietnam's ambition to be the dominant power in Indochina seems to be in abeyance while it is weak, it is still too early to say whether this ambition has been completely renounced. The leaders in Hanoi cannot be happy about Thai economic inroads into Laos and Cambodia and the still cozy relationship between Bangkok and Beijing. And the Thai military must still harbor suspicions about Vietnam's intentions after it modernizes its economy. There is also the possibility that mainland Southeast Asia may come to have a different set of priorities from that of maritime Southeast Asia.

The huge difference in levels of economic development between Vietnam and some other ASEAN states could also prove to be a formidable obstacle to cooperation. Already Vietnam is asking for a delay in complying with the minimal standards of the ASEAN Free Trade Area (AFTA). Vietnam is bound to want a variety of safeguards to protect its inefficient state industries and its infant industries. Moreover, the more developed ASEAN states, such as Singapore, are already expressing an interest in joining NAFTA (the North American Free Trade Agreement) and in linking NAFTA to the Pacific, while the less developed ASEAN countries are mostly against this idea.

Despite these and other obstacles to Vietnamese integration into

ASEAN, however, it seems likely that Vietnam will try very hard to play a constructive role in the region during the next decade. The two principal factors now driving Vietnamese foreign policy are economics and concern about China. On both counts, Vietnam needs the cooperation of ASEAN and could benefit by being a member of ASEAN in good standing. Vietnam is also likely to go out of its way to befriend several powerful states within ASEAN, particularly Indonesia, a state with whom it has long-standing ties.

The changing international environment will also help to maintain the unity of ASEAN. The end of the Cold War, the declining United States security presence in Southeast Asia, and the rising power of China all contribute to feelings of vulnerability in the region. There is therefore an objective need to strengthen security cooperation among the smaller states and eventually to incorporate all ten states in the region into an expanded ASEAN. The inauguration of the ASEAN Regional Forum in 1994 was one step in this direction.

Another reason for optimism about ASEAN's future is that ASEAN itself has a history of considerable resilience in the face of external challenge. Since its founding in 1967, ASEAN has generally been recognized as one of the world's most successful examples of regionalism. Two successes stand out. First, ASEAN has been able to overcome a variety of territorial and national conflicts among its member states and to affirm a commitment to a regional order based upon the territorial status quo, a commitment enshrined in the 1976 Southeast Asian Treaty of Amity and Cooperation (the Treaty of Bali), concluded, not coincidentally, one year after Saigon fell to North Vietnamese armies. This commitment met its most severe test during Vietnam's occupation of Cambodia from 1978 to 1989, but the ASEAN states focused the international community's attention upon this territorial revision by force of arms and helped to generate the pressure that ultimately forced Vietnam to withdraw from Cambodia, to sign the Treaty of Bali, and to seek normal relations with all of its ASEAN neighbors.

ASEAN's second success has been to provide a mechanism whereby the medium and small powers of Southeast Asia could influence the actions of the great powers, such as the United States, Japan, China, and Russia. By speaking with one voice on the most crucial issues influencing their region, the ASEAN states have been able to develop some leverage on the great powers, leverage that would have been unimaginable if they were acting separately.

In the past few years, ASEAN has begun to adapt to the post-Cold War era with surprising speed and imagination. It has included Vietnam in its membership. It has reached a consensus on bringing about a closer association of all ten Southeast Asian states. It has begun a security dialogue with the other powers in the region, including all of the great powers. And it is gradually moving toward expanded security cooperation through a "spider's web" of bilateral and trilateral security relations.

In sum, the ASEAN states recognize that with the end of the bipolar Cold War era, if they want to improve their economies and get better control of their own strategic environment, they will have to cooperate and to stand together. Vietnam shares these views.

Notes

1. Nayan Chanda, *Brother Enemy* (New York: Harcourt Brace Jovanovich, 1986), p. 135.
2. Donald S. Zagoria, *Vietnam Triangle* (New York, Pegasus, 1968).
3. Carlyle Thayer, "Sino-Vietnamese Relations: The Interplay of Ideology and National Interest," *Asian Survey,* June 1994.
4. For a brief history of the claims, clashes, and negotiations in the South China Sea dispute, see chapter V in this volume.
5. Phillip Bowring, "The Spratlys: China's Neighbors Are Losing Patience," *International Herald Tribune,* April 7, 1995.
6. Thayer, "Sino-Vietnamese Relations."
7. Ibid.
8. John Bresnan, *From Dominoes to Dynamos: The Transformation of Southeast Asia* (New York: Council on Foreign Relations Press, 1994), p. 83.
9. Ibid., p. 84.
10. Lee Kuan Yew interview with the Singapore *Straits Times,* May 13, 1995, reprinted in FBIS, East Asia, May 15, 1995, pp. 63–66.
11. Reginald Chua, "China's Moves in Spratlys Spark International Ire," *The Asian Wall Street Journal Weekly,* April 24, 1995, p. 1.
12. "Spratlys and the South China Sea," Statement by the Acting Spokesman, U.S. Department of State, May 10, 1995, in *PacNet,* no. 16 (Honolulu, Hawaii: Pacific Forum CSIS, May 18, 1995).
13. Chua, "China's Moves in Spratlys."
14. Ibid.
15. Ibid.
16. *The Nation,* Bangkok, July 23, 1994, in FBIS, East Asia, July 25, 1994, pp. 1–2.
17. Ibid.
18. Bresnan, *From Dominoes to Dynamos,* p. 18.
19. In U.S. dollars. Cited in William S. Turley, "Vietnamese Security in Domestic and Regional Focus: The Political-Economic Nexus," in Sheldon Simon and Richard Ellings, ed., *Southeast Asian Security in the New Millennium* (Armonk, NY: M.E. Sharpe, 1996).
20. Bresnan, *From Dominoes to Dynamos,* p. 21.
21. See World Bank estimates cited in *Far Eastern Economic Review,* May 4, 1995, p. 23.
22. My conversations with Southeast Asian specialists at the Japanese Foreign Ministry, Tokyo, November 11, 1994.

23. Annual ODA report from the Japanese Foreign Ministry, 1993.

24. My conversations in Tokyo, cited above.

25. This section draws heavily on Dan Thien Do, "Vietnam's Membership in ASEAN: Problems and Prospects," Washington, D.C.: Centre for Strategic and International Studies, July 30, 1994.

26. See Martin Gainsborough, "Vietnam and ASEAN: The Road to Membership?" *The Pacific Review,* 6, no. 4 (1993), pp. 381–387.

27. Ibid.

28. Do, "Vietnam's Membership in ASEAN."

29. Leszek Buszynski, "Thailand's Foreign Policy: Management of a Regional Vision," *Asian Survey,* August 1994, pp. 721–737.

30. Lee Kuan Yew interview, Singapore *Straits Times,* May 13, 1995, in FBIS.

The Responses of Japan and
the United States

8

Vietnam in Japan's Regional Policy

Yoshihide Soeya

Since the early 1970s Japan has placed a high priority on Vietnam in its overall Southeast Asia policy. Strategically, a stable and neutral Vietnam as well as a stable entire Southeast Asian region in the post-Vietnam War phase have been considered important for the security of Japan's vital sea-lanes of communication. Vietnam has been a key factor, not only because of its potential to become a regional power, but also because of its complex relations with Cambodia and Laos, the ASEAN countries, China, Russia, and the United States. Economically, not only are Vietnam's economic potential and human resources enormous, but the economic integration among Vietnam, Cambodia, Laos, and the ASEAN countries that Japan envisages will greatly enhance regional economic development as well as Japanese trade and investment in the region.

Less obvious for outside observers are political motives that cut across strategic and economic interests. At the beginning of the 1970s, when the United States began to withdraw from Indochina, Japan viewed Vietnam as an important country with which to pursue a somewhat "autonomous" political role, which would go beyond its traditional economic-centered policy. The aspiration was to bring about a stable regional order in Southeast Asia by cultivating good economic and political relations with both Indochinese states and ASEAN countries and thus serving as a "bridge" between Indochina and ASEAN. This new political role of Japan was conceived as the centerpiece of Japan's regional policy. It became the core of the Fukuda Doctrine announced in 1977 and continues to influence Japan's Indochina policy today.

In Search of a Political Role

The Fukuda Doctrine

The Fukuda Doctrine refers to a policy statement made by then-Prime Minister Takeo Fukuda in August 1977 clarifying the central policy of Japan toward Southeast Asia. The three aspects of the Fukuda Doctrine enumerated in Manila at the time were: (1) Japan is firmly committed to peace and is determined not to become a military power; (2) Japan will establish a heart-to-heart relationship of mutual trust with Southeast Asia, not only in political and economic areas, but in social and cultural realms; and (3) Japan will cooperate actively with ASEAN's efforts to strengthen solidarity and resilience and to develop relations with the Indochinese states on the basis of mutual understanding.

The major thrust of this policy, as its drafters recall, was reflected in the third point.[1] Its intention was to bring about greater stability in Southeast Asia by encouraging peaceful coexistence between ASEAN and Indochina, with Japan serving as a bridge between the two. Given Japan's peculiar situation, the driving force of that policy was understood to be economic assistance. Japan started to give official development assistance (ODA) to Hanoi soon after the fall of Saigon in April 1975: 8.5 billion yen as a grant in October 1975, 5 billion yen as a grant in September 1976, 4 billion yen as a grant in April 1978, and 10 billion yen as a loan in July 1978. In December 1978 it decided to give a 14 billion yen loan for the fiscal year 1979 but suspended the action when Vietnam invaded Cambodia in the same month.[2]

The International Context

Japanese initiatives toward Indochina stood out at the time, in part because the United States was rapidly becoming disenchanted with the region. In turn, America's low profile convinced Japanese policymakers that it was time to formulate a somewhat autonomous policy toward Southeast Asia without necessarily contradicting the fundamentally cooperative relationship with the United States. For instance, when U.S. President Gerald Ford announced the "Pacific Doctrine" in December 1975, Japanese Foreign Minister Kiichi Miyazawa did not fail to note the doctrine's lack of a clear policy toward Indochina. This suggested to him the important role that Japan might play as "a bridge between ASEAN and Indochina."[3] Later in 1977, when the Carter administration set out to negotiate diplomatic normalization with Vietnam, time seemed opportune for Japan to launch such a policy.

Significant changes in ASEAN also encouraged Japanese policymakers.

The anti-Japanese riots in Jakarta and Bangkok in January 1974 during Prime Minister Kakuei Tanaka's Southeast Asian tour revealed a continuing suspicion in the region. But in the years immediately following, when the United States pulled out of Vietnam and appeared to many in Asia to be withdrawing also from the region, the leaders in the ASEAN capitals began to look more favorably on Japan's potential role.[4]

Under these circumstances, ASEAN's rise as a collective regional actor was impressive. The first ASEAN summit was held in February 1976 in Bali. At the summit, ASEAN heads signed three important documents, signifying a new age of cooperation: the Declaration of ASEAN Concord, stating the objectives and principles of ASEAN cooperation "in the pursuit of political stability"; the Treaty of Amity and Cooperation in Southeast Asia, purporting "to promote perpetual peace, everlasting amity and cooperation"; and the Agreement on the Establishment of the ASEAN Secretariat.[5] In line with its new aspiration in regional affairs, ASEAN began to increase its collective voice, demanding that Japan play a positive role in the region and hinting at ASEAN's readiness to invite Japan to the second ASEAN summit, scheduled in 1977.

The fall of Saigon in April 1975 and the unification of Vietnam in June 1976 were also regarded by Japanese policymakers as providing an opportunity for favorable Japanese initiative. In 1976, to rebuild the country from the war's devastation, Vietnam embarked upon a very ambitious second five-year plan, aiming at an annual 14–15 percent increase in GNP. The requirement of trade, investment, and financial assistance was far beyond what the Soviet Union or China could provide, not to mention smaller socialist countries. With the U.S. refusing to provide the aid it had promised to consider under the 1973 Paris agreement because of Hanoi's violation of the Paris accords (its liberation of the South by armed force), Japan was the most significant potential source from the West.[6] To policymakers in Tokyo this meant that Japan was in a position to play a role in bringing Vietnam into a wider network of regional economic interdependence. The fact that ASEAN countries began to seek rapprochement with Vietnam at about the same time provided further encouragement for Tokyo.

Last but not least, none of the great powers, not China, the Soviet Union, or the United States, had yet crafted a clear policy toward Southeast Asia in the post-Vietnam War era.

Policy Formulation

In early 1976, an informal policy group was formed within the Foreign Ministry's Bureau of Asian Affairs consisting of four key members:

Yosuke Nakae, director general of the bureau; Sumio Edamura, deputy director general of the bureau; Takehiko Nishiyama, director of the Regional Policy Division; and Sakutaro Tanino, director of the Second Southeast Asian Division.[7] From the beginning, the group placed priority on two proposals: Japan's support of ASEAN's efforts to strengthen resilience and Japan's contribution to bringing about cooperative relations between ASEAN and Indochina. These proposals soon became the central thinking in the Foreign Ministry, as demonstrated by the Japanese ambassador to Singapore in April 1976 when he said, "Japan would do whatever possible to promote peaceful coexistence between ASEAN and Indochina."[8]

The focal point of Japan's new Southeast Asian policy had thus become clear before the election of Takeo Fukuda as prime minister in December 1976. But there was some opposition to an overt political emphasis on Indochina from both within the Foreign Ministry and outside, particularly by the Ministry of International Trade and Industry (MITI). Those who favored a low profile in the political scene tended to emphasize the importance of economic ties with ASEAN; this was the thinking behind the agreement to establish the Japan-ASEAN Forum in November 1976 to discuss economic cooperation, the first meeting of which was held in Tokyo in March 1977.

Nonetheless, basically political considerations stood out in the new Southeast Asian policy. Vietnam was its central focus. An active policy toward Vietnam had been supported by the Cold War "warriors" in the Foreign Ministry as early as 1973, when Japan normalized relations with it. One of their important considerations was that a strong commitment to the reconstruction of Vietnam and to its integration into Southeast Asia would help prevent the expansion of Soviet influence southward.

The fact that the United States under the Carter administration was probing diplomatic normalization with Vietnam also seemed supportive. As a first step in this direction, the Carter administration lifted restrictions on travel by Americans to Vietnam on March 9, 1977, and began talks with Vietnam on improving relations in May in Paris. Just as the United States embarked on this, Fukuda visited Washington for his first summit meeting with Carter. The joint communique issued on March 22 expressed concern about future developments in Indochina and hope for its peace and stability.

Simply put, Japanese policymakers expected that improved relations between Vietnam and both Japan and the United States would encourage Vietnam to maintain an independent position between China and the Soviet Union. Such a "strategic" positioning of Vietnam was understood to be the precondition for the success of Japan's new diplomatic initiative toward Vietnam in particular and Southeast Asia in general.

Of course, given the peculiar nature of Japanese domestic politics, it was almost impossible or even politically suicidal for Japanese leaders to highlight the importance of power politics and to suggest that Japan was taking action based on strategic considerations. For Prime Minister Takeo Fukuda, who formed the Cabinet in December 1976, therefore, politically safe and appealing slogans were important. From the early 1970s, Fukuda had expressed his determination to lead Japan on a "historically unparalleled path," attempting to make Japan an economic power without becoming a military power. The culmination of this vision was the announcement of an "omnidirectional diplomacy," by which Fukuda expressed his preference for a diplomatic role for Japan as a bridge between conflicting countries or subregions without depending on military imperatives and in such a way as to make military considerations less prominent.

Hisashi Owada, who was seconded from the Foreign Ministry as Fukuda's secretary, was instrumental as a liaison between Fukuda and the ministry. For Owada, Japan as a world power should have a major doctrine, and only the prime minister himself could declare it—at the right time and the right place. As Owada put it, the Fukuda Doctrine was "a serious attempt to define the future role of Japan with respect to this part of the world, and by extension, to a wider world, not in terms of abstract philosophy, but in terms of a specific policy direction for Japan to follow."[9]

An occasion for making such an announcement presented itself in Manila, the final stop of Prime Minister Fukuda's Southeast Asian tour. The tour was symbolic of a new era of Japan-ASEAN relations, because Fukuda's attendance at the second ASEAN summit meeting held in Kuala Lumpur on August 4–5, 1977, marked the very first meeting between a Japanese prime minister and the heads of the ASEAN countries in the postwar years.

To Japan's great satisfaction, the final communique of the second ASEAN summit stated, "The Heads of Government emphasized the desire of ASEAN countries to develop peaceful and mutually beneficial relations with all countries in the region, including Kampuchea, Laos and Vietnam."[10] In addition, the ASEAN-Japan joint statement issued on August 7 contained all the elements included in the Fukuda Doctrine: the intensification of "cooperation in the cultural and social fields"; Japan's support for "the efforts of ASEAN to achieve self-reliance and solidarity"; Japan's pledge "to follow a peaceful course and not to become a military power"; and, most important, the shared recognition that "the situation as it exists today presents an opportunity for the countries in Southeast Asia to shape new relationships, irrespective of differences in political, economic and social systems."[11] Thus, the "Manila speech," which had been drafted in late July by Owada and Nishiyama and presented to Nakae, was rewritten into the final version by Nakae and Owada during the Southeast Asian tour on August 15, three days before the announcement in Manila.[12]

As this policy-formulation process demonstrated, the essence of the Fukuda Doctrine was condensed in the third point, aiming at declaring a clearly defined, long-term foreign policy principle. The first and second points—a commitment to a nonmilitary path and an emphasis on "heart-to-heart" understanding—were basically statements of general principles and a reflection of Fukuda's preference. The third point, defining Japan's role as a bridge between Indochina and ASEAN, on the other hand, was the result of careful deliberations on the Japanese position in the post-Vietnam phase of regional politics and was propounded as a long-term principle of a new diplomacy of activism.

Frustration of the Fukuda Doctrine

There were two noteworthy characteristics of the Fukuda Doctrine. First, this Indochina policy reflected Japan's aspiration for a larger role in areas where there was no major conflict of interest with the United States. Japan was prepared to step back should any such conflict of interest arise. Second, the doctrine was fundamentally conditioned by Japan's postwar aversion to involvement in politically sensitive issues, not to mention in areas where the elements of strategic and military rivalry among the major powers were salient. In the second half of 1978, both of these factors gradually turned against Japan's wishes, and the Vietnamese invasion of Cambodia in December frustrated them completely.

First, in May 1978, the United States clearly shifted toward normalizing relations with China with the objective of checking Soviet adventurism in the Third World. Then, by October 1978, in order to complete the China transaction, the United States decided to suspend negotiations on diplomatic normalization with Vietnam.[13] American strategic interests and Japanese political considerations in Indochina began to diverge.

Second, the highly volatile strategic rivalry between China and the Soviet Union clouded the Indochinese situation toward the end of 1978. China stood firmly behind the Khmer Rouge regime in Phnom Penh, which had severed diplomatic relations with Hanoi in December 1977. In the spring of 1978, Sino-Vietnamese relations further worsened over the Vietnamese treatment of Chinese residents, and in July China decided to suspend all aid to Vietnam. On June 29, shortly before the suspension, Vietnam joined the Soviet-led Council for Mutal Economic Assistance (CMEA), and on November 3 it signed a treaty of friendship and cooperation with the Soviet Union. This was followed by the

Vietnamese invasion of Cambodia in December 1978 and the Chinese invasion of Vietnam in February 1979. Thus, the foundations of Japan's "omnidirectional" diplomacy and the Fukuda Doctrine were destroyed.

In the lead-up to the invasion, Hanoi engaged in exceptionally active diplomacy, and Japan was an important target. From December 1977 to January 1978, Foreign Minister Nguyen Duy Trinh went to Malaysia, the Philippines, and Thailand; and in July 1978, Vice Foreign Minister Pham Hien visited Singapore, Malaysia, Thailand, Australia, New Zealand, and Japan. While in Tokyo, Pham Hien made it known that Vietnam was now ready to negotiate normalization with the United States without preconditions, a position that he repeated in August to a United States senators' mission to Vietnam. Between September and October, Prime Minister Pham Van Dong visited all five ASEAN nations. In December, shortly before the Vietnamese invasion of Cambodia, Foreign Minister Nguyen Duy Trinh visited Tokyo and conferred with the newly established Masayoshi Ohira government.

Tokyo understood these moves by Hanoi according to its own expectations, that is, as demonstrations of Hanoi's intention to pursue an "independent diplomacy" and its willingness to open dialogue with ASEAN. Although Tokyo started to feel some concern over the political situation in Indochina, it continued to take Hanoi's pledges at face value and decided to give a 10 billion yen loan in July and a 14 billion yen loan in December. Tokyo was still hoping to carry out the Fukuda Doctrine, as demonstrated by Foreign Minister Sonoda's explicit request to Hanoi to purchase ASEAN's products as much as possible.[14] Thus, Japan was misled by its own aspirations.

The Vietnamese invasion of Cambodia was a decisive blow to Japan's nonstrategic posture. To Tokyo's further dismay, the Chinese ambassador to Japan thereupon asked the Japanese government in January 1979 to support the Khmer Rouge government in Cambodia in accordance with the "antihegemony" clause of the Sino-Japanese peace and friendship treaty signed in August the previous year.[15] Soon after, the Soviet embassy in Tokyo issued a statement saying that if Japan stopped aid to Vietnam, the USSR would regard it as a joint action with China based on the "antihegemony" clause of the treaty.[16] In February 1979, the Vietnamese party newspaper *Nhan Dan* began to talk about a "Beijing-Washington-Tokyo axis" and to criticize Tokyo.[17]

Tokyo's decision to postpone and eventually suspend economic aid to Vietnam was made in the middle of this highly political environment. Japan, together with the United States and other Western countries as well as ASEAN, supported the Khmer Rouge government's seat at the United

Nations and called for the immediate withdrawal of Vietnamese forces from Cambodia. After the Soviet invasion of Afghanistan in December 1979, the international community's opposition to the Soviet-Vietnamese alliance became unequivocal. Thus, contrary to its intention and expectation, Japan became entangled in Asian power politics. The Fukuda Doctrine became inoperable, at least for the time being.

Japan's Response to the End of the Cold War

A New Perspective on the US

In the formulation of Japan's new external outlook in the post-Cold War era, the United States is the most important factor for two interrelated reasons. First, the United States is at the center of systemic transformation of not only the Cold War but "Pax Americana." The relative decline of the American influence is the key concept, implying that the United States can no longer be counted on as the sole architect of a new order, though it continues to be the most powerful and important country. Second, a challenge to Japan in a new age is to diversify its diplomacy, which will amount to the reduction of dependence on the United States in relative terms, while its dependence on the United States will remain the greatest in absolute terms. In short, the United States-Japan partnership in a new multilateral setting is increasingly regarded as ideal for Japanese diplomacy in a new age. A report by the advisory group on defense issues, originally commissioned by Prime Minister Morihiro Hosokawa and presented to Prime Minister Tomiichi Murayama in August 1994, makes this assumption explicit.[18]

> There is little possibility that any major nation with both the intention and the capacity to challenge U.S. military power head-on will emerge in the near future. However, the United States no longer holds an overwhelming advantage in terms of overall national strength. . . . The question is whether the United States, its preeminent military power notwithstanding, will be able to demonstrate leadership in multilateral cooperation. [pp. 2–3]

> In order to further ensure the security of Japan and make multilateral security cooperation effective, close and broad cooperation and joint work between Japan and the United States are essential. The institutional framework for this is provided by the Japan-U.S. Security Treaty. [p. 10]

This new aspiration of Japan, however, is conditioned by a uniquely Japanese situation: the burden of the half-century-ago history still nullifies, both externally and domestically, the option of unilateral initiatives and highly political, not to mention military, actions. Externally, many nations still feel strong psychological resistance to Japan being overly present in the region. Domestically, the political situation remains divided between those who favor activist policies and those who are prone to minimalist policies. In defending their approach, the minimalists often cite the wartime aggression of Japan. Even for the activists, the wartime legacy of Japanese brutality and aggression leaves them with no other alternative than to seek Japan's active participation in international politics through multilateral arrangements.

What is new here is that Japan now seeks the object of "compliance" beyond its bilateral relationship with the United States, in multilateral arrangements in which, of course, the United States is the most important part. The rise of this new paradigm in Japanese diplomacy reflects three structural changes occurring in the U.S.-Japan relationship in the post-Cold War era.

First, the disappearance of the Soviet threat calls for a new rationale for sustained U.S.-Japanese cooperation. Now there is a broad agreement throughout the Asia-Pacific region that a stable relationship between the United States and Japan is crucial to the creation of a stable and prosperous post-Cold War order. The catchword reflective of such an expectation has been "global partnership." Already in 1990, the then-vice minister of foreign affairs of Japan argued that the reactive nature of Japanese diplomacy, which took the existing international order as given, was becoming less realistic. He called for the maintenance of Japanese security and prosperity through active participation in international endeavors for the creation of a new world order. In this connection he contended that the "global partnership" and the bilateral security system between Japan and the United States would constitute the cornerstones upon which both the United States and Japan would define their active presence in the Asia-Pacific region.[19]

The second change is the narrowing of the power balance between the United States and Japan. This trend has basically persisted since the time of Nixon-Kissinger diplomacy a quarter of a century ago, and an expanded international role for Japan and a reduced presence for the United States in the Asia-Pacific continue to be the premises for U.S.-Japan cooperation. If analyzed in a multilateral context, this shifting pattern of the relationship is an inevitable outcome of the postwar transformation of Pax Americana and thus ought to be the premise for the construction of a new international order as well as the U.S.-Japan relationship in coming decades.

Third, the demise of the Cold War framework and the narrowing power gap between the United States and Japan encourages a more active role for Japan in regional and world affairs. Japan is starting to establish an important presence of its own, and it will continue to diversify links to the international system. The United States is still the most important link, but no longer the only one.

Initiative toward ASEAN

Under these circumstances, Southeast Asia is one of the most important areas with which Japan aspires to forge a stable link, and there are signs of new activism in recent Japanese diplomacy toward the region. Indeed, Southeast Asia occupies a central place in Japan's new diplomatic agenda in the post-Cold War era, as demonstrated by its multilateral diplomacy toward ASEAN and its policy toward the Cambodian peace process.

Since the late 1980s, ASEAN has occupied a central place in the Japanese government's policy toward multilateral cooperation and the regional political and security dialogue in the Asia-Pacific.[20] From the beginning, Tokyo has attached foremost importance to the fact that geopolitical conditions and the security environment in the Asia-Pacific are intrinsically different from those in Europe. Tokyo's thinking has emphasized the flexible application of "multiplex" mechanisms, in which an effective use of existing relationships and institutions for regional cooperation is envisaged. Four major pillars that are considered to form this "multiplexity" in the Asian context are (1) regional economic cooperation, (2) efforts toward the settlement of sub-regional conflicts, (3) cooperative defense relationships, and (4) a political dialogue.[21]

Out of this multiplex thinking developed a "two-track approach," whose official version was enunciated by Prime Minister Kiichi Miyazawa in 1992 in Washington, D.C. Miyazawa stated at the National Press Club on July 2 that the Japanese approach to Asia-Pacific security is composed of Japanese efforts toward "the promotion of sub-regional cooperation to settle disputes and conflicts" and "region-wide political dialogue to enhance the sense of mutual reassurance."[22] Tokyo's judgment is that each conflictual case should be considered separately at each subregional level, although it admits that the trends for multilateral cooperation in the Asia-Pacific will have favorable impacts on subregional cooperation.

The Japanese government's initiative for a political dialogue was first articulated by then-Foreign Minister Taro Nakayama in July 1991 at the ASEAN Post-Ministerial Conference (PMC) in Kuala Lumpur. Nakayama expressed Japan's willingness to participate in a "political dialogue aiming at enhancing a feeling of reassurance [*anshin-kan* in Japanese] with each other" and proposed to utilize the ASEAN-PMC as a forum for such dialogue.[23] Nakayama suggested starting a "reassuring process" utilizing the existing regional frameworks of cooperation without entertaining European-centered concepts such as a Council for Security Cooperation in Asia (CSCA).

Although Nakayama's wording was carefully worked out so that he would not give the impression that Japan's political role is synonymous with an ambition for political control, the proposal aroused suspicion among many Southeast Asian nations that Japan was now preparing itself for a security role in the region. Indeed, a central purpose of the Nakayama proposal was to initiate the discussion of issues having regional security implications, including Japan's political role and the fear of its expansion into a military role, in addition to the security role of the United States, the future of U.S.-Japanese relations, and so forth.

The proposal was not immediately popular among ASEAN governments. But soon the idea of a political dialogue was promoted by ASEAN, and the Japanese government continued to encourage such an ASEAN initiative. In January 1992, the ASEAN's summit endorsed the idea, calling for the pro-motion of a political dialogue on security issues. The ASEAN's ministerial meeting held in July 1992 invited China and Russia as guests and Vietnam and Laos as observers, thus enlarging the basis of a political dialogue. In the same month, Japan and ASEAN agreed to elevate the Japan-ASEAN Forum, which was first convened in 1977 for cooperation in nonpolitical fields, to a forum for a dialogue on subjects including political and security matters. In July 1992, Prime Minister Miyazawa advocated in Washington, D.C., the necessity to create a regional framework for a political dialogue involving Russia and China. In February 1993, Japan and ASEAN agreed in Tokyo that a senior officials' meeting be held before the ASEAN-PMC to discuss political and security issues (the idea was initially proposed by Foreign Minister Nakayama in July 1991 when he proposed political dia-logue but was at the time rejected by ASEAN counterparts). In July 1993, the ASEAN ministerial meeting agreed to set up an ASEAN Regional Forum, whose first meeting was successfully convened in Bangkok in July 1994.

The Japanese government's choice of ASEAN as host reflected several factors: the inability of Tokyo to be the center of a bold regional initiative, a permissive environment in ASEAN that has become receptive to Japan's political role, and the increasing capability and confidence of ASEAN in the management of such a regional forum, which can accommodate all the regional countries concerned, including Russia, China, the United States, and Vietnam.

In fact, the idea of a political dialogue formed within the Japanese gov-ernment (to be precise, the Foreign Ministry) through the process of careful probing and contact with its ASEAN counterparts. An important turning point where Japanese and ASEAN positions converged was at its ASEAN Institutes of Strategic and International Studies (ISIS) meeting (annual meeting by the ASEAN countries' semigovernmental think tanks) in June 1991, which a senior official of the Japanese Foreign Ministry (Yukio Sato, then-director general of the Information, Analysis, Research and Planning Bureau) attended as an invited speaker. The meeting issued a proposal titled "A Time for Initiative," which called for an ASEAN initiative for "Asia-Pacific Political Dialogue" and an "ASEAN PMC-initiated conference" at the end of each ASEAN-PMC.[24]

According to several participants in this meeting, Sato played a signifi-cant role in the process of consensus formation regarding the necessity and the nature of a regional political dialogue. The gist of the consensus was that initiative should build upon existing processes and institutions, particu-larly the ASEAN-PMC, and that the specific characteristics and needs of the Asia-Pacific should be taken into full account. Foreign Minister Nakayama's proposal in July 1991 included all these elements.

The ASEAN governments' cool response to the Nakayama proposal, therefore, came as a shock to the Japanese government. One would think that ASEAN was not enthusiastic because the proposal was presented as a Japanese initiative. Most of the ASEAN specialists, including those who participated in the ASEAN-ISIS meeting in June 1991, however, do not believe so. According to them, ASEAN has long been encouraging Japan's active and constructive engagement in regional affairs. After all, ASEAN is not an organization that acts according to external powers' proposals. Even within ASEAN, a consensus formation among its member countries re-quires tremendous energy and consideration of each other. Moreover, a primary long-term goal of ASEAN has been to free Southeast Asia from the influence of major powers. It was highly unlikely, therefore, that ASEAN would jump at Nakayama's proposal even though its contents reflected ASEAN's preferences and thinking.

Japan's Role in the Cambodian Peace Process

Japan's policy regarding the Cambodian problem provides another illustra-tion of the new Japanese diplomacy under new strategic circumstances. First, the Cambodian issue was "the first case where Japan participated fully in the settlement of an international conflict."[25] The Japanese government recognized this as a test case for Japan's participation in the creation of a new international order. Also, this was perhaps the first occasion in postwar Japanese diplomacy in which Japan basically operated in an explicitly mul-tilateral setting, while carefully preserving U.S.-Japanese cooperation. As stated, this form of new partnership between Japan and the United States is increasingly regarded as an ideal type by many Japanese. Particularly, Japan's participation in the United Nations peace-keeping operations (PKO) in Cambodia was an unmistakable indication that Japan's balanced engagement in international affairs could best be promoted through multilateral arrangements.

Second, Japan's partnership with ASEAN countries also entered a new phase with the Cambodian problem, as demonstrated by the ASEAN countries' encouragement for Japan to assume a bigger role in the Cambodian peace process as well as by their relatively calm response to the presence of Japan's Self-Defense Forces (SDF) in Cambodia.

The initial Japanese interest in the Cambodian settlement was made public in August 1988 when the Japanese government invited Prince Sihanouk to Tokyo and at the Paris International Conference in the summer of 1989 when the Japanese delegation lobbied for a larger role and accepted the cochairmanship of the Third Committee, responsible for refugees and the reconstruction of Cambodia.[26] This interest of the Japanese government was further highlighted by a Foreign Ministry official's visit to Phnom Penh in February 1990. The purpose of the trip was to investigate possibilities of giving a little higher priority than had been given by the permanent members of the United Nations Security Council (Perm-5) to the "indigenous" elements in Cambodia, including the Phnom Penh government. This move culminated in the Tokyo meeting in June 1990 to which Prince Sihanouk and Hun Sen, Prime Minister of the Heng Samrin government in Phnom Penh, were officially invited.

Reportedly, initiatives for the Tokyo meeting came from Thailand; in April 1990, Prime Minister Chatichai Choonhavan suggested to the Japanese government the convening of a Tokyo meeting, and the agreement reached at the Tokyo meeting was based on the paper prepared by a Thai general, Chaovalit Yongchaiyut, in May. According to several sources both in Tokyo and Bangkok, however, the fact was that the Japanese government took an active part in drafting the Chaovalit paper. Prime Minister Chatichai collaborated with Tokyo because he wanted Japan to play a larger role in the settlement.[27]

The refusal by the Khmer Rouge to attend the discussion in Tokyo tarnished the image of the meeting. The Tokyo communique signed by Sihanouk and Hun Sen, however, became an important precedent to the half-and-half representation in the Supreme National Council (SNC) between the Phnom Penh government, on the one hand, and the Sihanouk-led National Government of Cambodia, comprising three factions lead by Sihanouk, Son Sann, and Pol Pot, on the other. Until this meeting, the discussion on the SNC, a proposed interim government in the process of the political settlement under United Nations supervision, presupposed an equal distribution of representation among the four warring factions, resulting in an unfavorable balance against the Phnom Penh government. This new formula was accepted by all the warring factions, including the Khmer Rouge three months later in Jakarta.

Subsequently, the Perm-5 adopted the "Framework" document[28] in August 1990 and the "Proposed Structure" document[29] in November 1990. The Japanese government continued to support the Perm-5 efforts toward the comprehensive settlement embodied in these proposed documents. It nonetheless continued to feel that the Perm-5 should listen with a little more sympathy to Phnom Penh's concerns about the Perm-5 proposal, which called for what amounted to the dissolution of the Phnom Penh regime into the SNC. The Phnom Penh government was also concerned about the demilitarization process stipulated in the proposal, which they felt would be difficult to apply to the guerrilla-based Khmer Rouge forces, and about the possible return of genocide with the legitimization of the Khmer Rouge as part of SNC.

It was about these considerations that the Japanese government attempted to mediate between the Perm-5 plan of the comprehensive settlement and the warring factions' initiatives led by Sihanouk, who was increasingly becoming interested in developing a bilateral channel with Hun Sen. For example, Japan proposed to the conflicting factions in February 1991 that the military demobilization process be verified by the United Nations' peace-keeping forces and that some UN-related institutions be established to prevent the return of genocide.[30]

In the end, the Perm-5 draft agreement on the comprehensive settlement was slightly modified and accepted in September 1991 by the SNC. The new initiatives by the Sihanouk-led SNC were certainly precipitated by the normalized relationship between China and Vietnam, which had acknowledged themselves as custodians of the Khmer Rouge and the Phnom Penh regimes respectively. The Perm-5 welcomed such initiatives of the SNC, and on October 23, 1991, the Paris Conference on Cambodia finally witnessed the signing of the "Agreement on the Comprehensive Political Settlement of the Cambodia Conflict" and related documents.

The United Nations Transitional Authority in Cambodia (UNTAC) was established to ensure the implementation of the agreement and began activities in March 1992 with the arrival of Yasushi Akashi as the special representative. Largely due to resistance from the Khmer Rouge, the demobilization process had to be suspended, and the Khmer Rouge boycotted the elections of May 1993. Nonetheless, the observation of the election process by international volunteers and PKO forces made possible the "free and fair" elections called for, and nearly 90 percent of the eligible voters literally rushed to the polling stations. The election results were recognized as legitimate by the international community.[31] Prince Ranariddh of the Funipec and Hun Sen of the Cambodian People's Party became co-prime ministers of an interim government, and the new constitution was promulgated in September 1993. Now the Khmer Rouge became the odd man out, back in the jungle; and Cambodia began fresh, but difficult efforts toward the reconstruction of the country.

In this process, Japan actively took part in UNTAC, dispatching volunteers, civilian police, and the SDF as part of the massive PKO activities, as well as in the reconstruction of Cambodia's war-torn economy. The Japanese government was firmly determined to pursue both tracks simultaneously, and it proved this in the difficult process leading to the adoption of the Diet bill on PKO and the successful convening of the International Conference on the Reconstruction of Cambodia in Tokyo, both in June 1992.

The primary consideration on the part of the Japanese government in the Diet debates over the PKO bill was to prove that Japanese participation in the UN PKO activities outside of Japanese territories would not be unconstitutional. This was not an easy task, primarily because of the sensitive nature of constitutional issues in Japan's domestic politics and in the national debate.[32] That the Japanese government chose, nevertheless, to take part in the Cambodian PKO demonstrated its determination to move in the direction of becoming a full-fledged participant in regional and world affairs.

Policy toward the New Vietnam

With the end of the Cambodian War, Indochina, particularly Vietnam, has resurfaced as a central focus in Japan's overall efforts to enhance economic interdependence and political stability in Southeast Asia and the Asia-Pacific.

Despite the regional context in which Japan is pursuing its new diplomacy, there are still widely held suspicions, mostly in the West if less so in Asia today, about Japanese economic intentions in Indochina, particularly Vietnam. Many writers mention the danger of Japanese domination of the region, the overpresence of Japanese businessmen, and so forth. In reality, however, Tokyo's conduct of its economic policy toward Vietnam contrasts quite strikingly with this general perception.

First, Tokyo was a close associate of the United States government in the American-led economic sanctions against Vietnam since the Vietnamese invasion of Cambodia, and it has fully supported the United States on the issues of prisoners of war and those missing in action (POW/MIA) despite the lack of genuine appreciation on the part of the Japanese public of American sentiments. After the Vietnamese withdrawal from Cambodia in 1989, many Japanese felt that it was time to end the embargo and adopt a policy of constructive engagement, but the Japanese government maintained support for the U.S. position of continuing the embargo. Of course, Tokyo was concerned about possible political backlash from the U.S. Congress in case Japan went ahead of the United States. Such an American political response in itself was considered to be a disturbing factor in an emerging stable environment surrounding Vietnam, and so Tokyo judged it politically wise to avoid such backlash as much as possible. Note that in this thinking the United States is considered important not only for the sake of the bilateral relationship, but even more in the context of an evolving regional system.

The conclusion of the Cambodian peace accords in October 1991 was regarded as providing an opportunity to resume ODA to Vietnam, but after some debate, the Foreign Ministry decided to assist the improvement of U.S.-Vietnamese relations first, which was judged to be indispensable for the integration of Vietnam into the Asia-Pacific region.[33] By that time, Vietnam had already become enthusiastic about normalizing diplomatic relations with the United States and asked for Japanese mediation with Washington. When a senior Liberal-Democratic Party (LDP) politician, Michio Watanabe, visited Hanoi in early May 1990, Vietnamese Prime Minister Do Muoi expressed his hope of normalizing relations with the United States and explicitly asked Watanabe, who would visit Washington in late May, to convey his message to Washington.[34]

The government's support for the U.S. position in the case of the POW/MIA issue is perhaps most impressive, because the Japanese public in general felt that this issue was basically a bilateral one between the United States and Vietnam and did not necessarily require such a response. In early March 1992, taking the opportunity of U.S. Assistant Secretary of State Richard Solomon's visit to Hanoi, Foreign Minister Watanabe sent a letter to his Vietnamese counterpart, Nguyen Manh Cam, encouraging Hanoi's cooperation with the United States.[35] Five months later, in August, a senior Foreign Ministry official visited Hanoi and pushed Vietnam toward full cooperation with the United States on the POW/MIA issues.[36] The same message was repeated to Prime Minister Vo Van Kiet in March 1993, when he visited Tokyo to meet Prime Minister Kiichi Miyazawa and other Japanese leaders. Vo Van Kiet in return expressed his appreciation of Japan's efforts to promote U.S.-Vietnamese relations.[37]

Several interviews both in Washington and Hanoi confirmed that United

States and Vietnamese leaders and policymakers were fully appreciative of Japan's initiatives, and in Hanoi there is even a perception that in this matter Japan exerted some influence over the United States. The leadership in Hanoi is apparently beginning to realize the utility of Japan in their diplomacy and overall external relations. Again, back in May 1990, the Vietnamese leadership had already expressed such sentiment when Foreign Minister Nguyen Co Thach said to Michio Watanabe that Japan should not fall behind the United States and China in dealing with the Cambodian problem, and that Japan should exert its own leadership without following the United States.[38]

Tokyo's resumption of official assistance to Vietnam in November 1992, which amounted to 45.5 billion yen for commodity loans, was realized alongside these mediation efforts and after a full and careful consultation with Washington, for which the U.S. government expressed its gratitude. By the time the second round of resumed ODA to Vietnam (amounting to 52 billion yen for infrastructure projects) was signed in January 1994, therefore, the basis for criticism was considerably eroded.

The same kind of gap between public perception and reality exists in the realm of private business. In reality, in 1991 Japan was by far the largest importer from Vietnam ($719.3 million) but was fourth among exporters to Vietnam ($156.5 million), and this made Japan the second largest trading partner of Vietnam behind Singapore, which imported $427.6 million and exported $722.2 million. In 1992, Japan imported $892.3 million from Vietnam and exported $237.0 million to it, while Singapore imported $496.5 million and exported $877.3 million.[39] Japan exports to Vietnam mostly industrial products (such as machinery, electric products, transportation equipment, and chemicals) and imports mineral fuel (such as coal and oil), food, raw materials (such as minerals and wood), and light industrial products.

As to investment, Japan was only ninth in total amount of investment in Vietnam at the end of 1991 ($106 million), after Taiwan, Hong Kong, Australia, France, Holland, the Soviet Union, Great Britain, and Canada. As of May 1993, Japan barely became the fifth largest foreign investor in Vietnam, with the accumulated total of $453 million, following Taiwan, Hong Kong, Australia, and France. That represented a share of only 7.5 percent of the entire foreign investment in Vietnam, which amounted to $6.05 billion as of May 1993.[40]

Japan has thus been returning to Vietnam in a measured way. This is not to suggest, however, that Japan will not eventually emerge as a major economic actor for Vietnam. The case will perhaps be the other way around (although detailed figures are not available at the time of the writing, Japan has become Vietnam's largest trading partner in 1994). Indeed, Vietnam's expectations for Japan's economic contribution are quite high. According to a Vietnamese economist:

> Experiences of the Japanese investment in South-East Asia show that, like most of the other South-East Asian countries, Vietnam can meet the main objectives of Japan's direct investments. . . . Vietnam is trying to attract foreign investments into areas in which Japan enjoys comparative advantages and in which Japan has done successfully in East Asia and South-East Asia.[41]

Regarding Japanese ODA to Vietnam, too, while acknowledging that "Japan is taking the lead in the process of upgrading the infrastructure of Vietnam," Vietnam expects ODA to encourage Japanese private trade and investment:

> It is hoped that Japan's aid to Vietnam will continue to increase considerably and will become one of the motivations for the cooperation between the two countries, especially in foreign trade and direct investment.[42]

Quite unsurprisingly, the Japanese business community appears keen on taking advantage of this enthusiasm in Vietnam. One week after the signing of the Paris peace accords on the Cambodian problem in late October 1991, for example, the influential Keidanren (Federation of Economic Organizations) sent its mission to Vietnam for the first time since the Vietnamese invasion of Cambodia in 1978. The mission, which visited Hanoi and Ho Chi Minh City from October 30 to November 3, came away with three impressions: Vietnam's potentials are quite huge; Vietnam is likely to have a difficult transition for some time, and it is not time to invest substantially; and Vietnam's expectations for Japan are big, and Keidanren should try to meet its expectations and work on the Japanese government.[43]

Subsequently, the Japan-Vietnam Joint Economic Conference was set up between Keidanren's Japan-Vietnam Economic Committee and Vietnam's State Planning Commission. Its first meeting was held in Hanoi in February 1993 and the second meeting in Ho Chi Minh City in April 1994. The meetings were devoted to the discussion of possible investment projects, problems in the investment environment in Vietnam (such as infrastructure, administrative procedures, the legal system, and investment incentives), and the experiences of Japanese and Vietnamese economic development.[44]

Given the exceptionally high expectations on the part of Vietnam and Japan's firm belief in Vietnam's huge potential, it is highly likely and quite natural that economic relations should continue to constitute the core of the bilateral relationship. What is new and more important over the long run, however, is the political ramification of the economic dimension—the prospect of integrating Vietnam into Southeast Asia and the Asia-Pacific.

Revival of the Fukuda Doctrine

This idea of integrating Vietnam and Indochina into a wider region was the essence of the Fukuda Doctrine, which is now reinvigorated by the post-Cold War imperatives. The revival of the Fukuda Doctrine was first announced by Prime Minister Toshiki Kaifu, who stated in Singapore in May 1991 that he believed that "true peace and prosperity in entire Southeast Asia would become enduring when peace comes back to Indochina and its exchanges with ASEAN expand greatly in the future." Even though Kaifu did not make a reference to the Fukuda Doctrine per se, the meaning of his statement was clear.[45]

The end of the Cambodian conflict in October 1991 led to a more straightforward proposal from Prime Minister Kiichi Miyazawa. His statement in Bangkok in January 1993 included the following:

> The conclusion of the Cambodian Peace Accords opens the way not only to Cambodian reconstruction but also to the promotion of the policy of openness by Vietnam and Laos. It thus makes it possible for Southeast Asia, which consists of the countries of ASEAN and Indochina, to develop as an integral whole. Such development has consistently been the goal of Japan's Indochina policy since 1977, when Prime Minister Fukuda articulated in Manila Japan's policy of contributing to the building of peace and stability in the whole of Southeast Asia by expanding the scope of mutual cooperation and understanding throughout the region . . . .
>
> Japan considers it important that these countries of Southeast Asia strengthen their organic cohesion and pursue the development of the region as a whole. With this in mind, Japan intends to extend its cooperation to the improvement of infrastructures, human resources development and other areas to assist in particular the socioeconomic development of Indochina. To this end, I should like to propose establishing a "Forum for Comprehensive Development of Indochina."

This is clearly a revival of the Fukuda Doctrine, and Miyazawa's proposal for the "Forum for Comprehensive Development of Indochina" is a concrete implementation of the Fukuda Doctrine. Miyazawa continued:

> This forum would be designed to formulate strategies for harmonious development of the entire region of Indochina, by bringing together the experience and wisdom of the experts from interested countries and international organizations and other qualified personalities encompassing both the government and private sectors. They are expected to hold free and constructive discus-

sions and exchanges of views on the way with which trans-border cooperation and regional development of the entire Indochina should be conducted.
Japan would like to host an international meeting in Tokyo around autumn
this year to make preparations for this forum.[46]

The preparatory meeting of the forum was held in December 1993 in
Tokyo as planned. Ambassador Nobuo Matsunaga summarized the theme
of the forum in three points: transnational programs and projects; programs
and projects with implications and effects spreading across national boundaries; and programs and projects that address issues common to two or
more of the three countries. In the ministerial meeting held in Tokyo in
February 1995, which was attended by representatives from twenty-five
countries and eight international institutions, it was agreed that aid donors
would share information about development projects in Indochina and
would coordinate priority projects.[47]

Thus, an important step has been taken toward an effective and balanced
development of the Indochinese region, which is believed to be indispensable for the political stability of Indochina and Southeast Asia.

Vietnam's "Japan Card"?

Still, the question remains as to the extent to which Japan has or has not
become a full-fledged political player capable of managing delicate balance-of-power games among major powers in the region as well as with
ASEAN countries and Vietnam. The end of the Cold War has provided
Japan with a relatively benign international environment, which allowed it
to use economic means for political purposes. But international politics is
still in a state of flux that is likely to continue for some time to come.

In recent years, both ASEAN and Vietnam have elevated their interest in
regional multilateral cooperation. Vietnam gained membership in ASEAN
in July 1995. One obvious reason for Vietnam's enthusiasm is that joining
ASEAN and becoming integrated into the regional economy would benefit
the process of economic reform and hasten Vietnam's development. Also
associated with Vietnamese enthusiasm, however, are highly political motives, and Japan has yet to craft a policy to cope with these.

First, as Vietnam goes through economic reform and development, it will
inevitably face, or may already have started to face, a contradiction between
the calls for political pluralism associated with economic liberalization, on
the one hand, and the desire of its leaders to maintain the current political
order under one-party leadership. ASEAN countries do understand this dilemma, a subject about which Vietnam is anxious to learn and ASEAN

leaders appear interested to teach. The greatest source of concern for the leadership in Hanoi in this regard is what they call "peaceful evolution," the pluralization and possible collapse of its regime as a result of external pressures on democracy and human rights, particularly from the United States.

Second, Vietnam has proclaimed its version of "omnidirectional diplomacy," under which it is trying to make friends with everybody, including its traditional arch rival, China. To promote the *doi moi* policy domestically, Vietnam requires a peaceful environment externally. China holds the key to this, precisely because it is Vietnam's major source of security concern. In this respect, Vietnam calculates that closer ties with ASEAN will strengthen its hand against China without contradicting its official policy of omnidirectional diplomacy.

Both of these political aspects of Vietnam's external engagement have direct bearings on Japan's relations with the United States and China, the two most important powers with which Japan has to maintain stable relations in order to become a balanced power. In turn, Japan's relations with the United States and China ramify politically throughout the entire region. Today, Vietnam counts on Japan's meeting those challenges. As a vice foreign minister remarked in Hanoi in August 1994: "We have problems with the United States and China, but not with Japan. We can improve our position [vis-à-vis] the United States and China by cooperating with Japan."

Japan's search for a political role thus entered a new dimension.

Conclusion

Postwar Japanese diplomacy has suffered an image problem both inside and outside of Japan. Despite much proof of effective United States-Japanese cooperation and Japanese constructive engagement in the Asia-Pacific, most general observers and even many of the informed have often perceived the record of Japanese active diplomacy as nothing significant at best or ill intentioned at worst. Sometimes conscientious efforts to correct "misunderstanding" have been greeted with cynical eyes or even with giggles, interpreted as being government propaganda.

This problem is no more characteristically demonstrated than in the case of Japan's Indochina policy. Japan's ODA policy toward Vietnam has had to fight against this image problem, despite the fact that Japan had clearly begun to delink ODA from parochial business interests and to use it as a diplomatic tool a long time ago. In 1994 Japan's ODA was 84 percent untied, and only 27 percent was contracted by Japanese companies. Such a record was not built in a day, but these facts themselves may be subject to a wide range of interpretations depending on one's prejudices. The close government-business relationship in the decision-making process concerning ODA has become an old story, and private Japanese businesses now complain about these changes and see the government's policy as serving U.S. interests.

The shift in Japan's Indochina policy has not necessarily been as dramatic nor has it been taken as seriously as the policymakers wanted, but the changes of the paradigm behind the subtle policy shift have been noteworthy. History shows that Japan has in fact changed significantly whenever the international system has undergone transformation: the Meiji Restoration followed the opening of the country, the rise of militarism followed in the wake of the Great Depression, and a pacifist Japan developed under Pax Americana.

In the postwar years, the pattern of Japan's external engagement came to be conditioned on a virtual lack of a political basis, both externally and internally, of bold initiatives. The uniquely strong and centralized system of Pax Americana provided Japan with a stable external environment, which fostered this minimalist tendency. The transformation of Pax Americana, however, became obvious with the Nixon-Kissinger diplomacy in the late 1960s and the early 1970s. The Fukuda Doctrine was Japan's response to the new international environment in the 1970s. It represented an aspiration for something more general, a new political role reflecting regional imperatives.

The impact of the demise of the Cold War system has been more profound. In Southeast Asia, ASEAN has become increasingly confident in its ability to handle its own affairs, including political and security issues. Vietnam joined ASEAN in 1995, which indicates that the integration of Vietnam in a wider Southeast Asian context is now irreversible. Accordingly, the scope of Japan's regional engagement is steadily becoming broader, and Japan's policy toward Vietnam and Indochina has greater political ramifications than before. In the 1970s, Japan's diplomatic aspiration was at the mercy of major power relations, which Japan simply attempted to avoid being entangled in. In coming years, Japan will probably have to deal with these highly political issues. There are clear signs showing that Japan is moving in this direction, including its bid to become a permanent member of the United Nations Security Council.

In Japanese domestic politics, the 1955 regime, characterized by the monopoly of power by the LDP and the perpetuation of the opposition, finally broke down in 1993, and massive reorganization of the political party system is under way. Even though it will require several elections under the new electoral system before a clearer picture emerges, politicians have began to talk about the substance of Japan's international profile. Eventually, contentious issues concerning the future course of Japan in the international community, such as constitutional revision, Japan's participation in multilateral peace keeping operations, Japan's response to a precarious situation on the Korean peninsula, and a policy to cope with an increasingly assertive China, may become an important source of both cohesion and division among political parties.

The future direction of these external and internal changes confronting Japan depends as much on the reaction of the United States as on Japan's choice, because of its influence, which after all is still formidable, the greatest in the world. Japan's external relations have now become diverse, and the U.S.-Japanese relationship, being the most important one, has come to be regarded as important in a wider international context. In the final analysis, Japan's coping with mounting regional challenges from China, Vietnam, and the embryonic ASEAN Regional Forum will not be successful without crafting a new partnership with the United States.

Today Vietnam has become a dynamic regional actor: in its relations with China, the ASEAN countries, Cambodia, Laos, the United States, and the other members of the ASEAN Regional Forum. In coming years, Japan's policy toward Vietnam will increasingly unfold in this larger regional context, with a view to facilitating the integration of Vietnam in the post-Cold War Asia Pacific.

Notes

1. Seki Tomoda, *Nyumon: gendai Nihon-gaiko* [Introduction to Contemporary Japanese Diplomacy] (Tokyo: Chuo Koron Sha, 1988), p. 58.

2. For details, see Masaya Shiraishi, *Japanese Relations with Vietnam: 1951–1987* (Ithaca: Southeast Asia Program, Cornell University, 1990), pp. 58–69; Juichi Inada, "Taietsuenjo toketsu wo meguru Nihon no seisaku to gaiko-teki imi" [Japan's Policy to Freeze Its Aid to Vietnam and Its Diplomatic Implications], in *Indoshina wo meguru kokusai-kankei: taiwa to taiketsu [International Relations Surrounding Indochina: Dialogue and Confrontation]*, edited by Tadashi Mio (Tokyo: Nihon Kokusai Mondai Kenkyu Jo, 1988).

3. Sueo Sudo, *The Fukuda Doctrine and ASEAN: New Dimensions in Japanese Foreign Policy* (Singapore: Institute of Southeast Asian Studies, 1992), p. 163.

4. Charles E. Morrison, "Japan and the ASEAN Countries: The Evolution of Japan's Regional Role," in *The Political Economy of Japan, Volume 2: The Changing International Context*, edited by Takashi Inoguchi and Daniel I. Okimoto (Stanford: Stanford University Press, 1988), pp. 418–419.

5. *ASEAN Summit Meeting, Bali, February 23–25, 1976* (Jakarta: State Secretariat of the Republic of Indonesia, 1976).

6. Masahiko Ebashi and Yasuhiro Yamada, *Shinsei Betonamu no keizai: hirakeyuku sono shijo [Economy of the New Vietnam: Its Developing Market]* (Tokyo: JETRO, 1978); Shiraishi, *Japanese Relations with Vietnam*, pp. 53–55.

7. For detailed examinations of this policy formulation process, see ibid., and Tomoda, *Nyumon.*

8. Sudo, *The Fukuda Doctrine and ASEAN,* p. 164.

9. Hisashi Owada, "Trilateralism: A Japanese Perspective," *International Security,* 5, no. 3 (Winter 1980/81), p. 24.

10. *"Final Communique, The Meeting of ASEAN Heads of Government"* (Jakarta: ASEAN Secretariat, 1977), p. 79.

11. "ASEAN-Japan Joint Statement, 7th August, 1977," ibid., p. 100.

12. For more, see Tomoda, *Nyumon,* and Sudo, *The Fukuda Doctrine and ASEAN.*

13. Sadako Ogata, *Normalization with China: A Comparative Study of U.S. and Japanese Processes* (Berkeley: Institute of East Asian Studies, University of California, 1988), pp. 66–71.

14. Sudo, *The Fukuda Doctrine and ASEAN,* p. 199.

15. *Asahi Shinbun,* January 17, 1979.

16. *Asahi Shinbun,* January 22, 1979.

17. Shiraishi, *Japanese Relations with Vietnam,* pp. 79, 129.

18. Advisory Group on Defense Issues, *The Modality of the Security and Defense Capability of Japan: The Outlook for the 21st Century* (August 12, 1994).

19. Takakazu Kuriyama, "Gekido no 90 nendai to Nihon gaiko no shin-tenkai" [The Turbulent 1990s and New Development of Japanese Diplomacy], *Gaiko Foramu,* no. 20 (May 1990).

20. For more on Japan's policy on multilateral security dialogue, see Yoshihide Soeya, "The Evolution of Japanese Thinking and Policies on Cooperative Security in the 1980s and 1990s," *Australian Journal of International Affairs,* 48, no. 1 (May 1994).

21. Briefing by the Foreign Ministry, July 24, 1991. See also Ministry of Foreign Affairs, ed., *Gaiko seisho, heisei 3–nenban [Diplomatic Bluebook, 1991]* (Tokyo: Okurasho Insatsukyoku, 1992), pp. 71–73.

22. "Address by Prime Minister Miyazawa at the National Press Club," Washington, D.C., July 2, 1992.

23. "ASEAN Kakudai Gaisho Kaigi Zentai Kaigi Nakayama Gaimu daijin sutetomento" [Statement by Foreign Minister Nakayama at the ASEAN Post-Ministerial Conference], Kuala Lumpur, July 22, 1991.

24. ASEAN Institutes of Strategic and International Studies, *A Time for Initiative: Proposals for the Consideration of the Fourth ASEAN Summit* (Jakarta, June 4, 1991).

25. Tadashi Ikeda, "Kanbojia wahei eo michi" [A Road to the Cambodian Peace], *Gaiko Foramu,* no. 80 (May 1995), p. 87.

26. For a detailed account of Japanese diplomacy toward Cambodia in this period, see ibid., and Seki Tomoda, "Nihon no kanbojia gaiko: seijiteki-yakuwari no jikken" [Japan's Cambodia Diplomacy: An Experiment of a Political Role], *Ajia daigaku Ajia kenkyujo kiyo,* no. 19 (1992).

27. Interview with Thai Foreign Ministry officials, Bangkok, December 15, 1990; interview with a former cabinet member of the Chatichai government, August 8, 1994.

28. "Framework for a Comprehensive Political Settlement of the Cambodia Conflict" (mimeo), New York City, August 28, 1990.

29. "Proposed Structure for the Agreements on a Comprehensive Political Settlement of the Cambodia Conflict" (mimeo), Paris, November 26, 1990.

30. Interviews with Foreign Ministry officials of Japan, June 20, 1992, and June 28, 1993.

31. The elections gave 58 seats to the Funcinpec, led by Prince Norodom Ranariddh, a son of Prince Sihanouk, 51 seats to the Cambodian People's Party of the former Phnom Penh government led by Hun Sen, 10 seats to the Buddhist Liberal Democratic

Party led by Son San, and 1 seat to Molinaka, the only one of 16 minor parties to gain a seat.

32. According to a survey conducted by the *Asahi Shimbun* during the debate, among 81 academicians specializing in the Constitution surveyed, 14 percent said Japanese participation in PKO in any form is unconstitutional and 67 percent said that Japan can participate only in nonmilitary operations of PKO and that taking part in the peacekeeping forces is unconstitutional. *Asahi Shimbun,* November 18, 1991.

33. *Mainichi Shinbun,* June 6, 1994.

34. *Asahi Shinbun,* May 8, 1990.

35. *Asahi Shinbun,* March 20, 1992.

36. *Mainichi Shinbun,* June 29, 1994.

37. *Asahi Shinbun,* March 29, 1993.

38. *Asahi Shinbun,* May 8, 1990.

39. Tran Hoang Kim, *Economy of Vietnam: Review and Statistics* (Hanoi: Statistical Publishing House, 1994), p. 183.

40. The State Committee for Cooperation and Investment (SCCI), *Foreign Direct Investment in Vietnam* (Hanoi: Office of SCCI, June 1993).

41. Do Duc Dinh, "Vietnam-Japan: Aid, Trade, Investment and Implications," *Vietnam Economic Review,* No. 4(26) (Hanoi: December 1994), p. 32.

42. Ibid., p. 30.

43. Keidanren, *Keidanren betonamu keizai chosa mission hokoku-sho [Report of the Keidanren Research Mission on the Vietnamese Economy]* (February 1992), pp. 5–6.

44. Keidanren Economic Cooperation Department, "Nihon-Betonamu Godo Keizai Kaigi no gaiyo" [Outline of the Japan-Vietnam Joint Economic Conference], unpublished paper.

45. "Kaifu sori no ASEAN-shokoku homon ni okeru seisaku enzetsu: Nihon to ASEAN—shin-jidai no seijukushita patonashippu wo motomete" [Policy speech by Prime Minister Kaifu on his visit to ASEAN countries: Japan and ASEAN—in Search of a Mature Partnership in a New Era], Singapore, May 3, 1991.

46. "Policy Speech by Prime Minister Miyazawa: The New Era of the Asia-Pacific and Japan-ASEAN Cooperation," Bangkok, January 16, 1993.

47. *Yomiuri Shimbun,* March 1, 1995.

9

U.S.-Vietnam Normalization— Past, Present, Future

Frederick Z. Brown

On July 11, 1995, President Bill Clinton announced that the United States would, at long last, establish diplomatic relations with the Socialist Republic of Vietnam (SRV). In 1996, although the U.S. relationship with Vietnam remains far from "normal," the groundwork for better bilateral cooperation has been laid and with the president's decision an important step toward closure of a painful chapter in American history has been taken.

In diplomacy, recognition does not constitute approval of one state by another, but the residual political and psychological impact of the Vietnam War on the United States rendered that textbook definition irrelevant. American politicians, skittish about confronting the only war the United States ever lost, viewed normalization not as foreign policy but as an intensely political domestic issue. It was not unlike the atmosphere that for decades surrounded relations with a China that U.S. politicians felt had been "lost" in 1949. There, rapprochement began with an exchange of liaison offices in 1973; the United States reserved diplomatic recognition for another six years before upgrading to embassies. The U.S. embargo on economic and trade relations with Vietnam had been lifted in February 1994, and liaison offices in Hanoi and Washington were subsequently approved. But there were highly sensitive domestic concerns to balance before formal recognition could be extended to Vietnam, largely because of Bill Clinton's decision as a young man to decline military service in Vietnam. The White House believed that recognition would gain few votes but could lose many. Inevitably, the timing of recognition thus turned on a judgment of political risk in the 1996 presidential election.[1] The November 1994 congressional elections, which had ushered in a Republican Congress for the first time in 50 years, altered the domestic American political climate and appeared to raise new fears about normalization. If normalization did not occur by the end of 1995, so the conventional wisdom went, it would be out of the question until mid-1997.

Senator Bob Smith, of New Hampshire, along with powerful allies including then-Majority Leader Bob Dole and Foreign Relations Committee chairman Senator Jesse Helms, resolutely pronounced the position that Vietnam had "not done enough" on prisoner of war and missing in action (POW/MIA) cooperation to qualify for diplomatic recognition. When the administration in spring 1995 signalled its intention to move in the direction of normalization, the senators pledged to offer a resolution expressly opposing normalization on the grounds of Vietnamese lack of cooperation. Variations of this resolution, which could have been attached to the State Department authorization bill or other legislation already on the calendar, criticized the Hanoi regime sharply and laid on demands beyond POW/MIA resolution (human rights and democratization) that would have to be met before normalization could take place.[2]

Senators John McCain and John Kerry, both decorated Vietnam veterans and the former a prisoner of war in Vietnam for five years, took an opposite position. They saw normalization as both a worthy foreign policy objective *and* as a way to heal grievous domestic wounds. Arguing that Vietnam's pattern of cooperation in recent years showed genuine determination to resolve the POW/MIA issue, McCain and Kerry—one a Republican, the other a Democrat—became prime movers in the bipartisan effort on Capitol Hill to establish full relations. Simultaneously, in the Congress and among the United States' friends and allies in ASEAN there was growing concern about China's preemptive claims of sovereignty in the South China Sea.[3]

With the chill in U.S.-China relations over Taiwan, human rights, and the South China Sea, a strategic argument for engaging Hanoi gained resonance within Congress.[4] In the end, this strategic argument tipped the balance among White House advisors. Secretary of State Warren Christopher came out publicly in favor of moving ahead with Vietnam. On the eve of Vietnam's entry into ASEAN, it was widely recognized that the United States needed to enter into regional security discussions with ASEAN and with Vietnam bilaterally, and for such conversations to have weight, diplomatic relations with Vietnam were necessary. Although congressional discontent continued, there was little public outcry against recognition following the president's July 11 announcement. Secretary Christopher attended the ASEAN Regional Forum discussions and subsequent ministerial conference in Brunei in early August 1995, during which the South China Sea and other security issues were frankly discussed. Christopher then visited Hanoi (stopping briefly in Phnom Penh) for discussions with the top Vietnamese leadership, thus inaugurating a new relationship between the United States and Southeast Asia, based in part on shared strategic interests.

With diplomatic relations between the United States and Vietnam finally established, five policy issues are preeminent in the bilateral relationship:

- economic relations, namely, the granting of nondiscriminatory trading (most favored nation—MFN) status and access to the U.S. generalized system of preferences (GSP);
- the POW/MIA issue;
- human rights;
- political change;
- last and by no means least, Vietnam as the seventh member of the Association of Southeast Asian Nations (ASEAN) and as a player in the strategic equations of the South China Sea.

Vietnam and the Cold War

Normalization of relations with the SRV was never some sort of magical moment that could be achieved by the stroke of a pen—it had always been a *process,* not a fixed destination. This fact was born of history, of our countries' distinct geopolitical situations, and of our different social value systems. The United States had never enjoyed anything approaching normal relations with any government of Vietnam, either North or South, or with the Vietnamese people. Until 1975, we had been effectively at war with half of Vietnam for the first 21 years of that country's independence from France. Mutual hostility between a unified Vietnam under communism and the United States had endured. Only with the end of the Cold War in the early 1990s did the environment begin to improve.[5]

One major obstacle to normalization—Vietnam's invasion and ten-year occupation of Cambodia—had been largely resolved when Vietnam, bowing to international pressure and the realities of the end of the Cold War, signed the October 1991 Paris Agreements on a Comprehensive Political Settlement of the Cambodia Conflict. During the tense peace-keeping presence of the United Nations Transitional Authority in Cambodia (UNTAC) from November 1991 through September 1993, Vietnam made good on its pledge to keep hands off the evolution of political events in Cambodia, thus satisfying the regional objectives of the United States, ASEAN, and China.

In 1993 and 1994, the SRV's relations with the United States moved in a positive direction precisely because of the Cambodia settlement and, on the larger post-Cold War stage, thanks to Vietnam's vastly altered strategic situation. The gradual relaxation of the U.S. embargo on trade with Vietnam after 1993 documents this movement. As far back as 1946, when the Truman administration made the decision to support France's reimposition of colonial control over Vietnam, the embargo's prime purpose was to obtain geopolitical advantage against the communist superpowers in the context of the Cold War. "Winning" in Vietnam was part of that syndrome. The ideas of Vietnam as a country and the Vietnamese as a distinct people were all but unknown in the United States; policymakers for the most part viewed Vietnam, North and South, not as an independent entity but as a strategic pawn on the global chessboard.

The U.S. embargo was first imposed against parts of Vietnam while the country was still a French colony.[6] The Trade Agreements Extension Act of 1951 required the U.S. president to suspend the most favored nation (MFN) status of communist countries as a sanction against their support of North Korea and China, then in armed conflict with the United States. The sanctions remained in place against North Vietnam after the country was divided at the seventeenth parallel by the Geneva Accords of July 1954. In 1964, the U.S. involvement in Vietnam escalated in support of its ally in the South. The embargo was reinforced by adding North Vietnam to the list of countries subject to the existing Foreign Assets Control Regulations. In 1975, the embargo was extended in the same way to all of Vietnam. The Departments of the Treasury and of Commerce implemented the embargo. Successive presidents extended the embargo year by year in a routine action that could have been reversed by the executive branch at any time under provision of the Trading with the Enemy Act (TWEA). The embargo also froze the Vietnamese government's assets in the United States. In 1994, these assets amounted to U.S.$325 million with accrued interest; the majority of U.S. claims against Vietnam, amounting to about $208 million, were from U.S. oil companies and, geographically, from California.[7]

The embargo's impact waxed and waned over the decades. From 1951 to 1954 it was intended to bolster France's military effort against the Viet Minh and to show the new communist government of China, which gave safe haven and material support to the Viet Minh after 1949, that the United States would resist international communist expansion by all means. Ideologically, embargoes in Vietnam and elsewhere symbolized the Cold War era. The support of the Soviet Union and China for their Vietnamese communist allies became one of the bitterest issue of those Cold War years. For Presidents John F. Kennedy and Lyndon B. Johnson, Vietnam was "our Asian Berlin." In fact, however, the embargo had little direct effect on the base areas of Ho Chi Minh's guerrillas before 1954 or on the course of the Second Indochina War, 1954–75, simply because the Soviet Union and China could (and did) supply North Vietnam with massive amounts of arms, food, and technical support to fight the South Vietnamese and their American allies.

Soon after the fall of Saigon in 1975, Vietnam was subject to a comprehensive regime of U.S. sanctions, including a prohibition on commercial and financial transactions and private investment in Vietnam. Most critically, the United States convinced other member-countries of the World Bank, the International Monetary Fund (IMF), and the Asian Development Bank (ADB) to withhold loans from Vietnam. The Carter administration, in early 1977, attempted to set the relationship on a fresh track; here again Cold War politics were part of the rationale. When the Soviets supported Vietnam's aggression against Cambodia in 1978, the U.S. embargo became a lever to force Vietnam to negotiate a settlement of the war on terms acceptable to the United States and ASEAN. With the end of the Cold War and dismantlement of the Soviet-Vietnamese strategic connection, the embargo's purpose evolved further to buttress the internationally sponsored Cambodia peace agreement and to speed resolution of the POW/MIA issue.

Throughout the decades of the 1970s and 1980s, the embargo—that is, the conditions under which it would be lifted—was used by both sides as a bargaining chip. In 1977, the Jimmy Carter administration in its negotiations with a unified Vietnam agreed to unconditional establishment of diplomatic relations, after which the United States would lift the embargo, support international financial institution (IFI) loans to Vietnam, and consider granting MFN status. Vietnam refused in the absence of economic assistance in the amount of U.S.$3.25 billion, which it claimed had been promised by President Richard Nixon as part of the 1973 Paris accords. For Washington, still smarting under the humiliation of its 1975 defeat, demands for reparations were unacceptable, if only because Hanoi's violations of the Paris Accords in 1973–75 had obviated any implied obligation under Nixon's "best efforts" pledge. The U.S. Congress responded to Vietnam's demand by passing legislation that categorically ruled out any aid to the victorious North. In September 1978 Hanoi withdrew the reparations demand, but the window of opportunity had closed. The Carter administration believed an opening to Hanoi would jeopardize the higher priority of securing normalization with China. In October 1978 Vietnam and the Soviet Union signed a mutual security treaty. The Vietnamese invasion and occupation of Cambodia two months later dashed any lingering hopes for normalization and an end to the embargo.[8]

The Cambodia Issue

The Vietnamese invasion of Cambodia in December 1978 and its subsequent ten-year military occupation heightened the rationale for the American embargo. Between 1979 and 1990, the members of the United Nations backed ASEAN's annual resolution in the General Assembly demanding Vietnam's withdrawal from Cambodia, and Vietnam found itself politically and economically isolated. The United States saw the Cambodia conflict both as aggression by Vietnamese communism and as a proxy war between China and the Soviet Union. Simultaneously, because of Vietnam's intimate links with the Soviet Union, the conflict became one more facet of the U.S.-Soviet strategic rivalry in the Pacific, exemplified by the Soviets' use of Cam Ranh Bay, the former American military facility. Cambodia became a key element of the "strategic relationship" between Beijing and Washington in confronting the Soviet Union and its surrogate, Vietnam.

The Ronald Reagan administration restated the U.S. condition for normalization: a complete and verified withdrawal of Vietnamese troops from Cambodia. The "pace and scope of normalization" would inevitably be influenced by Vietnamese cooperation in resolving the POW/MIA and other humanitarian issues. In 1985, the administration amplified this condition: the Vietnamese withdrawal would have to be "in the context of a compromise political settlement in Cambodia." As Cambodia peace negotiations commenced and the Vietnamese military completed its military withdrawal in September 1989, the administration became increasingly detailed about what Hanoi must do—namely, actively engage in a peace settlement and influence the "puppet regime" of Prime Minister Hun Sen (State of Cambodia, SOC) in Phnom Penh to do likewise—in order to begin formal U.S.-Vietnam normalization.

In April 1991 the U.S. administration announced a timetable for normalization of relations with Vietnam. The so-called road map for normalization was the administration's answer to critics charging that American policy toward Indochina was adrift. The road map attempted to codify a *quid pro quo* procedure whereby Vietnam knew what was expected of it and what benefits would accrue as reciprocal steps in the normalization process were taken. It was deliberately vague in parts, specific in others. The United States was the sole interpreter of when a given condition had been fulfilled. To critics, the road map was a unilateral, inherently unfair U.S. demand levied on Vietnam. To practitioners of *realpolitik,* the road map stated the obvious: that the United States held the whip handle. The road map stated unequivocally the U.S. positions that Vietnam had to accept as a practical basis for moving incrementally toward full diplomatic relations and a lifting of the embargo. Both camps were, of course, correct in their interpretations. The road map reflected an abiding American distrust of Hanoi's commitment to honoring diplomatic agreements. It also represented a crude political fact of life: while imperative for Hanoi, normalization was a low priority in the array of Washington's global foreign policy objectives.

In April 1991, few observers imagined the disintegration of the Soviet Union that would occur four months later. Vietnam, already under pressure to compromise on Cambodia and suffering from drastic reductions in Soviet aid, faced additional economic woes. It had little choice but to pursue normalization under terms set by the United States. One result of the global geopolitical sea changes of 1991 was Vietnam's signing of the United Nations-sponsored Cambodia peace accords, drafted by the Paris International Conference on Cambodia, together with Vietnamese-cooperation in their implementation since then.[9] A second result of these changes was increased cooperation from Vietnam on resolving POW/MIA issues.

The POW/MIA Issue

Vietnam had met U.S. demands regarding Cambodia. The George Bush administration, however, maintained that *all* requirements of phase one of the road map had not been completed, specifically on repatriation of MIA remains and access to all information the United States desired (for example, Vietnamese logs, maps, and provincial reports relevant to missing personnel). Recognizing *some* progress, in March 1992 the U.S. government pledged a $3 million humanitarian aid package in the form of scholarships to Vietnamese students coming to the United States, free shipment to Vietnam of NGO humanitarian assistance, and expanded aid in prosthetics and health care by U.S. medical teams on MIA field searches. Also, telephone communications between Vietnam and the United States were restored. High-level normalization talks were held in New York (November 1991) and Hanoi (March 1992), and working-level discussions continued. Commercial transactions meeting "basic human needs" criteria (such as prosthetics and other health care, assessment of education and training needs, and books) were routinely allowed; restrictions on U.S. NGOs operating in Vietnam were lifted. The game, however, was still *quid pro quo* as judged by Washington alone.

It was during this period that Vietnam changed its policy significantly and agreed to certain key U.S. requests on POW/MIAs. These included access to Vietnamese military records from the war and quick-reaction investigations into "live sighting" reports through the use of helicopters to go virtually anywhere in Vietnam in search of MIA remains or information.

The radically changed geopolitical scene dictated this shift. Japan had made clear it would not go against the United States regarding official development assistance (ODA) or in the IFIs while POW/MIAs remain a highly charged political issue during the election year of 1992. Vietnam received little comfort from Russia's President Boris Yeltsin, who, in an effort to win American favor, pledged Moscow's full cooperation—and muddied the waters further by stating that Americans captured during the Korean and Vietnam wars and Cold War operations of past decades might have been held in the Soviet Union or could even still be alive.

The April 1992 visit of the U.S. Senate Select Committee on POW/MIAs, led by Senators John Kerry (Democrat of Massachusetts) and Bob Smith (Republican of New Hampshire), impressed the Vietnamese leadership. The committee's final report issued January 13, 1993, stated, ". . . there is no compelling evidence that proves that any American remains alive in captivity in Southeast Asia." But the committee's contentious hearings and the public squabbles between factions within the U.S. government and among POW/MIA interest groups highlighted the intractability of this painful issue. Senator Smith retreated to his original negative position on Vietnamese cooperation. While better Vietnamese cooperation had been gained, the passionate discord on the American side regarding live sightings and alleged government conspiracies and "cover-ups" from the Vietnam War era prolonged the agonies.

The U.S. position, combined with Vietnam's inadequate legal framework and weak infrastructure and uncertainty about Hanoi's capability to implement reforms, had clearly dampened enthusiasm for international investment in the country. The withholding of approval for IFI loans continued to have a strong negative impact on Vietnam's economy. With the Cambodia problem removed as a regional irritant, the direct impact of the embargo on Vietnam's ability to engage in international trade and commerce began to diminish markedly. Commercial relations between Vietnam and Japan and the ASEAN countries escalated rapidly in 1992; the European nations no longer held back aid or trade. Foreign businesses were actually delighted that they did not face American commercial competition (some might have liked to see the embargo left in place). Nonetheless, all potential traders and investors in Vietnam, no matter of what nationality, saw the U.S. persistence in maintaining a de facto veto over IFI development loans as a hindrance to the creation of a viable investment climate in Vietnam. The U.S. embargo was viewed as primarily a weapon in POW/MIA negotiations, a bilateral matter that concerned only the United States and Vietnam, an emotional hangover from 1975 that ill befitted the world's only superpower.

Since 1975, during sporadic negotiations, both Hanoi and Washington had found it useful to characterize the POW/MIA issue as humanitarian rather than political: Hanoi did not care to be accused of trafficking in human remains for political gain, and Washington took the position that Vietnam was obliged to cooperate without any political compensation. In truth, both knew POW/MIAs were highly political. Vietnam became more responsive to American demands only when it recognized fully the domestic political importance of this issue to Washington and the blunt fact that relations would not get better until the issue was satisfactorily addressed from the American perspective. Hanoi's learning curve was further accelerated after 1991 by the rapid collapse of the Soviet Union, with all that event implied for Vietnam's strategic position vis-à-vis China. Since the Sixth Congress of the Vietnamese Communist Party in December 1986, the Hanoi Politburo had admitted the need to expand Vietnam's contacts with the noncommunist world. The decline and fall of the Communist Party of the Soviet Union brought real urgency to this diversification.

It was during the Reagan Administration that the National League of Families of American Prisoners and Missing in Southeast Asia had become prominent in the U.S. domestic political machinations on the POW/MIA issue. The league assumed the coordinating role for communication between the administration and the approximately 2,400 families with relatives missing in Southeast Asia, mainly in Vietnam or areas controlled during the war by North Vietnam. Building close contacts with staff members of the National Security Council and Department of Defense, the league's executive director became a member of the official U.S. government working group on the POW/MIA issue and accompanied government missions to Vietnam. Charging the Nixon, Gerald Ford, and Carter administrations with betrayal of the POW/MIA families and rallying the support of several veterans' organizations and conservative elements of the Republican Party, the league used its political clout to keep the Congress attentive to the POW/MIA issue, indeed so successfully that by 1988 few members of Congress would openly dare challenge the almost theological assumption that Americans might still be held prisoner in Vietnam.

The league's influence began to diminish somewhat under the Bush administration, as pressures increased from the U.S. business community to broaden U.S. policy beyond POW/MIAs and toward the commercial opportunities that Hanoi's accommodation on Cambodia (its withdrawal of the Vietnamese Army in September 1989) began to make possible. The league viewed Hanoi's increased cooperation on POW/MIA matters as helpful but by no means enough to justify any relaxation of the embargo. In the waning months of the Bush administration a sharp split emerged between the league and some parts of the Bush Administration (the Departments of State and

Commerce) over how to deal with the Vietnamese. The league's executive director went so far as to brand General John Vessey, former U.S. Army Chief of Staff and President Bush's special emissary to Hanoi on humanitarian affairs, as a traitor. In March 1995, the league flatly refuted statements by Secretary of Defense William Perry that Vietnam was cooperating fully and accused Assistant Secretary of State Winston Lord of "testifying in error" before the Senate Appropriations Committee on POW/MIA matters. The League sharply criticized business groups for lobbying Congress for expanded economic relations and remained adamantly opposed to any further steps toward normalization when President Clinton took that step in July 1995.[10]

It is worth noting that the United States had obtained remarkably permissive privileges and freedom of ground and air movement for POW/MIA search operations, including the stationing of American military personnel in Hanoi and access to archives—U.S. teams were even permitted to dig up North Vietnamese military graveyards. These search operations pumped millions of dollars directly into Vietnam's economy through helicopter rentals, wages for Vietnamese workers, provisioning, guides, excavation rights, and other support functions. The overall cost of the POW/MIA effort for 1994 was estimated at $11 million.

Loosening the Embargo

Beginning in 1992, there had been steady POW/MIA progress, thanks to joint field operations in many regions of the country by Vietnamese and American search teams. While not yielding spectacular results in terms of artifacts, remains, or information, these operations were indicative of Vietnam's seriousness of purpose and commitment of resources. Hanoi's decision in October 1992 to allow U.S. investigators to examine the war archives of Vietnam's Ministry of Defense for evidence on the fate of American servicemen seemed to be a major breakthrough. In December 1992, the Bush administration responded by partially lifting the economic embargo, allowing American companies to sign contracts on prospective commercial ventures—but not to implement them—and to perform certain other acts helpful in promoting the companies' commercial positions vis-à-vis their foreign competitors.

Rumors abounded that President Bush, in the waning days of his administration, would take further steps toward normalization, perhaps even lift the embargo entirely and agree to embassies in Hanoi and Washington. This hope proved vain. The Vietnamese, for whatever reason, had not chosen to go the last mile in providing information on the remaining one hundred or so "last known alive" cases that might have precipitated a favorable decision. But even had they done so, given the bitterness of the election campaign and Mr. Clinton's vulnerable position regarding the Vietnam War, the outgoing Republicans had no desire to spare the incoming Democrats the political misery of dealing with this delicate issue. President Clinton was left to make peace with Hanoi and to declare at some future date that the POW/MIA issue was finally resolved—and take the political heat.

Assuming office in January 1993, the Clinton administration endorsed the 1991 "road map" specifying the reciprocal steps that would be followed in the normalization process, most obviously the conditions that Vietnam would have to fulfill. The prime impediment to normalization remained a "satisfactory resolution" of the fate of American servicemen missing in Southeast Asia. After the POW/MIA issue, the road map's principle condition was continued Vietnamese cooperation on the Cambodia peace process. This condition has been satisfied by Vietnamese actions since the Paris agreements and subsequent relations with the Cambodian coalition government put in place as a result of the May 1993 national elections.

The new administration was slow to pick up Vietnam as a foreign policy issue, not only because of the political sensitivity of Vietnam for the president but also because of pressing policy problems elsewhere—Bosnia, Somalia, Russia, Haiti. On March 22, 1993, Secretary of State Warren Christopher noted the "strong business incentives" and said the United States was ready to move ahead "as soon as they [the Vietnamese] are forthcoming on the MIA issue . . . that is the only thing stopping us from lifting our sanctions." On March 31, in his hearing before the Senate Foreign Relations Committee, Assistant Secretary for East Asia and the Pacific Winston Lord elaborated on this theme but also hinted at yet another possible dimension to United States policy, namely, political change in Vietnam itself.

In April 1993, the political impact of an unconfirmed report that Vietnam had failed to release 614 American POWs at the time of the 1973 Paris accords prevented the administration from making good on the final step of phase two of the 1991 road map, that is, helping eliminate Vietnam's arrears to international financial institutions (IFIs). The administration postponed consideration of granting Vietnam access to IFI loans, which had been proposed by France and Japan for the April meeting of the IMF/World Bank. However, in June 1993, a congressional delegation returning from Hanoi argued in favor of forward movement, and the president then announced that the United States would no longer oppose IFI loans to Vietnam but that the embargo would remain in place (with the changes already made under the Bush administration).

The next six months demonstrated once more the dilemma for U.S. policy created by the emotions of the POW/MIA issue. Lifting the IFI veto *without lifting* the embargo put American businesses at an immense disadvantage in competing with foreign firms for major infrastructure projects that World Bank funds now made feasible. Yet the administration, and certainly the vocal POW/MIA lobbying groups, were unwilling to give up what was deemed the last real leverage in negotiating with Hanoi for greater access to sensitive files and tangible progress in the hundred or so discrepancy cases that the Vietnamese appeared capable of resolving. The period was marked by pressures brought to bear by dozens of leading American commercial firms (Boeing, Caterpillar, banks, major oil companies) seeking to participate in the Vietnamese market, on one hand, and against them the POW/MIA lobby supported by the American Legion and several smaller veterans groups who opposed any opening to Vietnam (the Veterans of Foreign Wars was divided but took a generally positive position on normalization).

Yet another administration delegation visited Hanoi in mid-July 1993 to press for more progress on POW/MIAs and provided more documentary evidence to help the Vietnamese resolve certain cases. In a July 21 appearance before the Senate Foreign Relations Committee, the delegation stated that the embargo should not be lifted without more progress on POW/MIAs—but they also underscored the potential commercial advantages to improved relations and the fact that other countries were beginning to dominate the Vietnam marketplace. President Clinton clung to a hard line on September 13, 1993, by signing a renewal of the embargo. The same month, however, the administration approved $3.5 million in humanitarian aid for Vietnamese orphans and prosthetics programs.[11] In December, the president changed course again and eased the embargo by allowing U.S. companies to bid on IFI-financed projects "pending a lifting of the embargo." By then, there was a sense of inevitability; the question was not "if" but "when."

On February 3, 1994, President Clinton ordered an end to the embargo, almost 47 years after its initiation against parts of Vietnam. The decision was taken after several months of intense negotiation with the Vietnamese government that reportedly achieved "tangible results," and a significant January 27 vote in the Senate that gave the president some political cover by urging that the embargo be lifted. The Senate language was attached to the House of Representatives Bill H.R.2333, and it was signed into law by the president as P.L. 103–236 on April 30, 1994. And on May 26, 1994, Vietnam and the United States announced that liaison offices would be established in their respective capitals "in two or three months."

Addressing the Constraints on Economic Relations[12]

With the lifting of the embargo and establishment of diplomatic relations, two sanctions against Vietnam remained in effect as of July 1996: the denial of nondiscriminatory (most favored nation, MFN) status with regard to Vietnam in its trade with the United States, and Vietnam's ineligibility for the U.S. generalized system of preferences (GSP). Some complicated steps must be taken to obtain MFN and GSP for Vietnam and also to gain access to benefits under the Export-Import Bank of the United States (Ex-Im Bank) and the Overseas Private Investment Corporation (OPIC).

Absence of MFN status means that the United States assesses customs duties on imports from Vietnam at the high rates enacted by the Tariff Act of 1930 rather than the substantially lower rates resulting from concessions granted to other countries since 1930. A U.S. statutory policy dating back to 1934 and codified in section 126 of the Trade Act of 1974 stipulated that concessionary rates granted in negotiations to any country are applied as a matter of general policy to imports from all U.S. trading partners. This policy was modified by section 5 of the Trade Agreements Extension Act of 1951, which required the president to suspend the MFN status of most communist countries as a sanction against their support of North Korea in its armed conflict with the United States. As described earlier in this chapter, "any part of . . . Vietnam which may be under Communist domination or control . . ." was included in this provision. The proscription was incorporated into the revised Tariff Schedules of the United States (1962), which contained a list of "Communist countries" denied MFN status under the schedule's General Headnote 3(a).

Without MFN, the kind of products Vietnam is most likely to export at this stage of its national development (inexpensive apparel, footwear, basic household equipment, and perhaps assembled electronic gear) cannot enter the American market at a competitive price; this has been the experience of such countries as Taiwan, Korea, Thailand, Malaysia, the Philippines, and others in Asia who have entered the American market in an earlier era. Two events relevant to Vietnam's eligibility for MFN status had occurred in early 1975. On January 3, the Trade Act of 1974 was enacted, which in section 401 mandated continued denial of MFN to any country denied such status at the time of its enactment, except as provided for in Title IV of the act. The other, based on the original denial language of the General Head-note, automatically extended suspension of MFN status to South Vietnam after its conquest by North Vietnam in April 1975. When the Harmonized Tariff Schedule was enacted under the Omnibus Trade and Competitiveness Act of 1989, reference to "Communist countries" was deleted, but Vietnam was among the countries specifically denied MFN status.

The evolution of these proscriptions enacted in 1951 and 1975 means that specific legislation may be required to grant MFN to all of Vietnam (that is, *restoration* to South Vietnam and *initial granting* to North Vietnam). The legislation could be one of two types: either specifically making restoration provisions of Title IV applicable to all of Vietnam, or granting outright to Vietnam regular (that is, unconditional and unlimited) MFN status. Either measure would have to be considered under standard congressional procedures and subject to approval by the House and Senate.

In the event that restoration takes place under Title IV, the procedure applicable by law to "nonmarket economies" (NME) requires compliance with the freedom of emigration under the Jackson-Vanik amendment and the conclusion of a bilateral trade agreement. The requirements of Jackson-Vanik can be fulfilled by either a presidential determination that Vietnam is in full compliance with the freedom-of-emigration requirements or a waiver if the president determines that the waiver will substantially promote the objectives of Jackson-Vanik. The *initial issuance* of a waiver does not require congressional approval nor is it subject to congressional disapproval, but it must be renewed semiannually and it is subject to disapproval by a joint resolution of Congress after the first year.

The trade agreement required by law must contain a reciprocal grant of MFN status as well as several safeguard provisions. Its implementation (for three years) must be approved by the enactment of a joint congressional resolution. Renewals are not subject to congressional approval or disapproval, but again political risk to the Clinton administration in the 1996 election year could be present.

Another provision of the Trade Act of 1974 (section 403) denies MFN status to any NME country that the president determines is not cooperating with the United States in accounting for, repatriating, or returning remains of U.S. personnel missing in action in Southeast Asia. With regard to GSP, Vietnam is currently denied the status of a "beneficiary developing country" (BDC), which permits an array of products of countries so designated to be imported to the United Status free of duty. Although South Vietnam pre-1975 was designated a BDC, it was omitted from the 1976 executive order implementing GSP; North Vietnam has never been designated a BDC.

Three conditions for BDC designation are relevant to Vietnam today. Designation is generally denied countries that (1) have not settled or are not in the process of settling expropriation or nationalization claims against it made by U.S. citizens; (2) do not afford internationally recognized worker rights to its workers; or (3) do not have MFN status, are not members of the IMF, or are "controlled by international communism." The claims question has already been settled during negotiations leading up to formal recognition announced in July 1995. The workers rights condition may be waived by the president; Vietnam is a member of the IMF; and "international communism" is no longer a relevant consideration. However, it seems quite possible that the Congress (Republican or Democrat) may adopt an adverse construction of "international communism"; if so, MFN status—and consequent eligibility for GSP privileges— will be difficult for Vietnam in the next several years.

Financing of U.S. exports to Vietnam through export credits from the Ex-Im Bank remains restricted in several ways until it is determined (1) that Vietnam is no longer a Marxist economy, and (2) that the requirements of Jackson-Vanik are satisfied. The principal programs affected are export credits and credit guarantees or insurance of the Ex-Im Bank and export credits of the Commodity Credit Corporation (CCC). The Ex-Im Bank is specifically prohibited from engaging in any transaction that benefits a "Marxist-Leninist" country, unless the president certifies that such transaction are in the national interest. Again, despite Hanoi's reforms in the direction of a market economy, the Clinton administration will be unable to make a convincing case that Vietnam is *not* a Marxist-Leninist country (Hanoi's rhetoric to its own people confirms that it is).

While there are no restrictions on U.S. private investment in Vietnam, such investment is in effect discouraged by two provisions affecting the investor's ability to use the OPIC facility. One is the NME provision of Jackson-Vanik; the other restricts OPIC operations in communist countries by virtue of OPIC legislation being part of foreign assistance legislation. Under existing legislation, the president is granted discretion in certifying that a country is "making progress" in key areas so that waivers may be granted to obtain benefits. For members of the Commonwealth of Independent States (CIS) making a political as well as an economic transition from communism, the "making progress" argument can be legitimately used. However, for Vietnam, it would be difficult for the president to certify positively at this time regarding two of the five essential criteria for waivers: freedom of association and genuine collective bargaining in Vietnamese labor unions.

Human Rights and the Future of
U.S.-Vietnam Relations*

In a very real sense, the "easy" part of normalization had been accomplished by 1995. Today, the bilateral relationship appears to have reached a certain plateau of accomplishment. From 1996 and into the next century, it is probably fair to predict that domestic political considerations extant in both countries seem likely to limit development of political relations.[13] The evolution of the relationship will be played out on a field where American and Vietnamese objectives are sometimes compatible, in other cases in conflict. For the United States these objectives include resolving the POW/MIA issue, establishing satisfactory commercial relations (particularly intellectual property rights protection), seeing Vietnam move toward greater respect for international human rights standards, and creating a strategic dimension to the relationship in the context of the ASEAN Regional Forum and relations with China. For Vietnam the key objectives are gaining MFN and GSP privileges, expanding U.S. investment, gaining access to technology, and using the American connection and ASEAN membership as a strategic lever with China.

The big question marks in future relations are conflicting positions regarding human rights and political change and the degree to which these differences will prevent progress in the commercial and other areas of mutual interest. Next steps on economic relations depend heavily on the acquiescence of the Republican Congress and its perceptions of Vietnamese actions on these questions, as well as continued cooperation on POW/MIAs.

Psychologically for Americans, there is no precise separation of human rights from "democratization." When a Vietnamese writer is imprisoned for advocating pluralism or "peaceful evolution," the two issues obviously merge. The American involvement in Vietnam occurred for a variety of motives, not the least being pure great-power politics and what we perceived as Cold War imperatives. Ingrained in these were concerns about human rights and what we saw as a desirable political order for a future

---

*The sudden death of Vice Foreign Minister of Foreign Affairs Le Mai on June 13, 1996, removes from the scene the architect of Vietnam's rapprochement with the United States. An astute judge of Vietnam's long-term foreign policy interests, Le Mai defended normalization against criticism by Vietnamese Communist Party conservatives. Le Mai was responsible for convincing the party of the necessity of responding to U.S. demands on POW/MIA matters. He also managed Vietnam's acceptance into ASEAN. Le Mai was slated to become foreign minister after the 8th VNCP Congress and was on the fast track to eventual Politburo membership.

Vietnam. The Wilsonian impulse in American foreign policy was part and parcel of our reasons for plunging into Indochina—in the words of John F. Kennedy's inaugural address, the United States was ready to ". . . pay any price, bear any burden, meet any hardship, support any friend, oppose any foe, to assure the survival and the success of liberty." From 1950 to 1975 the United States, as a foreign power and at a cost of billions of dollars and millions of Vietnamese and American lives, tried to shape Vietnam's human rights performance and to affect its political system. It is hardly surprising that, in 1996, the cleavage between the United States and a still-Leninist Vietnam has yet to be mended.

U.S. policy has the task of differentiating between what we might like to see happen in Vietnam and what is reasonable to expect in the bilateral relationship, at least in the short run. What degree of respect for human rights on the part of the Vietnamese government should the United States realistically expect today, and in what time frame? What is the most effective way to promote basic values Americans hold to be universal?

For Americans who have had close association with Vietnam over the decades since 1946, these questions are not easily answered.

Human rights were prominent in the Bush administration, yet were handled for the most part selectively and according to pragmatic policy requirements in specific bilateral circumstances. In 1992, continued MFN status for the People's Republic of China was justified in terms of using the free market and trade relations to fuel China's burgeoning economic development on the presumption that liberalization in politics would eventually follow. By withdrawing MFN, the United States would hurt the very forces advocating changes in the political sphere, so went the argument. On human rights, the Bush administration applied measured pressure on specific cases to gain Chinese cooperation, playing "good cop" to the potential strong measures of Congress, the "bad cop."

The Reagan administration had tested Hanoi early on humanitarian matters and gained remarkably good cooperation concerning Amerasian children, the Orderly Departure Program, emigration for former reeducation camp inmates, and repatriation of boat people to Vietnam without prejudice. Hammered out pragmatically and with little fanfare, these programs ended up working well, so well in fact that they are scheduled to be phased out by the end of 1996. The Bush administration was able to limit *political* conditionality in normalization to the issues of Cambodia and progress on POW/MIAs (the latter was disguised as "humanitarian" to suit the requirements of *both* Hanoi and Washington). Concerns about democratization and blatantly obvious human rights issues were deliberately finessed in deference to what were deemed priorities of immediate consequence.

At the outset of the Clinton administration, the issues of human rights ascended, at least rhetorically, to a prominent position in U.S. foreign policy.[14] In dealing with China, this policy proved to be disastrous initially. The administration's conditions for extending MFN in the spring of 1993 were subsequently ignored by China. When the time for MFN renewal came in 1994, Secretary of State Christopher made a high-profile personal demarche to the Chinese leadership. He was unceremoniously rebuffed in Beijing. China knew the United States was not prepared to jettison the valuable bilateral trade relationship, a fact of life every American chamber of commerce in Asia could have told the administration. Consequently, in June 1994, the Clinton administration was forced to retract its major human rights emphasis and declare that henceforth trade relations with China would not be held hostage to human rights considerations. The administration repeated this explanation in renewing MFN for China in 1995. Although U.S.-Vietnam bilateral trade is relatively modest, the experience with China is relevant to the future relationship in terms of balancing ideals with pragmatism.

The Vietnamese have been willing to enter into a formal dialogue with the Clinton administration on human rights with the proviso that they will brook no interference in Vietnam's internal affairs. That, obviously, is the rub in any dialogue of this sort. Particularly sensitive politically is the regime's repression of the Unified Buddhist Church of Vietnam (UBCV) and the imprisonment (or "pagoda-arrest") of monks who have resisted the Vietnamese Buddhist Church (VBC), a state-sponsored organization created specifically to give the government control of Buddhist activities. Suspicion of the Catholic Church is even more evident. The government restricts movement of Catholic priests, limits the number of young Vietnamese entering the priesthood, and obstructs the church's efforts to obtain religious teaching materials. As long as the government maintains this policy, it will be difficult to gain congressional support for MFN and other commercial benefits for Vietnam.[15]

The Dilemmas of Political Change

With regard to democratization, two schools of thought have debated the appropriate strategy toward a Hanoi regime that in many respects remained stubbornly Leninist. One was the "let them stew in their own juice," school, which saw no advantage in establishing a relationship with Vietnam's current leadership. It held that U.S. interests were best served by hobbling Vietnam's economic development and awaiting a Soviet-style upheaval, causing the downfall of communism. For proponents of this view, the longer the embargo stayed in place the better. The opposing view, which triumphed in 1994 and 1995, held that opening up Vietnam to the outside world through, among other steps, full normalization with the United States was the best means to bring about political change in Vietnam over the long run.

At the party's Seventh Congress in July 1991 and in the new constitution of the Socialist Republic of Vietnam, adopted in April 1992, the principle of democratic centralism and the leading role of the party as "the force leading the State and society" were reaffirmed. The party explicitly rejected the concept of political pluralism. Despite discontent stirring within its own ranks and in the population at large, political change outside the boundaries of the party was denounced as a mortal threat. "Stability" during difficult times was imperative and "peaceful evolution," that is, fundamental social change that takes place without the sanction of the party, was dangerous and intolerable. Yet, while all candidates for the National Assembly still had to be approved by the Communist Party's "mass organizations," the enhanced powers of the elected Assembly under the 1992 constitution would seem to provide indications of the gradual passage to a more representative system. The news media, which are controlled by the state, may vigorously criticize corruption and inefficiency but may not challenge the primacy of the party, seriously question government policies, or challenge "Ho Chi Minh thought." In sum, Vietnam has adopted an unyielding position on political change, and this can only signal coolness on one level of U.S.-Vietnam relations.

Despite the refusal of the Hanoi regime to admit political pluralism, the continued process of normalization of relations with Vietnam is nonetheless the rational way to facilitate the broad social trends the United States advocates globally as a matter of principle: wider political representation of different interests, respect for human rights, market economics, and civil freedoms in general. Although in the short run recognition may indeed work to the benefit of an authoritarian Hanoi regime perpetuating its power, establishment of full relations would also seem to be in the interests of the Vietnamese people north and south.

One of the passionate arguments currently under way within and outside Vietnam is whether Vietnam can achieve genuine, lasting economic improvements in the absence of greater openness in the political realm. No vast social upheaval along the lines of the former Soviet Union is likely to occur in Vietnam. Any political change will have to be evolutionary rather than revolutionary, if only because the party has made certain that the conditions for the creation of political alternatives are not present in Vietnamese society. Moreover, the economic benefits and, importantly, the psychological lift of "opening up" have indeed helped create the economic stability the Hanoi regime needs to maintain political control—from the beginning that was the rationale behind *doi moi,* Vietnam's policy of "renovation" or "renewal." The evidence since the Sixth Party Congress of 1986 suggests that as long as economic reforms bring benefits, as they have so far, the Vietnamese people may be willing to accept political limitations.

President Clinton's announcement on July 11, 1995, included not only the good news of normalization but also these words:

> . . . normalization and increased contact between Americans and Vietnamese will advance the cause of freedom in Vietnam, just as it did in Eastern Europe and the former Soviet Union. I strongly believe that engaging the Vietnamese on the broad front of economic reform and the broad front of democratic reform will help honor the sacrifice of those who fought for freedom's sake in Vietnam . . ."[16]

This blunt statement—the quintessence of "peaceful evolution"—stunned the VNCP and strengthened the hand of those conservatives who had warned of how the United States would use normalization, and everything that comes with it, to undermine the party's political control.

The Vietnamese Communist Party knows full well it faces a harsh dilemma. The party no longer appears to enjoy the "mandate of Heaven" in the eyes of the populace to the extent it did during the war, when ideology bonded with nationalism. *Doi moi,* the lifting of the embargo, the infusion of capital from international financial institutions, bilateral economic assistance programs from Japan and other international donors, and, above all, the corollary influences that come with a foreign presence have already had a major impact on Vietnamese society. Over the longer term, as Vietnam's society modernizes, receives information, and joins the outside world, it seems likely that economic change will beget greater participation in the Vietnamese political process. Certainly, ideology is already being eroded by science, education, cultural exchange, and the marketplace. These facts of modern life would appear to make peaceful evolution in Vietnam inevitable, an evolution initially to a softer authoritarianism and later to a more sophisticated participatory system of governance. One indicator of social change already under way is the restructuring of Vietnamese higher education away from Marxist orthodoxy and in the direction of Western standards, something that would have been unthinkable only five years ago.

An important element in normalization is the attitude of the Vietnamese American community, which constitutes about one-half of the *Viet kieu* (overseas Vietnamese) of two million persons. In 1995, *Viet kieu* remittances to their homeland were estimated at U.S.$1 billion, and this figure is expected to increase steadily through the decade. Although there are certainly pockets of expatriate resistance to better official relations, the majority of overseas Vietnamese seems to favor the idea of working constructively with the current Hanoi regime in order to facilitate the process of economic and political change toward a prosperous and democratic society. The *Viet kieu* represent an influential force in this direction, but, clearly, they are regarded as a threat to the stability of the country by some quarters in the VNCP.[17]

Looking to the longer term, it seems likely that Vietnam will move at its own pace away from the current Leninist system toward a peculiarly Vietnamese version of what Robert Scalapino calls "authoritarian pluralism," an amalgam of socialism and free-market economics kept in place by a structured political system that only gradually admits the existence of more than one party.[18] The experiences of South Korea and Taiwan are instructive in this regard.

So what official stance should the United States take regarding these fundamental issues of human rights and political change? In this writer's view, the United States should speak out quietly but firmly on human rights and on guarantees of freedom of religion, speech, and assembly. It should also make clear that an enlightened electorate and participatory—as opposed to an exclusionary—governance are the real foundation of stability. At the same time, the United States should not demand acceptance of an American perspective on human and civil rights as a precondition for further movement toward normalization; such a position could well retard the progress of the very values and institutions we favor. It would be shortsighted and hostile to our own national interests to make Vietnamese acceptance of American-style values and institutions the precondition for further movement. Under no circumstances should the United States—either the administration or Congress—lend support or encouragement to external Vietnamese groups seeking to overthrow the current Hanoi regime by force.

History has shown that the Vietnamese people are endowed with a strong spirit of independence. Events since 1945 have also left a bitter political legacy within Vietnamese society and as yet unhealed regional difference between North and South. Whether, over time, the Vietnamese collectively will be able to design a political system open enough to combine many points of view peacefully remains to be seen. Given the country's tortured history, this can only be a complex and drawn-out process, a process that will depend crucially on the Vietnamese Communist Party's willingness to admit pluralism.

The Strategic Importance of the
U.S.-Vietnam Relationship

Vietnam will never again be near the center of American foreign policy, as it was in the 1960s, nor should it be. Nonetheless, the United States has identifiable economic, political, and strategic interests in Vietnam. Although withholding diplomatic recognition, the United States after 1975 had accepted the SRV as a state under international law and acknowledged that the SRV exercises effective control within Vietnam and of the country's borders. Since 1989, the United States has dealt with SRV authorities routinely on a range of issues and, in practice, has more and broader contact with the Hanoi government than with many other states with which the United States enjoys "normal" relations. As noted above, the United States has obtained privileges and freedom of ground and air movement regarding POW/MIA search operations (including the stationing of American military personnel in Hanoi and access to archives) that are remarkably permissive.

Since the lifting of the embargo, trade and investment by American private business has risen steadily, if not dramatically. Two-way trade in 1995 totalled $460 million, with a four-to-one advantage for the United States. That figure is expected to double in 1996. American companies have joined the top ten investors in Vietnam, with $1.7 billion pledged for a variety of projects; Mobil Oil's growing operations account for a significant share of this total. Many "Fortune 500" companies have opened offices and, as expected, U.S. companies have been active in aircraft, energy, tourist, communications, and information-processing ventures. Vietnam's 73 million population, industrious work force, preference for American products, and rapid economic growth rate are viewed as a potentially attractive addition to Southeast Asia's thriving economic environment. At the same time, many American companies have experienced profound frustration in dealing with the omnipresent Vietnamese central and provincial bureaucracies, official corruption, and the inadequate administrative and legal framework for conducting business affairs in Vietnam. Vietnam remains in the early stages of working out the transition to what its leadership describes as free-market economics with a socialist orientation—a confusing concept that may be a major part of the country's problem.

It is in the realm of regional security that the national interests of the United States and Vietnam converge most significantly. During the Cold War, the Soviet Pacific Fleet was in competition with the U.S. Seventh Fleet for control of the Pacific Ocean. By 1978, the Soviet-Vietnamese security relationship was a potential threat to Southeast Asia, as demonstrated by the heavy Soviet investment in Vietnam's Cambodia adventure. During this period, it was in the United States' interest to have a weak, confined Vietnam.

With the collapse of the Soviet Union, this Cold War argumentation became null and void. A familiar and more durable strategic player has moved onto the scene: China, the "Middle Kingdom," a power always to be reckoned with in Southeast Asia. China's long-term intentions are unclear, particularly regarding the South China Sea, where China's sovereignty claims directly conflict with those of the Philippines, Malaysia, Brunei, as well as Vietnam. China's military capabilities (a blue-water navy and advanced long-range aircraft, submarines, and amphibious vessels) are improving steadily. In July 1995, Vietnam became a member of ASEAN and the ASEAN Regional Forum (ARF), where the South China Sea issue is prominent. Having been invaded many times by the Middle Kingdom over the past 2,000 years, the Vietnamese are painfully aware of their own China problem. Several countries in the region have for some time viewed Vietnam as a potential bulwark against an unpredictable China. The uncertainty of the current leadership transition in China makes it all the more important for the United States to develop a dialogue on regional issues both within the ARF and bilaterally. In doing so, the United States should not portray Vietnam as some sort of praetorian guard against a supposed Chinese aggression against Southeast Asians.

Yet, while one of the most fundamental American interests in Asia must be to build a sound relationship with China, building a parallel relationship with Vietnam on security matters is certainly a prudent course to follow. Vietnam is now increasingly plugged into the ASEAN economic and security grid, and it will be joined by the end of the century by Cambodia, Laos, and Burma. With the Cold War over, American national interest will be directly promoted by seeing Vietnam become economically prosperous and a genuine contributor to regional stability. This fact recognized—and it is a striking fact in the light of our history with Vietnam since 1945—lengthy, no doubt painful negotiations on many levels and sustained patience on the part of both countries will be required to move the bilateral relationship forward and, eventually, to realize the full potential of the Vietnam-United States connection.

Notes

1. Advisors favoring recognition argued that Clinton had already antagonized voters who were against further normalization. Consequently, he would lose few votes by

moving ahead. Moreover, by showing he was capable of making a tough decision on a sensitive topic, the president would counter his popular image of indecisiveness.

2. S.J.Res. 34 and H.J.Res. 89 (Rep. Gilman). See "Concerned Citizen Newsletter," June 19, 1995, National League of Families of American Prisoners and Missing in Southeast Asia, Washington, D.C.

3. See "Peking's Hop, Skip and Grab," *Far Eastern Economic Review (FEER)*, August 13, 1992, and "China's New Law of the Sea," *FEER,* June 16, 1994.

4. See testimony of Winston Lord, Assistant Secretary of State for East Asian and Pacific Affairs, before the House International Relations Committee on Asia and the Pacific, June 27, 1995.

5. An exception was the highly significant role of American nongovernmental organizations (NGOs) that were active in South Vietnam all during the war and that after 1975 developed a range of humanitarian and educational programs countrywide. The NGOs, private voluntary organizations, and (after 1992) the Ford and Fulbright foundations became, in effect, an unofficial "track" for normalization.

6. Vladimir N. Pregelj, Robert G. Sutter, Alan K. Yu, and Larry Q. Nowels, *Vietnam: Procedural and Jurisdictional Questions Regarding Possible Normalization of U.S. Diplomatic and Economic Relations* (Washington, D.C.: Congressional Research Service Report for Congress 94–633 S, August 4, 1994). For a broader analysis of postrecognition issues, see *U.S.-Vietnam Relations: Issues and Implications* (Washington, D.C.: General Accounting Office, April 1995).

7. On January 28, 1995, the United States and Vietnam signed an agreement settling claims by the U.S. government on behalf of the 192 private claimants for expropriated properties. A separate agreement settled the issue of U.S. diplomatic properties in Vietnam. The United States unblocked Vietnamese assets worth about $90 million. Source: *Indochina Digest,* February 3, 1995.

8. Nayan Chanda, *Brother Enemy: The War after the War* (New York: Harcourt Brace Jovanovich, 1986), and Frederick Z. Brown, *Second Chance: The United States and Indochina in the 1990s* (New York: Council on Foreign Relations, 1989).

9. "Agreements on a Comprehensive Political Settlement of the Cambodia Conflict, Paris, 23 October 1991," United Nations Department of Public Information DP/1180–92077, January 1992.

10. National League of Families of American Prisoners and Missing in Southeast Asia, *Concerned Citizens Newsletter,* March 24, 1995.

11. Other congressional maneuvering during the September-December 1993 period are detailed in Pregelj et al., *CRS Report for Congress,* 94–633 S.

12. See Pregelj, et. al., CRS Report 94–633 S.

13. For a cogent analysis of where the relationship currently stands, see Mark Sidel, *The United States and Vietnam: The Road Ahead* (New York: Asia Society Update, April 1996).

14. See speech by Anthony Lake, national security adviser to the president, "From Containment to Enlargement," at Paul H. Nitze School of Advanced International Studies, Washington, D.C., September 21, 1993.

15. See Adam Schwartz, "In God They Trust," *Far Eastern Economic Review,* June 27, 1996, which quotes the head of the Institute for Religious Studies in Hanoi as arguing that the Vietnamese government has the same right to crack down on the UBCV as American authorities had in using force against David Koresh and the Branch Davidian sect in Waco.

16. President's speech, "U.S. Normalizes Relations with Vietnam," reprinted in *Department of State Dispatch,* July 10, 1995.

17. See, for example, *The Economist,* June 22, 1996, p. 39, which states that the Free Vietnam Alliance, a Vietnamese exile group, ". . . has support not simply from exiles but from many Communist Party members in Vietnam, some of them holding senior posts." See also Le Xuan Khoa, "The Overseas Vietnamese Communities and Vietnam Today," *The Bridge,* Vol. 11, Number 4, Winter 1994–95.

18. Robert Scalapino, *The Last Leninists: The Uncertain Future of Asia's Communist States,* Washington, D.C.: Center for Strategic and International Studies, 1992.

10

Where Do We Go from Here?

Masashi Nishihara and James W. Morley

The Promising but Uncertain Future

The picture of Vietnam that emerges from this study is of a country on the move away from the war-prone, impoverished isolation of the past toward a future that is fraught with exciting possibilities—but is still problematic.

Renovation is flourishing. A nationally elected and newly empowered National Assembly is debating and enacting fundamental legislation. The doors are wide open to foreign ideas, and advice is being sought everywhere—without regard to its ideological origins. The push for collectivization has been halted. The peasants are now empowered to use the land as they see fit. Private enterprise is warmly encouraged. A free market is heralded. Efforts are being exerted to build the financial and legal institutions such a market requires. And the country is responding, driven by a powerful entrepreneurial drive, burgeoning particularly from Ho Chi Minh City.

The foreign policy of Vietnam has undergone equally dramatic changes. Vietnam has long since abandoned its failed thrust into Cambodia. It has brought its armed forces home, reduced their numbers by half, and assigned many of those remaining to economic development activities. At the same time, it has withdrawn from what is left of the international communist movement and is pursuing an overall policy of international cooperation, with an emphasis on economics. It has opened its doors to new ideas, and invited the international business community to come in.

It has made up with its erstwhile enemies, China and the United States. It has reinvigorated its ties with Japan, Australia, New Zealand, Canada, and the states of Western Europe. It has been invited by its regional neighbors into membership in ASEAN, the ASEAN Regional Forum (ARF), and the Asia Pacific Economic Cooperation (APEC) forum.

The benefits of the new course that Vietnam has set upon are everywhere visible. The people of Vietnam have been freed at last from the turmoil of collectivization and the burden of war. While the majority remain impoverished, the economy is taking off, infusing the country with a new spirit of hope; and ideas from abroad are injecting a new vigor into the intellectual and cultural life of the people.

The United States and Japan have especially benefited, particularly by the cooperative attitude that Vietnam has adopted toward the POW/MIA issue, the result being that the resolution of that issue is now within sight. This has enabled the United States to join the rest of the world in establishing more normal relations with Vietnam, and Japan has been freed from the restraints that it had imposed on its Vietnam relations in support of the American position.

Both Japan and the United States are at last able, as is the international business community at large, to share in Vietnam's economy. Traders, investors, and manufacturers are taking advantage of this open door, along with a growing number of individuals and humanitarian nongovernment organizations that are anxious to contribute what they can to Vietnam's progress.

The new course has also benefited the political and strategic interests of the United States, Japan, and their friends. For Vietnam's neighbors, the withdrawal of Vietnam's forces from Cambodia and its cooperation in the peace settlement has made an indispensable contribution to the easing of the tension that for decades tormented the Indochina peninsula and eventually drew in not only the other states of Southeast Asia but also all the major powers of the world. Its recent admission into ASEAN brings that organization closer to its aspiration to represent all the nations in Southeast Asia and enhances its capacity to strengthen the security of the region. At the same time, its entry into the APEC forum and the ARF brings it for the first time inside the tent of all the nations seeking, together with the United States and Japan, to build a wider Asia-Pacific community.

Vietnam's effort to find a peaceful, but somewhat distant accommodation with China, while keeping defensive forces on its border and drawing closer to the members of ASEAN and the rest of the Asia-Pacific community, has been a welcome change from the extreme policies of the era of "lips and teeth" diplomacy, when it collaborated with China, and of the more recent past when it engaged in war with China. This change would seem to be predicated on the conception that coping with China's immense size, expanding economy, strengthening military power, and traditional ethnocentrism will continue to be one of the central issues of international relations for many years to come. The policy that Vietnam has approved, that of engagement plus deterrence, would seem to be entirely consonant with the policies of Japan and the United States and indeed adds a valuable new geographical dimension to their approaches.

On the other hand, the picture is not without its dark spots. While the most dynamic forces at work seem to be driving Vietnam in favorable directions, the outcome is by no means certain. The obstacles that remain to be overcome are enormous: for example, the rural poverty, the broken welfare system, the inadequate educational system, the failed state enterprises, the lack of economic and legal infrastructure, the thinness and inexperience of the new elites, and the corruption that corrodes all efforts. Moreover, the Communist Party, which is trying to guide the reforms while it has lost its way ideologically and is appealing to the intellectuals to help it, continues to brook no open dissent. So far, its efforts to increase popular participation have been quite limited. These efforts give little promise yet of a program of systematic political liberalization, which Vietnamese society will increasingly demand if the economy is to continue to grow and the doors are to remain open to fresh ideas.

It is, therefore, not beyond the realm of possibility that Vietnam may fail in its present efforts, that "old thinking" will regain its power, that the promising program of marketization and openness to the world will come to naught, and that its foreign policy will revert to a nationalistic intransigence.

For the Vietnamese people such a collapse would be an unmitigated disaster. For the American and the Japanese people, and for their friends and allies, the failure of the reform movement would stand at least as a costly lost opportunity: the possibility of adding Vietnam to the global market and to the community of nations that are working toward a more cooperative, peaceful environment in the Asia-Pacific would, at least for the time, be lost. At worst, failure might provoke a violent popular upheaval or a reactionary coup that would confront us, once again, with a security problem of unforeseeable proportions.

It may be that we put the matter too starkly. Complete success or complete failure are probably not the realistic alternatives. The more likely course is somewhere in between. But it is important to understand that the degree to which the favorable prospects can be achieved is of immense advantage to the people of Vietnam and also to the world community, including Japan and the United States.

It is also important to understand that the outcome in Vietnam will depend, not only on the leaders and people of Vietnam, but on the actions taken by the world community, and given the strength and influence of our two countries, not least of all by Japan and the United States.

Vietnam has joined the world because it needs the world's support. Vietnam needs advice on development issues such as only the international financial institutions can give. It needs help in replacing its broken welfare system, which the international nongovernmental organizations are best equipped to provide. It needs capital and technology to rejuvenate its agricultural and industrial production, which can only come from abroad. It hungers to share in the world's culture, from which it has been cut off for so long. Above all, it seeks peace and acceptance.

As two of the wealthiest, most powerful, and most influential countries in the world, Japan and United States, therefore, are in a position to play a significant role in determining the course that Vietnam will take. Their fundamental interests in Vietnam, moreover, would appear to be common: to move it farther in a politically cooperative, market-oriented, and democratically inclined direction. The imperative then seems clear, that Japan and the United States cooperate to advance their common interests.

Managing the Alliance

But first a caveat needs to be entered. Having common fundamental interests does not mean that Japan and the United States do not and will not have differences in less fundamental interests, issues that are more tactical than strategic. It is also does not mean that our two countries will not at times differ in their approaches. A brief review of our past differences over Vietnam and how they were handled will help to illustrate the point.

Throughout most of the Cold War period the United States approached Vietnam primarily from strategic perspectives. In the 1950s and 1960s Washington saw Vietnam as a proxy of Chinese and Soviet communism. Soon after the Chinese Communist Party succeeded in taking power in 1949, the United States started to provide military assistance in support of the French forces fighting against the Ho Chi Minh-led Viet Minh forces struggling for independence. The subsequent "Americanization" of the war in Indochina is a familiar story. Even after 1975, when Saigon fell, the U.S. continued to look at Vietnam as a proxy for Soviet power. It then supported China partly to counterbalance the Soviet-Vietnamese alliance.

During the same period Japan's primary concern was how to recover its own position in Southeast Asia by concluding peace treaties and war reparations agreements and reestablishing trading relations. It early on formed the view that an economically prospering, politically stable Southeast Asia, including Vietnam, was in its interest; and since Japan believed its security role to be limited, it determined to contribute to the region by offering economic cooperation and building a relationship of interdependency. At a time when the United States was giving all-out support to South Vietnam, Japan limited its own relationship to that government to extending economic aid in the name of war reparations and loans.

Thus, there was a wide gap in the involvement of our two countries in Vietnam. Between 1960 and 1974 Washington expended a total of $5.447 billion, most of which was in military aid, while Japan's aid was exclusively economic in character and amounted only to $137 million, including $39 million for war reparations. Besides, between 1964 and 1973 the United States put a total of over 8.7 million soldiers into Vietnam and incurred some 58,000 deaths. Japan did not participate in the war at all.

During this period, three Vietnam-related issues in particular troubled U.S.-Japan relations. One was the difference in concern: Washington took the communist aggression very seriously, while Tokyo, beset by domestic antiwar movements, which were expressed by most of the Japanese media and student and labor movements, gave the U.S. efforts only limited public support. Another was the difference in trade policy: during the war years Japan's big trading companies, acting through dummies, continued to trade with the North, although on a small scale. Finally, there was the difference in diplomatic stance: while the United States was conducting painful peace talks with North Vietnam, the Japanese government in February 1972 secretly contacted Hanoi; and in September 1973, only eight months after the Paris peace talks were concluded, it established diplomatic relations with the government of the new, united Vietnam—with whom the United States continued to remain at odds for more than twenty years.

In the post-Vietnam War years, Japan and the United States continued along somewhat different tracks. The United States was primarily concerned about the safe entry of Vietnamese refugees into America and the collection of data on American prisoners of war and servicemen missing in action in the Vietnam War. Japan, on the other hand, seeing the U.S. diplomatic and military retreat form the region, took the opportunity to activate its diplomatic role there. It promoted its relations with the countries of Indochina, as well as with those in ASEAN, and announced its support for harmonizing the relationship and enhancing the cooperation between the two. It was the hindrance of this demarche that made the U.S. trade embargo a contentious issue between Washington and Tokyo until it was lifted in February 1994.

On the other hand, we should remember also that, notwithstanding these differences over Vietnam policy, the broader interests that drew Japan and the United States together and the conviction they shared in the value of their alliance caused them to show great sensitivity to each other's interests and kept them in a close working relationship. While Japan felt great hesitancy about supporting the U.S. war effort publicly, it did recognize the need that the United States felt for some kind of assistance. To that end it did provide quietly some logistical and procurement support. On one occasion, in September 1967 at the height of the fighting, Prime Minister Eisaku Sato made a visit to South Vietnam. In the post-Vietnam War years, while Japan felt frustrated by the U.S. trade embargo from pursuing its interest in Hanoi, it did observe that embargo, contrary to the action taken by many other states. The United States, for its part, although it wanted Japan's support, did not demand that it be given openly; and in 1972 it went so far as to meet Japan's demand for the return of Okinawa, even though the island had been useful for the war effort in Vietnam.

With the ending of fighting in Vietnam and in Cambodia, the course change in Vietnam itself, and the establishment in 1995 of U.S.-Vietnam relations, a new era has opened. But all differences in Japanese and American policies toward Vietnam cannot be assumed to have been swept away. Three areas would seem to require particular attention.

One is the difference in our readiness to engage the Vietnamese. The Japanese, after all, have been working for several decades to accelerate the economic development of the countries of Southeast Asia and link them with Japan in a wider Asia-Pacific community. Ever since the enunciation of the Fukuda Doctrine in 1977 that vision has included the rehabilitation of Vietnam and its inclusion in these communities. Government interest is high, a large economic assistance program is in progress, and business is heavily engaged. The Japanese-Vietnamese relationship is taking off.

The United States, on the other hand, is still moving up to the starting line. The United States is twenty-two years behind Japan in recognizing Vietnam; and a number of obstacles, involving, for example the continuing POW/MIA problem, trade restrictions, and human rights, still impede the "normalization" of the relationship. American businesspeople have been exploring the Vietnamese economy for the past several years, and a few of the larger corporations, notably the oil companies, are already active; but, so far most are still warming up and have not yet entered the race. Nongovernmental agencies are increasingly active, but there is no supporting economic assistance program. Given this difference in depth of interest and commitment, it is not difficult to imagine that frictions may arise.

A second area that will need sensitive handling is that of human rights. Both Japan and the United States place a high value on human rights and democracy and look forward to their ultimate triumph in Vietnam, as elsewhere. But it is also apparent from our experiences in China, Myanmar, Indonesia, and elsewhere in the world that while the United States has been inclined to take a hard-line position on these issues—to confront governments that violate human rights or deny democracy and often to try to coerce them into compliance by using trade embargoes and other pressures—Japan has preferred a softer approach—talking privately with officials to persuade them into agreement or relying on long-range economic support to bring about the changes in Vietnamese society that will result in stronger domestic pressures to realize these objectives.

A third area of potential difference is that of international security. Obviously both Japan and the United States want a secure international environment, and the two countries are clear on the need for a forward positioning of U.S. forces in order to keep a favorable balance of power in the region. But recent history shows that in threatening circumstances Japan is far more inclined to conciliate while the United States is more inclined to confront. Since Vietnam's future is clouded by disputes with China on its land border and also in the South China Sea and the Gulf of Tonkin, one needs to be aware that there may be differences in the responses of the United States and Japan to such disturbances over whether to bolster one side or the other or to remain aloof.

While these potential differences are not greater than the ones that were handled in the past, they do suggest that our two countries must proceed with sensitivity to each other's interests and approaches. We need to recognize that there may be times when joint or parallel action is not possible. It is, however, clear that the consonance of our interests in Vietnam today is without parallel in the past and presents an opportunity for cooperative action that should galvanize us into action.

Major Policy Recommendations to
Our Two Governments

We therefore recommend to Japan and the United States to:

1. Promote greater openness and international cooperation in Vietnam by encouraging Vietnam to participate more actively in regional and international meetings, both governmental and nongovernmental. It may be possible for our governments, for example, to provide financial and other assistance, as our private sectors have done in the past, to increase the

number of Vietnamese with English-speaking ability who are able to participate in or sponsor such meetings (ASEAN-related meetings alone, for
example, number about 250 a year, of which Vietnam is expected to sponsor 30 or 40).

2. Reinforce Vietnam's commitment to a market economy by opening
our own markets more widely to its commodities; facilitating our own
respective bilateral trade, investment, and technology transfer; extending
aid; supporting the activity of Vietnam in ASEAN and other regional economic groupings; and supporting the full engagement of international financial institutions, such as the World Bank and the International Monetary
Fund, in Vietnam. In extending our direct and multilateral investment and
aid to Vietnam, we should keep in mind that a balanced development of
northern and southern economies will be a key to national stability.

3. Support a greater respect for human rights in Vietnam and an acceler-
ation of the liberalization of its political system by making known our views
to the ruling elites and the people, encouraging the openness of the country
to external contacts, offering to help strengthen the legal and other systems
that an effective human rights regime requires, and strengthening the demand of indigenous social forces for these reforms by supporting the continued economic and social development of the country.

4. Develop broad security dialogues with Vietnam, urging Vietnam to
pursue a security role that is conducive to peace in the region by reducing
its armed forces to a size that is economically sustainable and commensurate with its defensive needs; to strengthen the professionalization of its
forces by establishing a stable and effective system of civilian control; to
help reduce the tensions in the area by joining its neighbors in the effort to
devise confidence-building measures, such as the exchange of military officers and military doctrines, measures for military transparency, and measures for regional maritime security; and to consider its future security
needs within the framework of ASEAN and the ARF.

5. Help Vietnam to improve its human resources by launching vigorous
programs of cultural exchange, offering to help improve Vietnam's educational system, particularly its agricultural and technical high schools. We
should also encourage our nongovernmental organizations to develop active
programs of their own in Vietnam to improve training in technical skills,
business know-how, medical services, and the like. And in parallel, we
should promote projects for bringing Vietnamese students to our own countries for more advanced education.

6. Make greater efforts to learn about Vietnam ourselves. Southeast
Asian area study programs were never strong in Japan and, since the end of

the war in Vietnam, have been allowed to wither in the United States. Each country needs to reinvigorate these programs and stimulate a greater engagement of its citizens in Vietnam's intellectual life.

7. Broaden and deepen the contacts between our own governments relating to Vietnam, as well as setting up policy discussion fora, business councils, and study projects between our two publics, so that by a greater sharing of our analyses and concerns we can capitalize on opportunities for cooperation and avoid unnecessary conflicts, thereby strengthening our alliance and enabling us to advance our common interests more effectively in Vietnam and in the wider Asia-Pacific community.

Index